Caribbean Inhospitality

Critical Caribbean Studies

Series Editors
Yolanda Martínez-San Miguel, Carter Mathes, and Kathleen López

Editorial Board: Carlos U. Decena, Rutgers University; Alex Dupuy, Wesleyan University; Aisha Khan, New York University; April J. Mayes, Pomona College; Patricia Mohammed, University of West Indies; Martin Munro, Florida State University; F. Nick Nesbitt, Princeton University; Michelle Stephens, Rutgers University; Deborah Thomas, University of Pennsylvania; and Lanny Thompson, University of Puerto Rico

Focused particularly in the twentieth and twenty-first centuries, although attentive to the context of earlier eras, this series encourages interdisciplinary approaches and methods and is open to scholarship in a variety of areas, including anthropology, cultural studies, diaspora and transnational studies, environmental studies, gender and sexuality studies, history, and sociology. The series pays particular attention to the four main research clusters of Critical Caribbean Studies at Rutgers University, where the coeditors serve as members of the executive board: Caribbean Critical Studies Theory and the Disciplines; Archipelagic Studies and Creolization; Caribbean Aesthetics, Poetics, and Politics; and Caribbean Colonialities.

For a complete list of titles in the series, please see the last page of the book.

Caribbean Inhospitality

The Poetics of Strangers at Home

NATALIE LAUREN BELISLE

RUTGERS UNIVERSITY PRESS
NEW BRUNSWICK, CAMDEN, AND NEWARK, NEW JERSEY
LONDON AND OXFORD

Rutgers University Press is a department of Rutgers, The State University of New Jersey, one of the leading public research universities in the nation. By publishing worldwide, it furthers the University's mission of dedication to excellence in teaching, scholarship, research, and clinical care.

Library of Congress Cataloging-in-Publication Data

Names: Belisle, Natalie Lauren, 1976– author.
Title: Caribbean inhospitality : the poetics of strangers at home / Natalie Lauren Belisle.
Description: New Brunswick, New Jersey : Rutgers University Press, 2025. | Series: Critical Caribbean studies | Includes bibliographical references and index.
Identifiers: LCCN 2024015380 | ISBN 9781978838291 (paperback) | ISBN 9781978838307 (hardcover) | ISBN 9781978838314 (epub) | ISBN 9781978838321 (pdf)
Subjects: LCSH: Citizenship—Caribbean Area. | Political participation—Caribbean Area. | Belonging (Social psychology)—Political aspects—Caribbean Area. | Tourism—Political aspects—Caribbean Area. | Tourism—Social aspects—Caribbean Area. | State, The.
Classification: LCC JL599.5.A92 B44 2025 | DDC 306.4/81909729—dc23/eng/20240813
LC record available at https://lccn.loc.gov/2024015380

A British Cataloging-in-Publication record for this book is available from the British Library.

Copyright © 2025 by Natalie Lauren Belisle

All rights reserved

No part of this book may be reproduced or utilized in any form or by any means, electronic or mechanical, or by any information storage and retrieval system, without written permission from the publisher. Please contact Rutgers University Press, 106 Somerset Street, New Brunswick, NJ 08901. The only exception to this prohibition is "fair use" as defined by U.S. copyright law.

References to internet websites (URLs) were accurate at the time of writing. Neither the author nor Rutgers University Press is responsible for URLs that may have expired or changed since the manuscript was prepared.

♾ The paper used in this publication meets the requirements of the American National Standard for Information Sciences—Permanence of Paper for Printed Library Materials, ANSI Z39.48-1992.

rutgersuniversitypress.org

To the little girl who walks with me. You are home.

Contents

Introduction: In the World, Not of It: On the Aesthetic of Caribbean Inhospitality   1

1   Deliberative Misdirection: The Non-Sense of Caribbean Community in Annalee Davis's *Migrant Discourse* and Ana Lydia Vega's "Jamaica Farewell"   23

2   Disoriented Citizenship: Misreading Puerto Rico in the Uncosmopolitan Elsewhere   51

3   Freelance Personhood: Living Off the Books in the Outer Spaces of Cuban Writing   79

4   Altered States: Bordering the Inhuman in René Philoctète's *Le Peuple des terres mêlées* and Pedro Cabiya's *Malas hierbas*   112

Coda: Loving Beyond (Sovereignty)   143

Acknowledgments   147
Notes   151
Index   175

Caribbean Inhospitality

Introduction

IN THE WORLD, NOT OF IT: ON THE AESTHETICS
OF CARIBBEAN INHOSPITALITY

Still Lives, Still Life | Not So Enchanted, an archival print ink series by Trinidadian photographer and artist Abigail Hadeed, inverts the paradisiacal lens of Caribbean tourism to reveal the alienating underside of a region mostly known for "sun, sand, and sea." In one still titled *Ghost Ship*, featured on the cover of this book, the silhouette of a cruise ship peeks from behind a dirty alchemy of haze and fog that coalesces into a thick wake that ribbons a tempestuous, dark blue sea. Yet it is the story behind the print series that clarifies the unseen human toll of the local hostility that is wedded to the Caribbean's world-renowned hospitality. Hadeed's images capture the Royal Caribbean's *Enchantment of the Seas* cruise ship, on which nearly three hundred native Trinidadian and Tobagonian hospitality workers were forcibly quarantined at the height of the COVID-19 pandemic in June 2020. For nearly a month, these workers were suspended on the turbulent waters of the Gulf of Paria, only paces from their homeland, as they anxiously awaited the ever-changing news of their uncertain repatriation. The conditions of legal citizens who work as *hosts* to the absent guests of a phantom ship that is not their home while being simultaneously dispossessed within reach of their native political community reframes the transhistorical significations of the ship as described in contemporary theories of the Caribbean and the African Diaspora.[1] Hadeed's visual figuration of what curator Marina Reyes Franco describes as a "highly racialized" visitor economy not just conjures the ghostly confines of ships that held enslaved Black Africans and indentured Asian laborers in a state of onto-juridical suspension.[2] Extending further into the past, *Still Lives, Still Life*, I contend, evokes the founding scene of Caribbean hospitality: Christopher Columbus's encounter with Caribbean natives whom he welcomed as *visitors* to his ship.

Hadeed's photographic rendering of the entangled spatiotemporalities of a Caribbean *hospitality* that paradoxically enshrouds what I call *inhospitality* informs this book's focus on Caribbean aesthetic responses to the political and juridical estrangement of Caribbean citizens and subjects from their homelands. While there exists substantive scholarship that explores how Caribbean peoples are mobilized in service to the region's visitor economy, this book follows a different approach guided by the critical intervention of Caribbean writers, artists, and intellectuals. It investigates how a logic of hospitality that largely underwrites the Caribbean nation-state also conditions the rights, practices, and obligations that govern belonging and membership in these nation-states. Depictions of the unreserved hospitality Caribbean nations offer up to foreign visitors elide the fact that Caribbean peoples also have lives that call upon them to vote, deliberate, speak, and be represented as citizens and subjects of the very nations and states that also provide escape, respite, and hospitality to foreigners. In what way does representation of the Caribbean's historic hospitality to foreigners inform and overlay the representative claims and possibilities of Caribbean peoples as citizens and subjects? What does it mean to be a *host* in a home that is not one's own? This book wrests Caribbean peoples from the decorative roles they have largely occupied in picturesque representations of Caribbean tropicality and foregrounds them in the vicissitudes of postcolonial sovereignty.

Caribbean Inhospitality: The Poetics of Strangers at Home recasts the Caribbean's legacy of hospitality to the world in the context of literary, filmic, and digital representations of Caribbean citizens and subjects who are estranged from the Caribbean nation-states they call "home." *Caribbean Inhospitality* argues that contemporary literary and cultural production from the Spanish, Anglophone, and Francophone Caribbean conceptualize forms of displacement, itinerancy, unworldliness, spacelessness, and depersonalization that confuse and unsettle the juridical distinction between the citizen of the nation-state and the "stranger" or guest. The representative texts under consideration in this book—Ana Lydia Vega's "Jamaica Farewell," Annalee Davis's *Migrant Discourse*, Yoss's *Se alquila un planeta*, the Alternative Cuban Blogosphere's clandestine narratives, Giannina Braschi's *Yo-Yo Boing!*, Eduardo Lalo's literary travelogues, René Philoctète's *Le Peuple des terres mêlées*, and Pedro Cabiya's *Malas hierbas*—register the failure of the Caribbean nation-state to guarantee the rights and conditions that contribute to citizens' sense of belonging in their home country. Namely, these texts expose how the Caribbean nation-state frustrates the practice of citizenship in specific ways addressed in this book's four main chapters: they foreclose meaningful political deliberation, dislocate citizenship from space and place, render the law illegible to citizens, and compel the racialized self-estrangement of the citizen under the pretext of juridical universality.

THE AESTHETICS OF POSTCOLONIAL CARIBBEAN CITIZENSHIP

At the heart of this book's thesis that Caribbean literary and cultural production elucidates a conflict between the lived experience of Caribbean citizens'

INTRODUCTION

estrangement from their home countries and the illusion of a Caribbean hospitality is a desire to rethink the significance of Caribbean aesthetics and cultural practices in the wake of the now less fashionable postcolonial discourse, which profoundly formed and shaped my own intellectual and scholarly formation in the early aughts. The Caribbean has been deployed as an archetypal expression of "hybridity," one of the key weapons in postcolonial theory's arsenal of discursive resistance to and unsettling of European colonialism's attempt to assimilate difference and instill racial purity, cultural imperialism, epistemological universality in the (neo)colony.[3] The Caribbean envisioned as a mode of postcoloniality threads seminal works of Latin American and Caribbean cultural theory, which demonstrate how the region's violent genesis from the "meeting" of strangers native to four continents is transmuted into "relational" and transcultural poetics that echo or "repeat" across nations fragmented by languages, geographies, and governmental forms.[4] As Shalini Puri outlines in her field-defining *The Caribbean Postcolonial*, the Caribbean and its key cultural discourses—such as *mestizaje, antillanité*, and creolization, to name a few—both instantiate and interrogate postcolonial hybridity.[5] Moreover, these cultural discourses work in a manner that is "conjunctural" to the Caribbean nation-state such that they make possible a pragmatic "politics of equality."[6] To be clear, and as I explore in chapter 1, Puri suggests that the conjunctural nature of these cultural discourses can equally serve progressive and conservative politics. But Puri's larger point, and one that I provisionally share, is that Caribbean literature, performance, and art mobilize a poetics and aesthetics of postcolonial hybridity that speak and write against the colonial impulse to purity while articulating a politics of representation.

Yet it is the discursive and representative dimension of postcoloniality that has been subject to vigorous reappraisal and skepticism, considering the failed promises of Caribbean postcolonial sovereignty with respect to citizens. The consensus among many scholars committed to a practical politics of Caribbean self-determination in both the humanities and the social sciences seems to be that, to echo Brian Meeks, there has been a "real-world evaporation of any vestigial space of sovereignty."[7] Without recapitulating all the terms and positions of this debate, there is an overarching sentiment among critics of postcolonial thought that the current crisis requires a deeper commitment to a praxis than what postcolonial criticism's singular focus on discourse, poetics, and aesthetics can offer. Taking a more tentative approach to postcolonial theory's impasse, scholars such as David Scott rightfully insist that "to make the political appear requires an attention to the relation between criticism" (what he relegates to the epistemological and cultural) "and strategy" (the ethical and political) in the "aftermath" of postcolonial sovereignty.[8]

Although the practice of citizenship, the exercise of nation-state sovereignty, and the law's codification and regulation of both are at center of *Caribbean*

Inhospitality, the book's key focus is contemporary Caribbean literary and cultural production in its relation to national, regional, and international law. Therefore, this book does not necessarily abandon or minimize the significance of the discursive and the aesthetic, as its focus on Caribbean literary, audiovisual, and digital narratives obviously suggests. Nor does this book presume to shelter the promise of a practical approach or a definitive solution to the crisis of Caribbean sovereignty and citizenship that it outlines. Rather, as I further explore, in its turn to the political and juridical it shows how this crisis is bound up with the aesthesis of hospitality.

Historically, contemporary Latin America and Caribbean literature has long had a keen investment in representing the law. In *Myth and Archive*, Roberto González Echevarría demonstrates that Latin American and Caribbean literature has traditionally mediated and critically assumed the form of hegemonic discourses, replicating and parodying, for example, the legal, classificatory, and scientific rhetoric through which Europe invented itself through the discovery of the New World Others. Moreover, González Echevarría explains, the form of Latin American and Caribbean narrative, such as the novel, shifts and responds to forces external to itself at the time of its emergence, beginning first and foremost with the law's rhetorical and enunciative force.[9] While post-emancipation and modernist Latin American and Caribbean novels mimetically incorporate legal rhetoric into their narrative framework, the literary, audiovisual, and digital narratives at the heart of *Caribbean Inhospitality* evince a decolonial skepticism both toward the law's rhetoricity and with regard to the historicization of the law's contemporaneity with the work of fiction that represents it. Instead, they demonstrate that the senses of the law do not necessarily follow.

Caribbean Inhospitality takes one of its cues from writer Jamaica Kincaid's *A Small Place*, a satirical and scathing denunciation of tourism. Addressing an anonymous yet ubiquitous foreign traveler, Kincaid notes that the tourist experience in her native Antigua—and, by extension, the Caribbean—is structured to delimit what the tourist does and does not *see*.[10] Effectively, Kincaid's text indexes an aesthetic regime that is specific to the senses of tourism as I discuss in chapter 1. There I borrow and revise Jacques Rancière's notion of the "aesthetic regime," which relates to how the senses (sight, sound, and taste, for example) are partitioned across a perceptual field that overlaps with and is identical to the regime of politics. According to Rancière, these overlapping sensory regimes disclose "who has a part in the act of governing and being governed."[11] For Kincaid, however, tourism conditions the tourist to intentionally erase from their perceptual field the spaces, places, and monuments to civil society through which citizens construct a sense of belonging, membership, and home—for example, hospitals, libraries, and schools.[12] Yet Kincaid's chief concern is not limited to the tourist's sensory experience. *A Small Place* points to the more pernicious implications of tourism on the experience and practice of citizenship. Her text signals how a world cohabited by both the foreign tourist (stranger) and the native citizen (host) must bend to the perceptual needs of the tourist, a necessary condition of the "hospitality industry" as an economic enterprise. In doing so, tourism disrupts the aesthetic regime or what Kincaid terms the "political perception" shared between the native Caribbean citizen and the nation-state.[13]

At first glance, *Caribbean Inhospitality* enumerates a set of political and legal concerns that might be perceived far outside the purview of literary and cultural analysis and far removed from if not inconsequential to the aesthetic conceit of literature and film, and less so of blogs—the three narrative forms analyzed in this book. Yet in attending to the aesthetic dimensions of inhospitality, this book underscores the centrality of Caribbean literary and cultural production not as mere representations of a political and juridical reality but rather as a terrain that is coterminous to the disfigured "political perception" between the citizen and the inhospitality of the nation-state toward them. While the Spanish, English, and Francophone Caribbean texts under consideration in this book use figures of speech and figural representation such as allegory, metaphor, and analogy to portray the predicament of citizenship and nation-state sovereignty in the contemporary Caribbean, the figurative is invoked to draw attention to the reality of a Caribbean inhospitality that is concealed by the illusion of hospitality the Caribbean nation-state extends to foreigners.

In "Bourgeois Universality and Anthropological Differences," Étienne Balibar helps clarify what I contend is the necessity of aesthetic and cultural criticism to decode and make legible the law in its figural and illusory workings. Turning to Marx's critique of the grammar that both sutures and differentiates the "rights of man" (the human) and the "rights of the citizen" (the political subject), Balibar signals the disjuncture between the utopian *ideal* of citizens' rights articulated in political writing, speech, and the law and the *reality* of the state's negation of these rights in a conflict that unfolds between those who own property and those who do not.[14] According to Balibar's reading of Marx, the "rights of man" acquire juridical universality insofar as they become the exclusive rights of the bourgeois property owner against all other political subjects, including the citizen, of the state. As I consider further ahead, especially in chapter 3, property and proprietorship condition the citizen and stranger essentially swapping places in the narrative of Caribbean inhospitality. In the meantime, however, I want to emphasize and suggest that Balibar's—by way of Marx— distinction of the ideal from real politics necessarily marks the law as discourse that always takes a figural or symbolic form. In other words, the law (as political rights) is illusory and operates at the level of an aesthesis (sense experience) that we associate with fiction. Thus, it can and must never literalize what it means less it expose the actual stakes of the conflict.

This book contends that the representative works of Caribbean literature, film, and digital writing under consideration do not merely rehearse the rhetoric of the law so much as interpret and expose the law's effects. Echoing Joshua Chambers-Letson, I understand the legal interpretation enacted by Caribbean literary and cultural texts as a performance of the law as it moves from a declarative statement to representational and aesthetic forms that contribute to the perception, recognition, and misrecognition of whom and what the law of citizenship and the law sovereignty actually define.[15] In a similar sense, my reading of these texts follows what Erin Graff Zivin, vis-à-vis Rancière, calls the "metapolitics of allegory," or how the figural dimension of these texts "performs, rather than thematize" the impossibility of the law's truth.[16] I understand the performative act of legal interpretation carried out by these Caribbean literary and cultural texts in three interconnected ways. First, in its denotative sense, interpretation entails the exegetical task of elucidating and explaining the law's conceptual and contextual meaning. In another sense, interpretation connotes translation, a term that is already coded with multiple significations. Lastly, *Caribbean Inhospitality* is concerned with translation not merely as the transfer of meaning between languages but rather as the conceptual and contextual signification of the laws that define sovereignty and citizenship as they interact within a system of international relations that we call the "world."

Spanning the 1980s to the 2010s, the Caribbean literature, film, and blogs analyzed in *Caribbean Inhospitality* locate the crisis of postcolonial Caribbean citizenship in the backdrop of a second global reordering that began in the twentieth century and, with it, the demand for the Caribbean nation-state to "world" itself—that is, to legitimize itself within an international political community and global (economic and cultural) market. If, as Michel-Rolph Trouillot has argued, the world first becomes global through the transatlantic flows generated by Europe's conquest and colonization of the New World Caribbean, this second global reordering of the world structures and dampens the emancipatory possibilities that the Caribbean nation-state holds for its citizens.[17] Moving from and between the present and the past, I delineate how this second moment of globality engenders a notion of worldly sovereignty that binds itself to the legacy of Caribbean inhospitality and political estrangement created in the first instance. To grasp how contemporary Caribbean literary and cultural production performs the nation-state's inhospitality toward its citizens, we must first apprehend how citizenship becomes redefined such that the Caribbean citizen exists not in relation to their fellow citizens nor the member state but, rather, relative to the global.

Citizenship is broadly defined as a juridical status that grants humans membership as legal persons in a nation-state that, in turn, confers upon them a set of reciprocal rights—voting, representation, and legal protection, for example—and civic responsibilities. Of course, as I elaborate in the cases of parliamentary

INTRODUCTION

republican Barbados and Guyana, nonsovereign Puerto Rico, socialist Cuba, and republican Haiti and the Dominican Republic, the meaning and exercise of these rights and responsibilities vary according to the political constitution and governmental form of the nation-state. Throughout this book I invoke the term "nation-state" while remaining attentive to the predicament of nonsovereign nations whose natives possess citizenship, albeit conditioned, as neocolonial subjects of a sovereign state, as in the case of Puerto Rico, or sovereign states that are members of political and economic associations, like the Caribbean Community (CARICOM), that extend legal rights and privileges to nationals of member nations.

The texts studied in *Caribbean Inhospitality* also respond to the juridical configuration of the postcolonial Caribbean nation-state and the Caribbean as a regional political economy as it becomes unevenly entangled, willingly or unwillingly, in a global political and economic order otherwise described as a system of "international relations." Within this system of international relations, there are two approaches to the idea of state sovereignty that are conceptually, if not legally, relevant to my reading of Caribbean inhospitality. In one instance, this system enforces and universalizes what international relations scholars call "methodological nationalism," the view that state sovereignty constitutes the only legitimate and globally recognized form of a self-determined political community. Accordingly, the state derives its legitimacy from the recognition of other equally "legitimate" sovereign states who form part of a hegemonic international political community. As one scholar has argued, methodological nationalism "sees our world as comprising of nation-states locked in competition" against other, ostensibly "illegitimate" and anarchical forms of political community that operate outside universal law and threaten the global order.[18] A system of methodological nationalism appears consistent within an international political framework that reconfigures the "world" as global politics. Yet the world within this system of international relations obtains juridical universality such that it deems political constitution outside of its discursive borders illegitimate. Another perspective closely related to methodological nationalism espouses a constitutive theory of statehood, which views the nation-state as a *person* of international law.[19] Thusly, the sovereignty of the state overrides the legal personhood of the citizen and subject, inasmuch as the sovereignty of the state is overwritten by a system of international relations. As Trouillot demonstrates, this world and the legitimacy of political communities that inhere within it are defined by what he calls "North Atlantic Universals"—words and concepts that "project the North Atlantic experience" ensuing from the first configuration of modern globality "on a universal scale that they themselves helped create."[20] These, Trouillot asserts, include words and concepts such as "progress, development, modernity, nation-state" and, undoubtedly, personhood and citizenship.

The worlding of state sovereignty law has resounding and pernicious implications on the life of the citizen who is captured by the particularity of race, gender, sexual orientation, and class. As Balibar outlines, the conflict between the idea and reality of citizenship reveals the anthropological difference inherent within the idea of citizenship, as various classes or forms of humanity within political modernity. According to Balibar, the fact that the human being (as a citizen) becomes abstracted to a "purely juridical universality" that can be embodied only by a *white, male proprietor* suggests that the state excludes the racial and gendered Other as part of the whole of citizenship and, by extension, the human.[21]

By considering the state's situatedness within the world as a system of international relations, I propose a slightly different reading of the Caribbean (native) citizen, who historically emerges as the signifier of anthropological difference—or hybridity and strangeness—par excellence of political modernity. This reading is deeply indebted to Aníbal Quijano's idea of *colonialidad del poder* (coloniality of power), a concept that explains how the modern world was constituted by a racial schema originating from the colonization of Latin America and the Caribbean and subsequently globalized (*se mundializa*) through the "nation-state" form, which, by definition, is always already European and, therefore, universal.[22] Such a reading underscores the subalternity and anthropological difference of the Caribbean nation-state within the juridically universal idea of "the world" constituted by a hegemonic international political community defined by the expansion of global capitalism, the consolidation of neoliberalism, and territorial capture and dispossession. Thusly, the postcolonial hybridity of the Caribbean citizen can never attain, resolve, nor bypass the juridical universality of citizenship because the postcolonial Caribbean nation-state must respond and conform to the universality of the world vis-à-vis international relations, in ways that compromise the nation-state's rights and responsibilities to its citizens.

Literature, art, and media have long portrayed the complexities and inner workings of international and foreign relations. These include alien invasion fictions, genocide stories, hostage accounts, fictions of diplomacy, and postutopian cybernarratives—the main genres investigated in *Caribbean Inhospitality*. One of the central claims of this book is that an aesthetics of hospitality, which engenders the New World Caribbean in the first global ordering of modernity, primes the worlding of the Caribbean nation-state and its citizens within the landscape of international relations. Indeed, this book insists that it is the narrative or poetic that legislates the Caribbean native's estrangement with respect to the Caribbean nation-state's positioning in the world in ways that antecede the formation of international relations. We can glean this by considering the founding discourses of Caribbean inhospitality that make possible the first global ordering of the world.

INTRODUCTION

(Re)visiting Columbus

To fully apprehend the aesthetico-political contours of inhospitality in contemporary Caribbean literary and cultural production, we must return to the scene that not only founds the Caribbean but, importantly, would perennially subject the Caribbean native to the foreign visitor as both *host* and *stranger*: the narratives of Christopher Columbus's encounter with the New World. Columbus's account of his "discovery" of the New World Caribbean and his first contact with its Indigenous population is a discursive, epistemological, and ideological enterprise that sets the stage for how the Caribbean would be read long after his voyage. The four main texts that collectively relate Columbus's journey to the insular and mainland Caribbean not only provide the religious and legal justification for the Spanish Crown's subsequent conquest and colonization of the Americas but also radically reorder early modern European understandings of the world and Europeans' place therein. The way Columbus—and, I would argue, the Caribbean—is read across time has been shaped by a discursive and ideological apparatus that far exceeds his pen, and that of the editors, corroborating witnesses, commentators, translators, and other respondents who supplement and amplify Columbus's not-so-innocent intent. For example, as Margarita Zamora demonstrates, the narrative is supplemented by the "decisive meditation" of Bartolomé de las Casas, Columbus's key "Reader."[23] This, she argues, produces a historiographic writing of the discovery—one that makes Columbus much more accountable as a writer and historical agent rather than a passive narrator and observer.[24] For readers today, however, the otherworldly and imaginative language that Columbus uses in the face of a previously undocumented, if not unseen, natural and human ecology shares a greater affinity with literary fiction than with the historiographic register through which it was read in Columbus's time.[25] Yet these transtextual readings of Columbus do much more than produce the genre of an event. Indeed, I argue, they make legible a hospitality/inhospitality dynamic that becomes embedded in the legal discourse and juridical framework of the postcolonial Caribbean nation-state. It becomes the task of contemporary Caribbean literary and cultural production, as I demonstrate, to expose the law as a genre and aesthetic of inhospitality.

Columbus's narratives inaugurate this dynamic by inventing the Caribbean as an uncomplicatedly receptive host to Europe and, by extension, the world. In a pivotal scene from his *Diaro del primer viaje* (Journal of his first voyage), Columbus recounts his reception by Hispaniola's natives (two months after his arrival to the Caribbean in 1492) in terms that confuse who is the *guest* and who is the *host* of the New World house. The confusion arises when Columbus describes the Taínos moving from land to sea, in their canoes and swimming, to his docked ship, where they greet and welcome him peacefully, bestowing gifts, and without incident:

Dize que aquella ora cree aver venido a la nao más de mil personas, y que todos traían algo de lo que poseen, y antes de que lleguén a la nao con medio tiro de ballesta, se levantan en sus canoas en pie y toman en las manos lo que traen, diziendo: "tomad, tomad." ... Juzgava que avían venido cinco señores e hijos de señores, toda de su casa, mujeres y niños a ver los cristianos.[26]

(He says that, according to his reckoning, a thousand people had *visited* the ship, all of them bringing something. Before they come alongside, at a distance of a crossbow shot, they stand up in the canoe with what they bring in their hands, crying out, "Take it! take it!" ... Among the *visitors*, five chiefs had come, sons of chiefs, with all their families, to see the Christians.)[27]

Couched in las Casas's third-person voice, the passage cunningly inverts and reorients the frame of relations when describing the reception *given to him* on his ship, the *Santa María*, by the Taíno. He strategically maintains his dominant position as the master of a ship, transmogrified in the Caribbean Sea into a host space that *receives* the Caribbean natives who, as we know, will be subjected as possessions of the Spanish Crown. Proliferating the ideological work of Columbus's words at the editorial hands of las Casas, royal geographer Clements Markham's 1893 English translation titles the passage with the heading "Hospitality of the Natives" and adds the noun "visitors," absent in the original Spanish text. This post-Columbian translational move captures the spatial and ontological position of Hispaniola's native population not only with respect to Columbus's ship but also, in the wake of the nineteenth-century "rediscovery" of Columbus, with respect to European and rising North American global hegemony. In the absence of the Taínos' perspective as Columbus's purported hosts, the ideological workings of translation not only bolster a myth of hospitality. To borrow a phrase from Gayatri Chakravorty Spivak, Columbus's text worlds the natives' "own world . . . by obliging them to domesticate the alien as 'Master' of the house."[28] The text foregrounds the native Caribbean subject as both host and stranger, in terms that underscore what Jacques Derrida observed to be an etymological multiplicity that inheres with the concept of hospitality and, with it, the fundamental inseparability of the hospitable and the inhospitable in the domain of the law.[29]

Columbus's depiction of native hospitality stands in sharp contrast to the well-known images of the hostile, bellicose, and cannibalistic Caribe Indians, who are mentioned only as a menacing specter in the *Diario* before the threat of their appearance is made real in the *Relaciones* of his second and third voyages to the Caribbean. Ironically, it is from Hispaniola's hospitable Taínos that he learns about the cannibals, whom he later misreads and conflates with the Caribe that, in his second voyage, he encounters on the same island.[30] Columbus's *Diario* and *Relaciones* set up a series of ontological equations—the Taínos as hospitable, the Caribe as hostile—that would lay the foundations of raciality that order the modern world. That Columbus previously encountered hospitable natives does not erase the threat of the savage Caribe. Instead, the Columbian narrative of the savage Caribe would, as Zakiyyah Iman Jackson has argued, produce the "ontological disfigurement of the 'Native'" who would later be replaced by the Black as the abjected Other of the New World.[31] Blackness, as this book examines across its four main chapters but particularly in chapter 4, would be estranged from and rendered inhospitable to Caribbean nations and states.

Revisiting the ideological and discursive workings of Columbus's narratives of discovery, *Caribbean Inhospitality* emphasizes how they found and naturalize a substitutionary relation between the native Caribbean host and the stranger, which exceeds both the space-time of the colonial and the strictures of mere historical and literary (or aesthetic) representation. Sylvia Wynter clarifies the transhistorical *legislating* effects of Columbus's voyage on the ("Euro-American") ordering of the present world, via the expansion of the nation-state form and the West's techno-economic mastery of the globe.[32] In "Columbus, the Ocean Blue, and Fables that Stir the Mind: To Reinvent the Study Letters," Wynter tracks how Euro-America's rehabilitation of Columbus in the nineteenth century would recast the separation between "nature" and "culture." Prior to Columbus's voyage, European orthodoxy held that the earth was divided into "habitable and uninhabitable regions, and the universe was divided by an ontological difference of substance between the unchanging and incorruptible perfection of a celestial realm . . . and the degraded fallen realm of the terrestrial."[33] The aftermath of his voyage would demand a revolutionary, epistemological corrective that recognized the physical homogeneity of the earth and the continuity of the laws of nature therein. Yet, Wynter notes, this corrective to the natural and physical sciences would be extrapolated to the order of *culture* whereby Europe asserted itself as the universal. That is, like the universal laws of nature, so too "would the laws of culture hold in the same way for the now hegemonic and globalized cultures of the techno-industrial West."[34] What Wynter calls the "laws of culture" is the Word itself—the fictions we invent to describe our origins and who we are. Euro-America's ongoing encounter with human non-homogeneity, narratively instituted by Columbus's encounter with the natives (replaced by racial Others), would be the dominant narrative as retold in literature, film, and those aesthetic forms belonging to the universal order of culture. As Wynter discusses elsewhere, these narratives behave in a "law-like manner," a guiding concept throughout her oeuvre that defines the (behaviorally and cognitively) regulating function of storytelling in the aesthetic mode.[35] Wynter's reading of the law-like manner of narrative reframes the regulating function of storytelling in the aesthetic mode. But what if the storytelling also regulates the order of legal discourse? If Columbus's narrative inaugurates a discourse of Caribbean hospitality, would it not also regulate actual juridical systems? What if the law is itself a legal fiction that is regulated by the founding discourse of Columbian hospitality?

This book reads Caribbean sovereignty and citizenship as legal fictions that, respectively, legitimize the state to the world and legitimize the citizen as a member to the state in the world. Reading sovereignty and citizenship as fictional constructs that are legislated narratively, I recall Barbadian sociologist Linden Lewis's suggestion that Caribbean sovereignty is "built on a foundation of myth and illusion" insofar as Caribbean political communities simply conformed their governmental structures to a notion of sovereignty passed down from Westphalian Europe and thus an extension of the very foreign forces that colonized the region.[36] Lewis queries what it means to implement a political form derived from the place from which one was emancipated. Writing of Haiti's newfound freedom, Colin Dayan frames the contradictions of this conceptual leap in rather appreciable terms, noting that Haitians had to transmogrify themselves ontologically—from slave and savage (Black) to sovereign and civilized (white)—as political subjects "while remaining black."[37] As Aaron Kamugisha claims, Caribbean self-government and self-determination have been articulated either as a desire to validate the humanity and agency of Caribbean subjects "within the coordinates established by European social and historical experience" or as *reactions* and *responses* to the (foreign) forces of modernity.[38] As the Other of the Western European nation-state form, the Caribbean nation-state must legitimize itself as such in terms that ultimately contravene the difference represented within. According to Trouillot, the globality of the contemporary nation-state sovereignty as the universally dominant and acceptable form of political community conceals its emergence against the background of colonialism and planetary imperialism, at the center of which lies the historical experience of the Caribbean's development.[39] Nation-state sovereignty is conceptualized even as Europe, to echo Immanuel Kant's words, behaves inhospitably in the Americas—denying the sovereignty of the people it colonized. What Trouillot wants to draw attention to is the fact that modernity and its attendant concepts—the nation-state and sovereignty—required the creation of an Other that is fundamental to colonialism. What does it mean then to assume a political form in which one is always outside? One might wonder how the situation described here is specific to the Caribbean and not the general condition of international relations in which recognized nation-states find themselves today.

This book tracks the inscription of the Columbian narrative of Caribbean hospitality according to what Denise Ferreira da Silva calls the *elementa* or raw material of coloniality in juridical-economic forms such as the nation-state.[40] It reads hospitality as an elemental disposition that ontologizes Caribbean subjects as strangers to European modernity and two of its attendant concepts—nation-state sovereignty and citizenship. *Caribbean Inhospitality* tracks the colonial foundations of hospitality and reframes it, beyond its traditional

INTRODUCTION

association with the service economy and tourism. It defines hospitality as a logic and disposition that structures Caribbean nation-states' primary orientation toward the interests of a "world" that is hostile to the racial, gendered, cultural, linguistic, and classed difference of Caribbean peoples. This world is made up of an international political community, a global economy, political constitutions, ideologies, and discourses that are wedded to the notion of state sovereignty bequeathed to the Caribbean from post-Enlightenment Europe and transformed under globalization and neoliberalism. *Caribbean Inhospitality* insists that we must trouble the conceptual inheritance of juridical categories and political philosophies translated from Europe to the New World Caribbean, whose capacity to engage in rational thought necessary for articulation of a sovereign will and self-possession was undermined and suspect to European thought.

THE INHOSPITALITY OF THE PROPER

This book's titular concept, *inhospitality*, signals Immanuel Kant's theory of hospitality as "cosmopolitan right," a concept that since its Enlightenment bequeathal has generated considerable reappraisals as it pertains not only to contemporary political theory but also to world literary studies. Whereas Kant's doctrines of right present his theory of cosmopolitan right as it relates to international law, it is in his Third Article "To Perpetual Peace" that he defines and identifies hospitality as cosmopolitan law that opposes the "inhospitableness" of European colonialism.[41] Kant's oft-cited Third Article defines hospitality as the *human right* of foreign aliens to present themselves before a foreign country without being treated with hostility as "an enemy."[42] Hospitality, he clarifies, guarantees not "the right to be a *permanent* visitor" but rather "the *right to visit*" in order to make commerce.[43] This right, he affirms, "belongs to all men by virtue of their common ownership of the earth's surface." Having presented the conditions for the exercise of hospitality, Kant turns to provide two instances of hospitality's less commented antithesis. In the first case, he condemns the "inhospitableness" of "coastal dwellers" (North African pirates) and "desert dwellers" (the Arabic Bedouins) who "rob" and "plunder . . . contrary to natural right."[44] In the second, Kant addresses European imperialism and settler colonialism: "Compare this with the *inhospitable* conduct of civilized nations in our part of the world, especially commercial ones: the injustice that they display *towards* foreign lands and peoples (which is the same as conquering them) is terrifying. When discovered, America, the lands occupied by the black, the Spice Islands, the Cape, etc., were regarded as lands belonging to no one because the inhabitants were counted for nothing."[45] It bears noting that Kant appears to issue a much harsher condemnation of Europe's inhospitableness—in the New World, Asia, and Africa—presumably because they should have known better as *civilized nations*, compared to the uncivilized North Africans and Arabs. That is, because cosmopolitan law as an amendment to international law—and, by extension, the right of hospitality—is contingent on humans overcoming their state of nature to live as a community or "totality of men" in the nation-state.[46] As Peter Niesen discusses, there is considerable debate, which exceeds the thematic constraints of this book, concerning whether noncitizens living in non-state forms can make claims to a Kantian hospitality.[47]

Noteworthy, however, is that Kant ascribes inhospitableness to European nations' conduct abroad on the basis of their unsubstantiated claim to land vis-à-vis the Roman principle of *terra nullius*, or no-man's-land. Prior to this, Kant had just told readers that the right to visit and "associate" as men (that is, as members of a political community) is a universal (cosmopolitan) right based on men's common possession of the earth, to which no one ostensibly has a greater right.[48] This common ownership is not just a human right but rather a human fact based on our natural scattering across the earth.[49] Thus, Kant's critique of European imperialism and colonialism rests on the fact that it treats its Others abroad as *not* men, ascribing to them an ontological strangeness that not only exceeds the foreignness of the alien but also dissolves the common right to possess the earth.

Yet an even more consequential and surprisingly overlooked aspect of Kant's critique—and one that is particularly relevant to this book—is the sly conceptual inversion that allows him to ascribe inhospitableness to the European foreigner's behavior *outside* of Europe. Indeed, most contemporary rereadings of Kant's Third Article "To Perpetual Peace" consider the inhospitality of Europe toward a certain class of strangers—refugees and immigrants, who tend to be racialized minorities—arriving to its doorstep. But if hospitality entails the act of *receiving* and welcoming a foreigner without hostility in one's political home as a *host*, how does *inhospitality* suddenly become the conduct of the *guest* in a home that is not theirs?

What patently elides Kant in his anti-imperialist naming of European inhospitality—and thus what would call into question the post-Kantian cosmopolitan discourse mobilized by Europe's Others—is the coloniality of race. That Kant allows Europe to assume the position of the *host* might be understood in the light of his views concerning human geography and Black enslavement. Robert Bernasconi's paratextual analysis of Kant's Third Article through the lens of the German philosopher's broader oeuvre suggests that while Kant "recognized that love for others embraces the whole human race," his cosmopolitanism was neither "the answer to racism" nor a means of giving the human races equal weight in the world.[50] In particular, Kant's ambivalent attribution of human (racial) difference to "differences in climate," which could be overcome with race mixing, betrays the insidious side of cosmopolitanism.[51] Extending Bernasconi's reading, the implication—one of profound relevance to the Caribbean—would be that Kant's ideal of the human race gradually coming "closer and closer together in a cosmopolitan constitution" could be accelerated through the disappearance of Blackness into whiteness.[52] Furthermore, according to Bernasconi, Kant's denunciation of inhospitableness seems equivocal in light of the philosopher's removal from the published version of "To Perpetual Peace" of what in an earlier, unpublished draft is his assertation that "the trade in Negroes is in itself a violation of hospitality."[53] This ambivalence would enable what I contend are two divergent senses of inhospitality in "To Perpetual Peace"—one rooted in the barbarism of the non-European, racialized subject and another arising from a founding, sovereign mastery that acts in surplus of itself. In this sense, we might reconsider how Kant's aesthetic theory of taste as *sensus communis* puts pressure on his theory of hospitality. How does Kant's cosmopolitan ideal of the human race—brought together in the common world of nation-states—contend with what he maintains is the "common sense" of taste and "shared sense" of a universal aesthetics from which, as Rizvana Bradley and Denise Ferreira da Silva explore, the Other, the Black, and the Savage are excommunicated?[54]

While Kant's work posits hospitality as inhospitality's antithesis, *Caribbean Inhospitality* proposes the inextricable entwinement of hospitality with inhospitality on the basis of the European guest's presumed founding mastery. My reading of this entwinement deeply engages with and reconsiders Jacques Derrida's interventions on Kant's cosmopolitan law, as they apply to our contemporary world, in his seminars on hospitality. Notably, Derrida's oeuvre signals the aporia that is inherent to hospitality, owing to both the concept's etymological multiplicity and the mastery required to actualize hospitality as a politic of the nation-state. Conceptually, Derrida demonstrates, hospitality would be the purview of the "host" and "guest" and even the "enemy," for hospitality discloses the crossing and confusion of the etymologically related Latin roots *hospes* (landlord, master, and host) and *hostis* (enemy, guest, and stranger).[55] Arguably, this unity of opposites would extend into the ethics and politics of substitution that are at the heart of hospitality. From an ethical standpoint, for hospitality to truly be hospitable without condition, the host must be willing to give of themselves—to exchange places with the guest (*hostis*), who feels and acts *as if* they are the host (*hospes, hostes*) of the house. For example, the law of hospitality is commonly enacted by the provocation to "make yourself at home." Such a provocation, however, is rarely taken as a literal enticement to abandon the rules of propriety, a term that not only denotes standards of acceptable behavior but also signals the behavior of one who possesses and owns oneself as *property*. From a political-juridical standpoint, it is precisely at this juncture that Derrida locates the limiting conditions of Kantian hospitality as a right deployed by the nation-state. The offer of hospitality presupposes not a "common ownership of the earth" but, rather, as I discuss in chapters 3 and 4, the possession of a self (personhood and citizenship) and a house (the state)—a gesture closer to John Locke than to Kant.[56] "No hospitality, in the classic sense, without sovereignty of oneself over one's home," Derrida declares in his reading of a conditional hospitality that is wedded to the law of the state.[57] The necessary propriety of hospitality not only betrays the violence of cosmopolitan right executed as a world constitution of sovereign states but also exposes the inhospitality toward the unwelcomed foreign guest as a *stranger*.

Although *inhospitality* has been generally theorized as a political and ethical practice—as legally defined conduct and habits between foreign peoples and nations—this book conceptually amplifies *inhospitality* to an aesthetic regime that binds itself to the state, in its representative relation to the citizen. In this regard, this book both embraces and slightly diverges from Derrida's deconstruction of hospitality by considering how the logic of inhospitality disentangles self-possession (as personhood and citizenship) from belonging to the nation-state and, in certain cases, from the possession of home as a property outside oneself in the context of the Caribbean. Along these lines, this book unsettles the notion of *home* within the political theoretical and philosophical discourse of Western modernity. I consider the meaning of *home* in three connotations: first, as a relation of property to and possession of oneself; second, as the legal dwelling place of the citizen and subject; and third, as the sensory and psycho-affective experience of dwelling or being at home with oneself, one's humanity, and, especially, one's fellow citizens and neighbors. I demonstrate how the logic of inhospitality that dispossesses the proper both from property and from dwelling produces the paradox I call the *stranger at home*.

To wit, the Caribbean literary, cinematic, and digital texts explored in this book disclose the citizen's political and juridical constitution as a stranger *inhospitality*, a term that, as I use it here, prepositionally marks the entanglement of the hospitality/inhospitality as a dyad. This paradoxical estrangement echoes W. E. B. Du Bois's existential query in *The Souls of Black Folk*: "Why did God make me an outcast and stranger in mine own house?"[58] Written during the post-Reconstruction period in the United States, Du Bois's question articulates a political theology of strangerhood that anticipates Carl Schmitt's Judeo-Christian reconceptualization of the modern political sphere as a delineation of the "enemy" (the *hostis* as what is foreign to the interests of the state) from the "friend."[59] For Du Bois, the outcast and stranger are not hostile foreign forces; they are created within the house, whose foundations were built by the unacknowledged labor of Black people, considered to be counted as *no one*. In rather explicit terms, Du Bois pointedly captures the raciality of inhospitality that is absent from Kant's critique of inhospitable. Although Du Bois's political theology of estrangement concerns the Black American experience in the United States, we know from the work of political theorists such as Juliet Hooker that he often theorized the problem of Blackness and, broadly, of race in the United

INTRODUCTION

States hemispherically with an eye toward Latin America and the Caribbean.[60] His thinking provides a framework for understanding the raciality of inhospitality that threads this book's four main chapters.

While the figure of the stranger in a strange land, particularly the intellectual as a stranger, has often been either tinged with certain romanticism in literary, ethnographic, and philosophical writing or invoked as the embodiment of a Freudian uncanny (the strangely familiar, the unhomely), *Caribbean Inhospitality* reads the stranger as a rather ordinary and quite familiar being. The stranger is the fellow citizen, the neighbor, the businessperson, and the worker who imbue life with familiarity even as they are misrecognized by the state. This is the stranger Georg Simmel conceives as the "member of the group itself" who, nevertheless, makes what is distant feel near by virtue of the fact that the stranger "imports" qualities that are foreign to the group.[61] Simmel's diagnosis of the stranger has significant implications for understanding the meaning of citizenship and sovereignty in the Caribbean. Balibar qualifies Simmel's stranger as an "inner foreigner"—"constituted by his or her very 'foreignness'—ascribed various causes (essentially race and culture)—is the one who 'should not be where he is,' and who functions both to reveal collective identity to itself and to call into question, if not to threaten it."[62] What if citizenship is not enough to "naturalize" the Caribbean subject into nation-state sovereignty as conceptualized and bequeathed from Enlightenment Europe, for the Caribbean subject always carries something that estranges them? To be clear, I am not suggesting that Caribbean people possess some type of essential difference or alterity. Rather, the Caribbean citizen-stranger or stranger at home exposes sovereignty's fundamental strangeness in its failure to be universal.

Inasmuch as *Caribbean Inhospitality* troubles the conceptual inheritance of nation-state sovereignty and citizenship, it is concerned with the ethical and political possibilities of the aesthetic mode, in the form of Caribbean literary, cinematic, and digital narratives that are at the center of this book. I call this aesthetic mode "the poetics of strangers at home," a gesture to and departure from Martiniquais philosopher, writer, and poet Édouard Glissant's theory of "poetics of Relation."[63] For Glissant, "poetics of Relation" describes the narrative mode (albeit not limited to poetry) par excellence of peoples originating in the historic and genealogical vacuum of modernity—beginning with the dispossession of the Indigenous and deracination of Black Africans—for it opposes the genealogical and filial historical mode of the West. Accordingly, Glissant suggests, the Caribbean's poetics of Relation is a means of creatively and inventively managing and suturing the historic and political "leap" from colonialism to emancipation.[64] Where Relation constitutes a nonidentitarian ethos of "solidarity" among peoples rooted in the "right to difference" and the "right to opacity," a poetics of Relation rejects the totalizing and universalizing impulse of the West contained in "le monde comme livre, le Livre comme monde" (the world as a book, the Book as world).[65] But there is a caveat. According to Glissant, "La Relation n'est pas d'étrangetés" (Relation is not made up of things that are foreign).[66] That is, Relation gives a symbolic, cultural citizenship to the "Other."[67] Nevertheless, in betraying and contesting a Caribbean inhospitality, Caribbean literary, audiovisual, and digital texts studied in this book disclose a politics of *nonrelationality* and a poetics of strangeness that exceed and belie Relation's refusal to contend with the legal and political.

CHAPTER OUTLINE

Although focused on the aesthetic modalities and creative expression of Caribbean writers and artists, *Caribbean Inhospitality* is a fundamentally cross-disciplinary book that reads Caribbean literary and cultural production in its direct engagement with law—in the form of treaties, statutes, declarations, acts, civil cases, and other legal and political discourses that regulate the meaning and practice of belonging and membership in the contemporary Caribbean. I understand the law not as rationality that merely makes procedural declarations of what is and what is not. Rather, as Dayan stresses, the law invents and calls things into being. It has the capacity to change the meaning and appearance of a thing and alter our perception of it, including what we deem to be the normative categories of Western modernity: sovereignty, nation-state, the citizen, personhood, the human being, and even the meaning of life and death. Reading the law as a legal fiction that makes possible the nation-state's inhospitality toward its citizens, *Caribbean Inhospitality* underscores the "shared sense" that binds the legal and the aesthetic. This book reads Caribbean literary and cultural production as both an interrogation of jurisprudence and a means of decoding the law's figural circumlocutions as it concerns the meaning of citizenship in the Caribbean.

This book develops a somewhat idiosyncratic method of reading that is not beholden to a singular critical tradition, although heavily informed by my training in Latin American and Caribbean postcolonial criticism and cultural studies. In postcolonial studies, I found a method of reading literature that deeply spoke to my innate critical sensibilities and my interests in history, anthropology, philosophy, and the law. Postcolonial criticism and cultural studies taught me to fluidly move from the close reading of textual rhetoric, form, and content to larger questions about literature's embeddedness in social formations. Yet what this book endeavors is to engage with the laws that underwrite such social formations and their structures of feeling by way of the aesthetic model—a task from which postcolonial criticism and the current permutation of cultural studies have largely absented themselves. In its reading of the law's production of an inhospitable Caribbean nation-state, *Caribbean Inhospitality* turns, heavily in some parts, to continental (European) political thought because of its historical

INTRODUCTION

investment in conceptualizing the North Atlantic Universals that are citizenship and sovereignty. But it exposes its aporias through its commitment to the critical posture of Black Studies, Caribbean theory, and decolonial thought and, especially, Caribbean literature, art, and media, which I read as theory and a form of political thought that does not espouse a totalizing idea of belonging, membership, and home.

The first chapter, "Deliberative Misdirection," tackles tourism from the perspective of Caribbean citizens and subjects making deliberative pleas to the nation-state. The protagonists of the book's first chapter are contemporary Caribbean regional integrational projects, namely the Caribbean Community (CARICOM), which turned to and promoted tourism as the primary economic engine through which Caribbean regional sovereignty could be fortified as a trade bloc. Against this backdrop, the chapter examines the appropriation of "Caribbean discourse"—theories that affirm a historically unified Caribbean— within the political economy of the Caribbean's regional tourism and hospitality industry. I explore how this encounter between antithetical projects is uniquely exemplified in two creative works—Barbadian visual artist Annalee Davis's experimental documentary *Migrant Discourse* (2006) and Puerto Rican raconteur Ana Lydia Vega's short story "Jamaica Farewell." My reading of Davis and Vega's texts suggests that discourses of Caribbean cultural unity are conflated with representations of Caribbean harmony in regional tourist narratives such that Caribbean citizens' political appeals are distorted and rendered senseless. Davis and Vega's texts transform the Caribbean's natural ecology, reinvented and replicated for tourists, into sensuous forms of "Caribbeanness." My reading is attentive to how both Davis and Vega's texts mobilize and even command the sensory faculties—sound, touch, taste, and even smell—in their depiction of Caribbean citizens' failed oral appeals within spaces that are engulfed by the sensory logic of Caribbean hospitality. "Deliberative Misdirection" also brings together a diverse body of thinkers—among them Danielle Allen's post-Aristotelean reading on politics, the undertheorized writings of Walter Rodney on rhetorical grounding as an antidote to the myth of Caribbean unity, Édouard Glissant's work on rhetoric, the political aesthetics of Jacques Rancière, and Jacques Derrida's reading of the senses of hospitality.

Chapter 2, "Disoriented Citizenship," contends with Latin American and Caribbean appropriations of cosmopolitanism as a means of accessing world literariness in view of the senselessness and illegibility of Puerto Rico's status. The Caribbean's cross-cultural history has been interpreted as an instantiation of a cosmopolitan hospitality, reconceptualized as postcoloniality's sibling theory or, perhaps, its sequel. That is, insofar as the Caribbean has historically been a dwelling place for foreigners, strangers, visitors, and exiles, it is understood to house within itself all the cultures and places of the world. In many instances, what is perceived as the Caribbean's foundational hospitality has been extrapolated to define the universal experience of strangerhood that conditions our contemporary global order, marked by transnational displacement, tourism mobilities, and migrancy.[68] Through Giannina Braschi's *Yo-Yo Boing!* and Eduardo Lalo's literary travelogues *Los países invisibles* and *La inutilidad*, this chapter interrogates the representation of Puerto Rico and the (world) literary market as a landscape that is inhospitable to the Puerto Rican writer and Puerto Rican literature writ large. The chapter situates Puerto Rican writers' sense of placelessness among an absent readership considering the unintelligibility of Puerto Rico's status as an Estado Libre Asociado (ELA), or "Free Associated State." The chapter theorizes what I call Puerto Rico's juridical and cartographic "disorientation" as a result of its legal status. The chapter delineates how Puerto Rico's dis-orientation, in turn, produces misreadings of Puerto Rico and Puerto Rican literature in the U.S. mainland, in insular Puerto Rico, and globally. The chapter interrogates what Lalo suggests is a crisis of Puerto Rican literature in the late twentieth and early twenty-first centuries—a crisis arising out of market logics of world literary studies and the development of national canons, which, the chapter shows, cannot be disentangled from a country's juridical legitimacy. At the same time, the chapter considers whether Lalo's critique of writers—and, in particular, his illegibility—is rooted in a particular definition of "literature" and "readership" that does not account for the ways in which Puerto Ricans today, especially after Hurricane Maria, engage in alternative aesthetic practices that demand a type of readership that does not privilege the paper or the book.

Chapter 3, "Freelance Personhood," is about the relationship between space, self-proprietorship, and personhood in postsocialist Cuba. Extending the discussion of tourism and its effects on political practice in the first chapter, the third chapter turns its attention to Cuba's Special Period. It considers as its starting point Cuba's reopening and qualified accommodation to neoliberalism and the global market to mitigate the economic and moral crisis that befell Cuba following the fall of the Soviet Bloc. Specifically, I focus on a central feature of these economic reforms: the development of denationalized tourist spaces designated exclusively for use by foreigners and, conversely, sealed off to Cuban citizens. The chapter considers how the affirmation of a collective people—against the singular person—within Cuban socialist legality falls apart as Cuba opens itself to the global. Cuban citizens are forced to engage in a liberal form of self-proprietorship as a means of survival. Chapter 3 contends that the confrontation between two discordant political economies, socialism and neoliberalism, created the conditions for Cuban citizens to develop what I call "freelance personhood"—a prosthetic, salable persona—made possible by "off-the-books," flexible labor that brought citizens in contact with foreign spaces from within Cuba. Reframing neoliberal notions of self-proprietorship as the delineation of a space that shores up the *proper* of the *person* against the stranger, the chapter explores how Cubans dislocate and disembody their personhood in space

INTRODUCTION   21

through inventive alliances with foreign entities and foreign infrastructure. The chapter reads two narratives that trouble the reconceptualization of the meaning of the freelancer—both as a mercenary, according to its original usage, and as a self-employed subject. First, I analyze how sex tourism enables the Cuban sex worker to host within her body a questionable form of personhood in the short story "Trabajadora social" (Social worker) from *Se alquila un planeta*, a collection of science fictional tales by Yoss, the nom de plume of José Miguel Sánchez Gómez. Then, I consider how the dissident social media collective that became known as the Blogósfera Cubana Alternativa (Alternative Cuban Blogosphere) exploit the possibilities of Cuba's expanding internet restructurer to "host" their personhood in digital spaces constituted outside the territorial borders of Cuba. I conclude the chapter by considering how the silencing of Cuban artists, writers, and intellectuals leading up to the uprising of July 11, 2020, enables us to see the etymological kinship between hospitality, the host, and the hostage in action as the Cuban state places artists, writers, and intellectuals under house arrest.

The book's fourth and final chapter, "Altered States," examines the figure of the unwelcomed neighbor—the border crosser, the shapeshifter, and the passing subject—in two speculative texts: Haitian writer René Philoctète's marvelous real novel *Le Peuple des terres mêlées* and Puerto Rican–Dominican writer Pedro Cabiya's zombie novel *Malas hierbas*. "Altered States" considers how the bridge of "naturalization" that would normally join the human being to the citizen in post-Enlightenment philosophy is fractured by the taxonomies of race that have shaped and differentiated the meaning of sovereignty and citizenship in Haiti and the Dominican Republic. Revisiting the history of internecine conflict between Haiti and the Dominican Republic, this chapter investigates how Philoctète's and Cabiya's novels expose and unsettle what I call the dermal politics of the inhuman. As the Dominican state imposes on its citizens a fictive racial-juridical skin, Philoctète and Cabiya's novels explore how Haitian-Dominican border subjects shift in and out of altered states of consciousness and being that cause them to see each other and themselves as impostors, passing subjects, and fundamentally inhuman. Bringing together neurophenomenology, philosophy of mind, and theories of racial ecologies drawing on the work of Frantz Fanon and Sylvia Wynter, this chapter asks not what it means to be a living, human being but rather how one can know with certainty that one is human and alive.

"Loving Beyond (Sovereignty)," the coda of *Caribbean Inhospitality*, returns to the endings of *Le Peuple des terres mêlées* and *Malas hierbas* as part of the book's brief closing reflection on the relationship between love and freedom and what it means to love "beyond" the structures of an institutionalized sovereignty that, albeit weakened, persists thanks to weapons (and I mean this in a very literal sense) of capture and dispossession. While much of *Caribbean Inhospitality* presents a critical and, arguably, pessimistic view of both sovereignty and the practice of citizenship in the Caribbean, the coda looks to alternative forms of community, belonging, and membership that Caribbean people can develop even as they live and work within the confines of the nation-state. In the ending of *Le Peuple des terres mêlées* and *Malas hierbas*, I find a vision of this alternative community—whether in Philoctète's adaption of the biblical Exodus to the promised land to depict allied Dominican and Haitian fugitives crossing into Haiti or in Cabiya's depiction of the zombie who is resurrected from the curse of living death, and thus from his delusion, as a result of giving himself over to the touch of a Haitian woman, an experience he describes as a stranger arising in him. In both texts, a new community and life arise from subjects lovingly and fearlessly giving themselves over and into that which they had refused or had been refused as impure, tainted, and untouchable. In light of these two texts, the book's conclusion proposes a need to encounter the stranger from within— the stranger who exists within all of us—as the precondition for any return to an unconditional hospitality in the contemporary Caribbean. The impulse to make criticism—and, therefore, the cultural, the aesthetic, and the poetic— accountable to political strategy partially foregrounds the turn in Latin American and Caribbean studies away from postcoloniality and toward decoloniality. As I discuss in more detail in the book's coda, decoloniality entails a reckoning with and overturning of colonialism's persistent afterlife, understood as the operation of "coloniality," which presently structures and reproduces the "world" as such through modes of racial/gendered dispossession, displacement, and capture that operate at the level of the nation-state. Consistent with decolonial theory's pivot to the work of Frantz Fanon, the cultural, the aesthetic, and the poetic do not merely resist coloniality but, as Fanon suggests, carry out a total (and violent) replacement ("substitution") of the colonial "species" of knowledge and being with ways of knowing and being Otherwise.[69] *Caribbean Inhospitality* registers how representative works of contemporary literature, art, and media that do not in every instance articulate a decolonial posture do anticipate, if not invite readers to ponder, the move toward a decolonial politics given the failure of citizenship to guarantee the rights and representation of all citizens.

CHAPTER 1

Deliberative Misdirection

THE NON-SENSE OF CARIBBEAN COMMUNITY IN ANNALEE DAVIS'S *MIGRANT DISCOURSE* AND ANA LYDIA VEGA'S "JAMAICA FAREWELL"

In the twenty-first century, the Caribbean continues to be perceived and defined through the sensorium of tourism. Thus, it is still hard to imagine that the Caribbean is home to people who are historically rooted in the region and who have meaningful, self-contained lives not designed to offer a benevolent welcome to an endless circuit of strangers more fortunate than they. But, as observed by Jamaica Kincaid and Derek Walcott, two of the most outspoken critics of tourism in the Caribbean, the hospitality industry's hold over the Caribbean produces a system of representation that delimits and clouds the sensorium of everyday life. In *A Small Place*, Kincaid repeatedly underscores that the tourist experience produces, if not necessitates, a certain escapist blindness and an overall perceptual impairment of her native Antigua and, by extension, the broader Caribbean. Walcott offers a similar indictment of tourism in his 1992 Nobel Prize lecture, "The Antilles, Fragments of Epic Memory," noting that tourist brochures collapse the visualization of the Caribbean's environmental and topographic diversity through "high-pitched repetition of the same images of service that cannot distinguish one island from the island."[1] Read as an ensemble, Kincaid and Walcott's texts point to an even more troubling implication: the deceptively reductive sameness of the Caribbean portrayed in the tourist image also reproduces a distorted notion of Caribbean regional harmony.

Indeed, a certain idea of Caribbean cross-cultural unity that is the basis of Caribbean cultural theory is also espoused in Caribbean regional politics, such that it may be tempting to conflate the conceptual intent of the former with the practical implementation of policy by the latter. Notwithstanding the region's linguistic and geopolitical fragmentation, Caribbean poetics highlight the shared history of Indigenous, enslaved African, and Asian peoples who, dispossessed of land and kin by the violence of coloniality, converged as strangers to birth a New

World transculture. The sociocultural manifestations of this racial synthesis have been described through a prolific conceptual framework that, as scholars have noted, has produced notable theories for reimagining radically innovative forms of belonging, relationality, and affiliation in the Caribbean.[2] Likewise, expressions of multiracial and multilingual harmony have been marshaled by both nationalist and regionalist projects, even as these have been immured by impasses and derailments that have left citizens feeling more disaffected than unified. But while the idea of a transcendent cultural unity allows for Caribbean poetics to theorize alternative communal modalities that break with the political philosophical tradition of the West, the rhetorical instrumentalization of such an idea within the postcolonial Caribbean state and regional projects, which have as yet been unable to shake off Western influence over their political and economic sovereignty, risks obscuring the political reality.

In his 1969 treatise, *The Groundings with My Brothers*, Guyanese historian Walter Rodney offers a noteworthy admonishment against an uncritical invocation of Caribbean unity by governmental forces. The text outlines Rodney's racial politics, rooted in a sense of global Black empowerment, in the wake of his being banned from Jamaica for inciting rhetoric perceived as a threat to Jamaica's strategic mythologization of national unity. Rodney devotes significant attention to analyzing how the governing elite conjures a false ideal of cultural and racial unity to stifle civic expression among the country's exploited Black population. Citing the example of Jamaica's instrumentalization of this ideal—by way of its national motto, "Out of Many, One People," a celebratory proclamation of the country's multiracial harmony—Rodney argues that this is a "hypocritical claim of the state regime," which obscures the racialized inequality "between the 'haves' and the 'have nots.'"[3] More specifically, Rodney reads the state's invocation of this myth as a rhetorical strategy designed to "confuse the people" so that it will not be challenged by the country's "clearly black" economically devastated population. Providing both an analytic and a corrective to the exclusion of Jamaica's Black citizens from the political decision-making process, *Groundings* also constitutes a sorely undervalued contribution to the practice of political deliberation and communication in the Caribbean.

In this latter regard, Rodney's text serves as a brilliant prelude to Édouard Glissant's more thoroughgoing dissection of the discursive means by which the idea of Caribbean unity engenders confusion. In "Le délire verbal," a seldom studied section of *Le discours antillais*, Glissant engages in a rhetorical analysis of communicative practices that have all but become legal custom—or what he calls "consuetudinary verbal delirium"—in the French Caribbean. In her reading of Glissant's concept, Celia Britton explains that verbal delirium expresses a psychopathology that enables the "occultation of social relations" in Glissant's native Martinique, where the system of neocolonial domination has been displaced to an elsewhere (France).[4] This avoidance strategy, argues Britton, explains the normalization of abnormal speech in French Caribbean society. For Glissant, verbal delirium attempts to salve the traumatic contradiction between who Martinicans are and "who they say they are" in the form of a compensatory linguistic excess—what in Spanish is referred to as "verborragia"—that is, "the art of saying nothing" while speaking a lot.[5] Effectively, Glissant also seems to be proposing a novel methodological account of Caribbean rhetoric.[6]

Given Glissant's theoretical acumen and his consistent, albeit critical engagement with the philosophical tradition of the West, in my view, his delineation of verbal delirium as a rhetorical art form suggests a debt to Aristotle's *Art of Rhetoric*, which Glissant naturalizes to the Antillean condition. It is generally agreed that the *Rhetoric*, although subject to considerable scholarly debate, serves as a manual on the most effective means of persuasive speech in deliberative communication. But whereas Aristotle's rhetoric presupposes the use of rational speech as a "faculty" to ascertain how to get people to agree on a given subject, Glissant notes that Antillean verbal delirium dispenses with the need to establish a coherent method, relying instead on the illusion that arises from the disorderly yet persuasive conflation and accumulation of words, ideas, and concepts.[7]

In a noteworthy passage in *Le discours antillais*, Glissant offers a damning instantiation of the compensatory rhetoric of Antillean hospitality, citing a 1979 article published in France's daily *Le Monde*, published by the former mayor of Guadeloupe's Gosier commune. In the article, Hélène waxes poetic about tourism in Guadeloupe and likens it to the "innate sense of hospitality" that birthed the Antilles as a multiracial and cross-cultural convergence of "multidimensional peoples."[8] Hélène's assessment of Guadeloupean hospitality relies on a notion of blood quantum that ascribes what one might call a biological cosmopolitanism to Guadeloupeans. In other words, given the Caribbean's multiracial constitution as a "meeting place of cultures," Guadelopeans, by extension, are therefore genetically predisposed to offer hospitality to (white European) tourists, whose blood they too share. Swiftly folding the present into the past, Hélène transmogrifies the forging of the Caribbean—through the violent colonial encounter of European settlement, Africans' enslavement, Indigenous dispossession, and Asian indentureship—into a harmonious narrative of Caribbean cosmopolitan hospitality that welcomes tourists with a "warm, fraternal reception." In turn, by citing Hélène's narrative as an example of verbal delirium, Glissant's text also elucidates how Caribbean hospitality operates through historical misdirection.

Overall, Kincaid, Walcott, Rodney, and Glissant's commentaries on the discursive construction of an illusory Caribbean that diverges from the everyday, lived experience of civil life on the ground suggest a deeply entangled relationship between Caribbean regional politics that are ostensibly attuned to citizens' interests and the logic of tourism. This chapter pursues these entanglements, but it does so by moving away from readings of Caribbean tourism as a practice that either solely centers on foreigners' consumption of the Caribbean or emphasizes Caribbean citizens' participation in the tourist labor economy as mere hosts. The experimental documentary *Migrant Discourse* (2006) by Barbadian visual artist Annalee Davis and the short story "Jamaica Farewell" (1982) by Puerto Rican raconteur Ana Lydia Vega are unique in their exploration of tourism not as a playground for foreign visitors to the Caribbean but rather as a regional political economy that seeps beyond the tourist spaces into the daily lives of Caribbean people who seek to exercise their right to be seen, heard, and counted as citizens and lawful subjects of the nation-states they call home. My readings of Davis and Vega's texts investigate how they play on the myth of a harmonious Caribbean that is mobilized by Caribbean regionalist projects to fuel the political economy of tourism that selectively re-presents Caribbean life and only works to confuse, distort, and silence what Caribbean subjects have to say about their lived experience.

This chapter revisits the idea that political representation is both a practice and right that fundamentally mobilizes the senses—hearing, sight, sound, touch, and even taste—as part of the process of making deliberative appeals. At the heart of *Migrant Discourse* and "Jamaica Farewell" is citizens' inability to make politically and juridically meaningful and consequential speech due to a constant distortion of the sense by the same Caribbean ecology enjoyed by tourists and navigated by Caribbean citizens alike. A paradisiacal Caribbean condensed into ambient sound challenges the intelligibility of the testimonies of undocumented Guyanese subjects depicted in Davis's film. Intoxicating material, gleaned from the environment and cultural objects, overwhelms the senses so as to derail the deliberative process of Caribbean delegates in Vega's story. In both works, elements of the Caribbean's cultural and natural ecology—music, sea, sunshine, singing birds, and food—are framed both in terms of their disruptive potential to the five senses and as a representative version of the Caribbean sold to tourists. This is not to say, however, that the local culture and environment are somehow foreign to Caribbean people, who, in fact, create and cultivate these for their own personal enjoyment and daily existence. At the same time, the foreign tourist is, for the most part, absent from both Davis and Vega's works, even as they gesture implicitly and explicitly to the invisible hand of tourism that extends its reach into national and regional Caribbean politics. What these texts illustrate, however, is how local culture, landscape, and environment are repackaged as sensuous forms of "Caribbeanness" that disorient Caribbean people's discursive constellation as citizens and policymakers. This capacity of citizens is described as the "space of appearance" in Hannah Arendt's *The Human Condition*.[9] It is not merely a space where one shows one's face for representation's sake but rather a space of speech that, in turn, leads to action.

DELIBERATIVE MISDIRECTION

In *Migrant Discourse* and "Jamaica Farewell," regional representational politics are fraught. They are disruptive. They are a far cry from the image of harmonious Caribbean peoples. And, especially, they are inhospitable to Caribbean citizens and even the leaders charged with representing them as the people and speaking on their behalf. Yet, as Davis and Vega elucidate in their works, the logic of hospitality produces a distorted sensory perception of Caribbean reality, and its hold over the very political economy that sustains Caribbean life likewise misdirects the perception of Caribbean subjects' spoken demands. Even more so, *Migrant Discourse* and "Jamaica Farewell" elaborate a connection between the sensorium of tourism and the sensorium of Caribbean politics, as they specifically pertain to the political expression of Caribbean citizens.

"THE SENSES DECEIVE"

Walter Ong famously defined the sensorium as the way in which different cultures relate to and make meaning of the world through the senses and, in particular, by organizing the senses to correspond with ways of perceiving, knowing, and being in the world. According to Ong, "The differences in cultures which we have just suggested can be thought of as differences in the sensorium, the organization of which is in part predetermined by culture while at the same time it makes culture."[10] That is to say, different cultures give priority to different senses by establishing a "ratio or balance of the senses."[11] But the terms "ratio" and "balance" may be misleading since they, in fact, denote not an equal division of the senses but rather their weighted import in a given culture based on a hierarchy of perceptual relevance. Of course, it is by now established that the sway of Western metaphysics over Western modernity presupposes "the privileging of sight and hearing over the other senses."[12] Because the philosophical tradition of the West demands that sense (meaning, understanding, knowledge) be made out of the sensations that originate in the sensory faculties, the ephemeral and subjective nature of taste and smell—and to a much less degree touch—means that they cannot always be counted on to offer the most reliable impression about an object of perception.[13]

The ratiocinative apportionment of the senses within a given culture's sensorium also extends to the dimension of politics. It is in the work of Jacques Rancière that the senses are reformulated within the domain of politics by way of his notion of the *partage du sensible*—the partitioning or, as it is more commonly translated, the "distribution" of the sensible that, Rancière argues, is constitutive of politics. Like Ong's "ratio," the semantic referent of "distribution" may give the impression that the senses share a more or less equal weight in the political domain than what Rancière's thinking actually denotes. The sensory nature that Rancière attributes to politics comes from the acute connections he weaves between aesthetics, the representational form of the faculty of sense, prefigured in the works of Plato, Aristotle, and, most importantly, Kant. Given the thematic constraints of this chapter, I attend to how Rancière makes these philosophical connections in three parts. First, he calls attention to the fact that in the *Politics* "Aristotle states that a citizen is someone who *has a part* in the act of governing and being governed."[14] More specifically, those who have a part use speech (logos) to make moral judgments. Second, he links Aristotle's political partitioning to his teacher Plato's "partitioning of the individual soul," which "was a partition of the collective social, which as a partition of the classes in the city."[15] In particular, Plato's division of the individual soul into reason, appetite, and emotions corresponds, in Rancière's terms, to a division between those who share in the governing of the common through reason and those "who cannot be put in charge of the common" because they are preoccupied with satiating the lower parts of the soul (appetite and emotion) through work. Last, this political partitioning fundamentally dictates "what is *seen* and what can be *said* about it, around those who have the ability to *see* and the talent to *speak*."[16] Ultimately, although Rancière locates in the partitioning of those who cannot speak, be heard, or seen in the common a radical "supplement"—the staging of politics as an interruption of the hierarchical ordering of humans—his distribution of the sensible nevertheless remains tethered to the primacy of sight and sound.

Still, when all is said and done, it becomes clear that the sensorium of politics is not so distinct from the sensorium of tourism in the Caribbean. Scholarly and narrative commentary on Caribbean tourism betrays a similar distribution of the senses. Recalling my point at the start of this chapter, the sensory reduction of the Caribbean premises both Jamaica Kincaid's and Derek Walcott's critiques of tourism. As if to drive this point home, Kincaid repeats in almost obsessive terms what the tourist sees—"you have not seen . . . you have seen . . . you see yourself."[17] This perceptual enclosure "must never cross" the tourist's mind."[18] Walcott's reference to tourist photography also centers on the ocular. Certainly, these entail a paradigmatic representation of what John Urry famously characterized as "the tourist" gaze.[19] Nevertheless, in these instances, the natives, for the most part, recede to the background, and when they do appear, they are filtered through the tourist's sensory perspective.

Davis's *Migrant Discourse* and Vega's "Jamaica Farewell" open up fresh and novel readings of the tourist sensorium at work in the Caribbean by showing how it structures and disorders the partitioning of political and juridical expression. To be clear, Davis and Vega are not merely rehearsing the truism that tourism, like nearly every cultural practice, is inherently political. Rather, if we redefine tourism as a partitioning of the senses through the disruptive work of pleasure that allows for the tourist to take a break from their reality, in my estimation, Davis and Vega also call for a redefinition of Caribbean regional politics as fundamentally touristic insofar as they mobilize the illusion of Caribbean unity—a rupture with political reality—by partitioning citizens' sensory faculties in ways that render their speech ineffective.

If, thus far, I have emphasized that the thematic of this chapter has *regional* implications, it is because *Migrant Discourse* explicitly and "Jamaica Farewell" more implicitly constitute critiques of the Caribbean's integration projects, specifically consolidated in the late twentieth century by the Caribbean Community and Common Market (CARICOM) and the related Caribbean Single Market Economy (CSME). Founded in 1973, at a time when most countries in the Caribbean had achieved formal political independence from their colonial metropoles, CARICOM sought to fortify the region's economic sovereignty through an intraregional trade bloc of member states.[20] By unifying the smaller economies of individual Caribbean countries, who "agreed upon a planned economic division of labor that encourages specialization in particular crops and industries,"[21] CARICOM could offset uneven competition between states, which were primed for exploitation by a rapidly globalizing market in which the lion's share of resources had been centralized in North America and Western Europe. Out of CARICOM, the CSME was birthed in 1989 to deepen regional socioeconomic integration and liberalize trade by promoting the free movement of people in the forms of "goods," "services," and "skills." This reduction of the Caribbean and its people according to their strategic usefulness does not seem that different from Aristotle's suggestion that a good society should be partitioned according to the contributions that its members make. This view is recapitulated in the context of the neoliberalization of Latin America and the Caribbean as a result of the United States' consolidation of its political and economic influence in the region through the aforementioned integration initiatives. Because tourism—and the hospitality industry writ large—fuels the political economy of the region, it shapes intraregional political practices, including the way CARICOM and CSME frame the rights of their member nations' citizens, who unavoidably navigate tourist spaces in various capacities, whether to make a living, socialize, or attend events that have an impact on Caribbean daily life.

In what follows, I investigate how Davis's *Migrant Discourse* and Vega's "Jamaica Farewell" compellingly challenge the idea of Caribbean unity and its rhetorical instrumentalization by these regional projects. Davis and Vega challenge the ideal of regional harmony through their depiction of the disruption and partitioning of the representative process, whether in the form of political speech or political deliberation, of Caribbean subjects. Moreover, their texts elucidate that this interruption occurs precisely because the economy of tourism controls and defines the system of regional political representation—perhaps in a much more insidious manner than the aforementioned regional integration projects are willing to concede. However, this is not, per Rancière, the promise of a radical interruption that brings forth a more authentic political community that makes itself seen and heard in new terms. This chapter is as much about listening and its associated difficulty as it is about speaking and the failure to cohere into what I call a senseful politics. Inasmuch as hearing and the cognition of what is heard are necessary for political speech to be of consequence, the disorderly system of representation disclosed by *Migrant Discourse* and "Jamaica Farewell" abandons the hierarchical distribution of the senses—most notably, its privileging of the ocular—that pervades the sensorium of Western cultural modernity. The sensorium of these texts draws from Caribbean material and sonic culture, gastronomy, landscape, and the environment, which activate the senses in ways that depart from the conventional tourist gaze as a means of both misdirecting the listening ear and distorting the spoken word.

Because this book is fundamentally about the estranging nature of citizenship in the Caribbean, one of the goals of this chapter is to bring to bear the sensory effects of the neoliberalization of the Caribbean, via tourism, on citizen representation. To this end, although *Migrant Discourse* was produced thirty-five years after the publication of Vega's story, I turn first to Davis's experimental documentary. I examine the Barbadian visual artist's transformation of the Caribbean ecology—sold in visual form to tourists as a representative ideal of the Caribbean—into non-diegetic, ambient sound that distorts the oral testimonies of Guyanese citizens living as undocumented workers in Barbados. Reading the film in light of Davis's own statements about the estrangement of Caribbean people by their own, I argue that the only way for Davis to represent this estrangement is through the film's dissonant coupling of the myth of regional harmony and the sensorium of tourism. I consider how the inhospitable treatment of Guyanese citizens, whose right of movement is supposedly guaranteed by CARICOM, discloses the aporia of hospitality in the form of tourism.

From my analysis of Davis's film, I take a backward glance at the early 1980s setting of "Jamaica Farewell," which more explicitly tackles the limitations of the regional integration projects that took shape in the Caribbean in the late twentieth century. Whereas Davis's film centers on the political speech of citizens, Vega's story focuses on group dynamics in its rehearsal of a scene of political deliberation between delegates from democratically aligned countries in the Caribbean as they attempt to negotiate economic and political outcomes on behalf of their respective nations. The idea of Caribbean unity and harmony appears as the ethos that is supposed to drive deliberate processes, even as reality rears its ugly head in the story's denouement to reveal the ethos as an illusion. The illusion, I contend, is conjured through the intoxication of the senses under the political self-interest of North America. I analyze the allegorical significance of the story's setting in a Jamaican tourist resort as the site of the partitioning of the senses. Overall, the spectator of *Migrant Discourse* and the reader of "Jamaica Farewell" will find themselves so drawn into the distorted sensory experience mobilized by these texts such that it becomes possible to read them as allegories of failed political discourse and deliberation.

Migrant Dissonance

Annalee Davis's eight-minute, thirty-second experimental documentary film *Migrant Discourse* has an arguably odd opening.[22] In the film's first five seconds, its soundscape grabs our attention with the faint roll of crashing ocean waves and the whistle of birds. It is an odd beginning because what we *see* during these first five seconds does not correspond with what we *hear*. In the film's visual frame appears a still image of four individuals—two men and two women—separated into four quadrants from indeterminate locations that disclose neither the presence of birds nor proximity to the sea. The stillness of the visual frame breaks when the first of these individuals speaks. From this point until the film's end, all of the other individuals break their silence and stillness in alternating fashion. From the accounts of two of them, we glean that they are all from Guyana but live in Barbados with fear and uncertainty due to the precarious nature of their illegal status. Their faces are notably indiscernible. Moving clockwise, from the upper right quadrant (see figure 1.1), an Afro-Guyanese woman holding a CARICOM brochure sits facing the camera, which hovers in the space between her lower bust and her knees; across from her, an Indo-Guyanese man appears at times blacked out as a shadow and at other times with his back turned toward us; below him sits another Afro-Guyanese woman under a mosquito net; across from her sits the Afro-Guyanese man, whose voice we first hear, with his back facing the camera as his shadow looms large against the stark white-walled room. Their concealment seems intentional and practical, for as undocumented Guyanese migrants in Barbados, their risk of exposure carries with it the penalty of detainment and deportation.

When we approach *Migrant Discourse* in its totality, however, it becomes hard to discern whether the experimental documentary's focal point is the story of its human subjects or the story of its soundscape, the latter of which occupies a larger-than-life role. As the film's undocumented migrants alternate in sharing their harrowing accounts of legal, economic, and sexual exploitation at the hands of Barbadian civilian authorities, businesses, and traffickers, ambient sounds of nature and the urban landscape—ocean waves, birds in flight, the faint crow of a rooster, footsteps in the sand, and the barely discernable passing of a transport vehicle—interpolate the documentary narrative from seemingly nowhere. Like the film's undocumented Guyanese subjects, its ambient sound is disturbingly out of place.

The ambient soundtrack of *Migrant Discourse* shares an uncanny resemblance to the ambient music trend, which has proliferated globally in the past decade or so. In their study of Australian ambient music, John Connell and Chris Gibson describe ambient music "as a means through which a very particular geography of landscapes and nature is constructed and vicariously experienced" through the production of generic and real sounds ascribed to places that are

Figure 1.1. Annalee Davis, *Migrant Discourse*, edited by Omar Estrada (2010, 8:27 minutes). https://www.youtube.com/watch?app=desktop&v=yA_VGjiy6AQ.

"both mythical and real."[23] This sonic vicariousness dates to the genre's emergence in the 1970s, in response to tourist demand for authentic "aural souvenirs" of remote places. The marketing of these aural souvenirs by certain host countries, as a form of sonic tourism, facilitates a certain construction of nationhood.[24] Connell and Gibson's analysis of ambient music betrays the genre's particular appeal to the nontraveler, who engages in a kind of passive, stationary tourism through which they sonically access a sensuous pleasure and relaxation ascribed to the experience of certain geographies and landscapes without necessarily having seen those places or even knowing the source of the ambient sound. Likewise, if we engage in a sensory experiment and bracket *Migrant Discourse*'s ambient soundtrack from the visual and spoken content of its undocumented Guyanese subjects, the film's ambient soundscape enacts a troublingly pleasing sway on the senses. Closing our eyes and ears to the film's testimonial narrative, an act the experimental documentary seems to demand of its audio spectators in order to distinguish its distinctive sonic registers, the ambient soundscape transports us to the scene of a tropical beach—a Caribbean beach many of the film's spectators have probably visited and experienced many times over.

Something otherwise unsettling and disorienting happens, however, when this sonic bracketing is foreclosed, and the film's ambient soundscape imposes itself upon the audiovisual frame of its speaking subjects. A sensory crisis ensues. It was once the case, as espoused in conventional film theory, that sound should settle us into the film's geography. Sound, traditional film criticism argues, binds the moving image to a place. And as Catherine Elwes recounts, sound was traditionally interpreted as a film's affective blueprint, "telling us how to feel about what we see."[25] This, according to noted film theorist Michel Chion, forms the basis of "the audio-visual contract"[26]—a symbolic contract in which the listening spectator understands and consents to sound's supporting role as "an added-value" to the visual.[27] This supporting role, Chion argues, derives from the now-debunked illusion that there exists a "natural harmony" between the visual image and sound.[28] Put another way, this more conventional understanding of cinematic sound discloses a sensorium that is in line with Western modernity's privileging of the ocular. Ambient sound, however, not only constitutes a genre separate from a film but also organizes a separate geography that takes shape in the imagination of the listener as a passive tourist. Thus, when it is coupled with the undocumented narrative of *Migrant Discourse*, in which visible persons make oral appeals about their geographic displacement, we experience a sensory crisis. And this crisis raises a series of questions. How do we listen? How do we listen *ethically*, responsibly, to the pained testimonies of Davis's undocumented subjects? For testimonies of this nature call for responsible listening. How do we avoid being displaced to a Caribbean elsewhere by the lull of the ambient soundscape, whose pleasing quality distracts from the pain of the speakers? How do we also make sense of the fact that the speakers are visually fragmented—in fact, symbolically decapitated?

I argue that Davis intentionally stages this sensory crisis to allegorize the out-of-placeness of the film's undocumented migrants and, in particular, the dislocation of the testimonial speech of the Guyanese nationals, who should, ostensibly, be protected under CARICOM's charter. My reading of *Migrant Discourse* analyzes how Davis stages this out-of-placeness as a form of sensorial dissonance between the sonority of non-diegetic ambient sound, the audibility of undocumented subjects' oral testimony, and the visual partitioning of the undocumented subjects' bodies on the screen. Furthermore, I investigate how the film's interpolation of ambient sound intercepts the spectating listeners' perceptual identification with the undocumented subjects' afflicted voices, expressed through their testimonial speech, which further underscores their transient nature as undocumented subjects. That their voices, their speech, and their physicality compete with the film's ambient soundscape for the audio viewer's somewhat frustrated attention allegorizes the partitioning of the senses within the logic of hospitality. These distinctive ecological sounds that coalesce to form the film's ambiance are representative of an idea of the Caribbean that is not only marketed to tourists but also constitutive of the shared experience of Caribbeanness described in Caribbean cultural theory. If, as I argue in this chapter, Caribbean hospitality is enacted through a sensorium that gives the illusion of Caribbean unity, the violent disharmony between the visual image and the sonic registers produces a disruption in sensorial perception, which, in turn, constitutes the nature of what I call Caribbean in/hospitality.

The sensorial dissonance of *Migrant Discourse* can be fully appreciated and grasped in light of the evolving critical space that Davis's aesthetic oeuvre dedicates to the uses and misuses of Caribbean discourse as an expression of a shared cultural and historical experience, with the Caribbean's regional political economy. A survey of Davis's work reveals a deeply attuned "visual artist, cultural instigator, educator, and writer" who is also a meticulous student of some of the Caribbean's most significant expositors of this shared historical and cultural experience.[29] This includes her Barbadian compatriot, Kamau Brathwaite, whose poetry, Michelle Stephens notes, is central to Davis's "critique of Caribbean unity" in a longer experimental documentary film *On the Map*.[30] In less explicit terms, it is also clear that Davis's critical aesthetics are informed by the likes of Glissant, who most notably codified the idea of a "Caribbean discourse,"[31] as well as his fellow Martinican writers Jean Bernabé, Patrick Chamoiseau, and Raphäel Confiant, whose *Éloge de la Créolité* canonized the Caribbean panegyric through their elucidation of *Creolité* or Creoleness as the emergent Caribbean cultural form resulting from the racial aggregation of arrivants to the region from Europe, Africa, Asia, and the Levant.[32] Davis's project, however, arrests the eulogistic vision of Caribbean cultural discourses through her gathering of the voices of Caribbean peoples who have been fragmented from the common and thus bespeak a "migrant discourse."

Migrant Discourse was spawned from two earlier works: the now-defunct *Project 45*, which subsequently morphed into the experimental documentary *On the Map* (2006–2007), both of which challenged the contradictions inherent in CARICOM's discriminatory immigration policies toward citizens of its member nations. The title of *Project 45* was a reference to Article 45 of the Revised Treaty of Chaguaramas, a 2001 emendation of CARICOM's founding charter. Article 45 commits CARICOM members "to the goal of free movement of their nationals within the Community."[33] Reading further, however, we discover that the promise of Article 45 is conditioned by Article 46, which not only prioritizes "university graduates, media works, sportspersons, artists, and musicians" but also engages in a dehumanizing reduction of the movement of people to the "movement of skills."[34] A thirty-two-minute film that features interviews from Barbadian officials, documented citizens, and Guyanese undocumented subjects whose stories Davis extracts to create *Migrant Discourse*, *On the Map* explores how the ideal of a shared Caribbean experience is sullied when co-opted by the integrationist promise of regional sovereignty buttressed by CARICOM. *On the Map* is not necessarily a disavowal of cultural theories of Caribbean unity. Rather, as Stephens argues in her study of the film, "it renders regional integration as being distinct from and detrimental to the work of community-building that is motivated by desires for decolonization."[35] Highlighting CARICOM's reshaping of the region through "neoliberal markets and mobility regimes," Stephens questions whether the Caribbean is an exemplar of cosmopolitanism, given that CARICOM's policies enact a politics of mobility that "privileges a cosmopolitan elite."[36] In light of proponents of a Caribbean cosmopolitanism, like Stuart Hall and Karen Fog Olwig, who respectively note that the region's "creolization, the cultural mix of different elements" signals its "openness to strangers," *On the Map* interrogates the import of such a concept in light of anti-immigrant sentiment toward Guyanese migrants in Barbados.[37] The film traces Barbadian people's ambivalent attitudes toward intraregional migrancy to the economic anxiety and precarity experienced by both Afro-Barbadians and Afro-Guyanese under British colonial domination.[38]

On the Map "debunks the myth of a unified, 'laid back' Caribbean culture" by contrasting "images of beach, golf course and paradise with the reality of Caribbean living, victimization and abuse," as Davis details on her personal website.[39] I hesitate on Davis's aforementioned statement, for I find the specific terms with which she maps her overarching project evocative, if not deliberate, to the extent that they locate intra-Caribbean disunity at the nexus of a semiotic dislocation between the *image* and the *reality* of a Caribbean enshrined by *myth*.

As Roland Barthes elucidates in *Mythologies*, myth does not necessarily conceal reality but rather produces a "certain knowledge of reality" that is divested of its historical context.[40] Expanding Saussure's structuralist interpretation of myth, Barthes shows that myth unfolds as a "second-order semiological system" instead of an uninterrupted equation from a signifier to signified that, in turn, produces a sign.[41] Expanding the semiotic chain of mythification, Barthes argues that "myth is depoliticized speech" that discloses a meaning, form, and concept.[42] The "meaning" of myth is its denotative, literal content, its "sensory reality" as we grasp it with our eyes. Taking *On the Map* as an example, myth's meaning is the image of beach, golf course, and paradise. However, when myth's meaning assumes a particular form—a statement, a story, or an image—it is drained of history.[43] For Barthes, this form is a distortion of the meaning. Accordingly, when "the myth of a unified, laid-back Caribbean culture" takes on the form of an image of Caribbean beach, golf course, and paradise, this image is divested of the history that Davis identifies as the "reality of Caribbean victimization and abuse," which has fundamentally colonial underpinnings. Barthes's semiotic chain is particularly compelling, given that the French theorist explicitly evokes colonialism—as both history and metaphor—to show how the propagation of the mythical form produces a clouded and distorted concept of postcoloniality.[44] Thus, Barthes states, "myth . . . is a robbery by colonization."[45] Barthes suggests that myth defers and distorts our interpretation of its full, historical meaning by robbing that which it represents of the capacity to provide contextual language. If the form drains myth of its history, the signified concept absorbs this history and allows for "a whole new history . . . to be implanted in the myth."[46]

Let us further consider Barthes's colonial metaphor by way of Davis's invocation of "the myth of the unified, 'laid-back' Caribbean culture." This myth takes the form of what we might collectively call Caribbean discourse—those ideas about the Caribbean that, as Davis argues, are "fashionably debated in first world academic centers" or, notably, the political rhetoric of the Revised Treaty of Chaguaramas. This mythical speech about the Caribbean emerges as concepts that, following Barthes, "distort" their full meaning. The form of Caribbean discourse distorts the fact that "the unified, 'laid-back' Caribbean culture" can exist only when certain Caribbean subjects are excluded from the promise of integration. It distorts the discontent that Barbadians feel about certain Guyanese migrants. This distortion, I argue, is made possible through the geopolitical concept of Caribbean hospitality.

In *Paradise and Plantation: Tourism in the Anglophone Caribbean*, Ian Strachan productively situates the discourse of Caribbean paradise as hospitality within a colonial mythology rife with stark contradictions. The pleasure experienced by Columbus and his crew of Spaniards in their encounter with the Caribbean's otherworldly beauty later compelled the extraction of its material resources via the "blood and sweat of the Taino and African."[47] Importantly, Strachan likewise emphasizes how Columbus and his European heirs laid the ground for the extractive enterprise of coloniality by imputing on this paradise a sense of unconditional hospitality. Paradise is paradise because it raptures and seduces its European "guests" with accommodating and uncritical welcome. *Paradise and Plantation* tracks the colonial bequeathal and transformation of this paradisial discourse within the contemporary Caribbean tourist industry, as exemplified by the propagandistic romanticization of the charming, cheerful, and acquiescent demeanor of the industry's overwhelmingly Black service workers in places like the Bahamas and Barbados.[48] According to Strachan, these representations of Black hospitality workers resemanticize the history of the plantation and the labor of enslaved Blacks who are held at the level of myth, thereby clouding the reality.[49] This chapter considers how the mythification of paradise clouds the senses of Caribbean delegates who unknowingly adopt the sensibilities of tourists with respect to the interests of their respective nations.

This mythical transmogrification of Caribbean paradise within the economy of modern tourism has been primarily fortified, as work historian Krista Thompson shows, by a visual regime that, beginning in the late nineteenth century, deployed the medium of photography to portray the Caribbean as a zone of idyllic exploration and pleasure to fuel "the seminal period in tourist development."[50] Drawing on the work of J. Michael Dash, Frances Aparicio, and Susana Chávez-Silverman, Thompson describes this visual regime as *tropicalization* or *tropicality*, "complex visual systems through which the islands were imagined for tourist consumption and the social and political implications of these representations on actual physical space and their inhabitants." Accordingly, within the regime of tropicalization, tourism promoters developed and used staged, picturesque images of the Caribbean island landscape that they "purported to be realistic representations of the islands when ideals of the tropics had long transformed, indeed constituted, the environment featured in the photographs."[51] These images atomized the geographic and demographic diversity of the Caribbean—in a manner described by Walcott—collapsing both inorganic and organic matter such that the Caribbean becomes iconized as natural ecology, as sea, as fauna, as landscape. Likewise, Caribbean people represented in these images are mapped onto Caribbean topography and absorbed by the landscape such that their personhood becomes secondary and inconsequential.

If the myth of Caribbean hospitality flourishes through a visual regime in which Caribbean people are reduced to landscape, *Migrant Discourse* constitutes an act of demythification insofar as it engages in a sensory partitioning of this regime in a twofold manner. First, *Migrant Discourse* draws out and differentiates Caribbean people—the undocumented migrants—from the natural ecology, allowing them to exist as self-contained subjects with bodies and voices. Second, Davis transforms the Caribbean's natural ecology, what is normally configured through a strictly visual regime, into what Pierre Schaeffer and Jérôme Peignot call "acousmatic sound"—sound that is heard without the ability to see or identify its source. In *Treatise on Musical Objects*, Schaeffer argued that the acousmatic calls for "pure listening," a type of focused listening that allows the listener to discover that the inferences made about a given sonic object are "in reality, merely seen, and explained by context."[52] Such inferences create confusion about the nature of what we are hearing. Certainly, when ambient sound overlays the oral testimonies of the undocumented speakers, *Migrant Discourse* demands pure listening. Because the sounds come from seemingly nowhere, *Migrant Discourse* also demands a constant reorientation and inclination of the body toward and away from the screen to discern and make sense of what exactly these ambient sounds are. At the same time, this act of pure listening can go for only so long, as it is hard to overlook the visual presence of the film's speaking subjects. Because myth, per Barthes, entails the depoliticization of speech through a contextual robbery, contra Schaeffer, I propose that *Migrant Discourse* enacts a demythification of the myth of Caribbean unity by reorienting the contextualization of these ambient sounds in relation to the visual and sonic presence of its undocumented Guyanese subjects.

This is a fundamentally phenomenological reorientation of the senses as they are conventionally organized and categorized within the neoliberal sensorium of Western postmodernity. Experimental documentary films like *Migrant Discourse* have been recognized for their capacity to challenge what philosopher of sound Salomé Voegelin calls the "sovereignty of the visual . . . within the philosophical tradition the West."[53] By turning the image into a soundscape, *Migrant Discourse* enables us to apprehend how the visual image is a distortion insofar as ambient sound disrupts our ability to listen to the speakers' testimony. It is here that we see the discursive opposition between Caribbean discourse and what

Davis calls "Migrant Discourse." By moving from the visual to the audiovisual, the intercalation of overpowering ambient sound disrupts the reality principle undergirding the testimonial narrative. Thus, as the speakers tell us about their experience of inhospitality, the sonic overpowers their speech; it constitutes a distortion in our ability to hear *as understanding*.

As a subject of *Migrant Discourse*, the ambient sound has its own history and worlding that both is contained within and exceeds the history of Caribbean migrant mobility in the documentary. The presence of the oceanic in the film's soundscape conjures the historical gravity of sea and water, writ large, in the symbolic repertoire of Caribbean poetics. "The sea," Derek Walcott declares in his monumental poem, "is history."[54] Water, in the words of Trinidadian-Canadian writer Dionne Brand, is "another country" that harbors the painful inheritance of those in the African diaspora.[55] This same sea, in Aimé Césaire's *Notebook of a Return to the Native Land*, rolls on the "shins of the beach."[56] Thinking through the symbolic space of water in Caribbean art, Elizabeth DeLoughrey and Tatiana Flores observe that "Caribbean literature and cultural practices have long engaged with the ocean as both dystopian origin and aquatopian future: a space of origins of the transatlantic Middle Passage."[57] In the recent present, they continue, "these oceanic imaginaries of unification must also be placed in dialogue with how migration crises position Caribbean Sea as space of loss and fragmentation." The oceanic speaks to the history of those who have come ashore, not necessarily as tourists but as dispossessed and displaced strangers. Although the undocumented Guyanese subjects of *Migrant Discourse* arrive to Barbados not by water but rather by plane, the oceanic soundscape blurs time and space in the geography of Caribbean tourism. Glissant's poetics of the beach in *Poétique de la Rélation* recapitulates this transhistorical transmutation of the sea: the tidewater that expels enslaved Africans, identified by Glissant as deportees, from the cargo of ships onto the shores of the New World Caribbean also flows and coalesces into the tourist beach, "collapsing in the end into the pleasures of sand."[58] The pleasure of the tourist beach dissipates, however, when we attend to the distressed speech of the contemporary migrant subjects of Davis's film.

Six seconds after the film's opening, an unnamed Afro-Guyanese man utters the film's first spoken lines: "Well, I leave my country hoping that it would be better here because things was tough back then. I had two kids to support. I remember when I first came here. And I started working as a carpenter. And I was only earning about two hundred dollars a week and another carpenter told me they were getting a hundred . . . a hundred dollars a day and so on." As he speaks, unseen ocean waves faintly fill the soundscape. Their cadence suggests a continuous oscillatory roll into the shore and a recession. The accompanying sound of birds singing remains steady but low, as if riding sonically high above the ocean waves, which have now grown more powerful. The birdsong becomes increasingly louder as it synchronizes with the sound of rapidly flapping wings

DELIBERATIVE MISDIRECTION

that supplement the final part of his statement: "a hundred dollars a day and so on." The motility implied by the sonority of the birdsong of birds and ocean waves corresponds with and even augments this man's story of migrant movement from his native Guyana to Barbados. The dissonance between his speaking voice and an ambient sound with no source of origin underscores the dissonance, implied in his statement, between his weekly salary of two hundred fifty dollars compared to that of a carpenter, more than likely from Guyana, earning a hundred dollars a day. As he concludes the first segment of his testimony, the ocean waves and the song of birds in flight, now at a higher pitch, escort his voice away from our sonic perception, returning him visually to a motionless state.

This same high-pitched singing of the birds ushers in the film's next speaker, an Afro-Guyanese woman, hidden under a long, suspended mosquito net and seated in the foreground of trees. Situated in the lower-right quadrant of the screen, the veiled woman admits, "I would like to say that being illegal is scary. It is hard." When she expresses that "being illegal is scary" the singing temporarily stops and we simply hear the roar of the ocean crashing; when she continues, "It is hard," the singing of birds resumes alongside the short-lived and barely perceivable crow of a rooster. This concludes her first line. And with it, the flapping wings of birds in flight grows louder. Her hands can be seen moving below the net before she returns to stillness. Later, she clarifies the nature of her angst: "It is very scary in the sense that . . . you are always wondering if something's going to happen." She is besieged by a constant sense of uncertainty about the unknown and, specifically, by the threat that the unknown poses to her already precarious status. Her life, like the sporadic flapping wings of birds interwoven into the soundtrack of *Migrant Discourse*, is up in the air. The sentiment of fear expressed by this unsettled, undocumented Guyanese woman, coupled with the ambient sounds of fleeting nature that permeate the film, calls attention to the particularly sensorial dissonance of this experimental film. Elements of this sonic pattern repeat, with slight variations, as each of its four undocumented Guyanese subjects breaks their stillness to provide alternating accounts of helplessness in the face of juridical exploitation.

If oceanic sound suggests the ever-so-faint distinction between the dystopian migrant crossing of Caribbean peoples and the pleasureful beach enjoyed by tourists, in my view, the sound of birds in flight belies the promise of sovereignty. In the political mythology of the West, birds often symbolize independence. Their song articulates a cry of freedom that is iconized visually by their flight. But they often foretell disaster, as in the case of modern cinema's most iconic depiction of avian horror, Alfred Hitchcock's *The Birds*.[59] In Hitchcock's film, the seagulls that herald what has been described as the "civilizational collapse" of a seemingly tranquil California seaside town emit a garish whistle that produces an almost equal amount of discomfort as the pecking that ensues when they rain down on the town's inhabitants. The birds force those who are fortunate enough to elude their attacks into a state of indoor confinement. Inasmuch as Hitchcock's birds constitute "a symbol of anarchic and spiraling violence," they also portend the loss of freedom, sovereignty—that most coveted and promised right conferred by Western modernity.[60] The birdsong in *Migrant Discourse* contrasts with the pained cry held back from the camera by the Afro-Guyanese woman's cracked voice and tears. Like the terror brought on by the birds, "being illegal is scary" for this Afro-Guyanese woman because her freedom hangs in the balance.

Scholars of both film and voice are keen to distinguish between the sound produced by the human voice and speech as the articulation of logos. Moreover, when one speaks of "sound," this term must be provisionally qualified, for as film theorist Michal Chion notes, sound consists of a broad category constituted by speech (that which is produced by a human voice), music, and noise.[61] Aristotle posited the logos of humans as the articulation of speech possessing a moral character, which is distinguished from voice that elicits pleasure and pain common to animals. In *For More Than One Voice*, Adriana Cavarero underscores that Aristotle's inheritance of Western political philosophy makes it so that "through discussion and deliberation, the citizen of the democratic *polis* shows himself to be a *zoon logon echon*—one who knows full well the political role of speech."[62] This is the self-revelatory nature of speech theorized more contemporarily by Arendt. Speech reveals the citizen-subject, sonically and visually.

One is left to wonder to what extent the oral testimonies of *Migrant Discourse*'s subjects could even be considered speech, or how revelatory is their speaking, considering that their heads are removed from the frame. Indeed, I contend, *Migrant Discourse* enacts a failed deliberation not only through the distortion of their oral testimonies by the intercalation of ambient sound but also through the very fact that the undocumented subjects articulate that they are not being listened to. For example, the film's Indo-Guyanese subject states, "He went for me at the airport. I gave him all my documents. I gave him all of my documents to look after my work permit under the influence that I was being looked after." Describing the person who picks him up upon his arrival to Barbados, he recapitulates what is ostensibly the failed promise of Articles 45 and 46 of the Revised Treaty of Chaguaramas. But this impression that he would be looked after also suggests a belief in the idea of Caribbean unity espoused by the regional integration project. He continues, "When I went, he told me that he knows people in the immigration office that would look after me . . . he have contacts. When I asked him for a letter he refused and put me out of his yard." This statement affirms the denial of the recognition of speech but also the denial of hospitality. His words, like those of the other three migrants, never coalesce into *logos*, politically consequential speech worthy of recognition. While he's talking, you hear the ocean waves and the sound of birds singing. It remains as voice, suggesting his and the others' dehumanization as undocumented.

How, then, do we simultaneously listen to and see dissonant subjects whose constitution in the film demands that we listen to and see them separately but interrelatedly? In certain moments, the speakers disappear from my gaze as I attempt to both earnestly listen to what they are saying about their experiences and capture the sonic expression of ambient sounds in constant flight. This way of listening is a consequence of the film's sonic composition: the recording of the speakers—their bodies, voice, and speech—has its own ambiance that does not match the recording of the ambient sounds, which appear blatantly unrealistic.[63] The tension between pleasure and pain, between *Migrant Discourse*'s sonic mixed messages, makes perceiving and apprehending the discursive content of *Migrant Discourse*'s undocumented subjects rather uneasy. It is uneasy because it suggests a complicit disregard for the fundamental violence that Davis intends to highlight. It requires sensorial disharmony. This, I argue, is the violence of Caribbean hospitality, which renders the undocumented Guyanese subject inhospitable to the gaze and the ear.

Political Intoxication

In "Jamaica Farewell," writer Ana Lydia Vega also develops a critique of the failure of political deliberation in an even more direct manner, given the story's recapitulation of what it may have been like for Caribbean countries to negotiate their rights and responsibilities as part of the Caribbean Community's efforts to consolidate the region's capacity for democratic self-government. In the deliberative process depicted by Vega, the transmutation of speech into politically decisive action is foreclosed by a series of interruptions. My close reading of "Jamaica Farewell" attributes these interruptions to sensuous material that is intentionally introduced in the deliberative process to distort and misdirect the communicative process. We glean that this sensory material marshals all the five senses in a matter that could be aptly described as "political intoxication." Thus, Vega asks us to think about the deliberative process in terms not exclusive to sight and hearing, the traditional metaphors for knowledge and understanding, respectively.

Vega's story is set in late 1980 Jamaica, where, under the auspices of the United States, delegates from countries in the Greater and Lesser Antilles (with the notable and intentional absence of Cuba and Grenada) have gathered to iron out their differences with the goal of forging mutually beneficial economic agreements. Amid the negotiations, "Jamaica Farewell" fixes on its central character, Martinique's delegate, who appears more like a Western tourist than a native Caribbean subject. His political investment in the gathering is constantly sidetracked by folkloric and atavistic expressions of Caribbean unity and harmony.

Following the meeting's closure, the Martinican delegate wanders the streets of Kingston while musing, enraptured, that "el Caribe era, en verdad, una sola patria" (the Caribbean was, indeed, a single homeland).[64] No sooner than making this pronouncement does the menacing shadow of a shabby, dreadlocked Rastafarian thief appear to quash the fantasy of Caribbean harmony. With the mugger's knife pressed against his neck, the delegate attempts to reason with his demand for money, rattling off in Kreyol, French, Spanish, and English, "Nou fwè we brothers, Caraïbes, Caribe, West Indies . . . Understand?"[65] Frustrated by his victim's meaningless and patronizing chatter, the thief presses the knife deeper, insisting a second time, "Shit, man, give me money." Closing the story with this line, Vega strategically deprives readers of witnessing the delegate's reaction to the robber. Leaving us to ponder instead the monetary demand that is simultaneously a denial of a filial politics of recognition, Vega lays bare the material asymmetries that divide Caribbean nations and cast a shadow over the political valence of narratives of cultural Caribbean synthesis. It is us as readers, then, who come to the realization that it is a narrative built on illusion.

If Vega's depiction of the Martinican delegate's violent encounter with the Caribbean "reality" of the street recalls the contrast between the paradisiacal Caribbean of the beach and the reality of Caribbean hardship in Davis's film, it is because Vega too wants to highlight how intra-Caribbean hospitality traffics in a shortsighted version of the myth of Caribbean harmony. The story's depiction of the Martinican delegate's distorted perception of this also belies what appears to be a more or less affable gathering, with a few minor but expected hiccups, among Caribbean delegates at a Jamaican hotel. Yet this encounter, in fact, illuminates the more nuanced instances of unresolved misunderstanding and disagreement that, although attenuated and pushed under the rug of diplomatic pleasantries, bespeckle the entirety of Vega's story. Following the Martinican delegate's wandering outside the comfort of the tourist resort allows us to see more clearly what is really at stake when we turn our attention backward. The inhospitable streets of Kingston, where the *real* Caribbean is unveiled and where the delegate receives no understanding or welcome as a "brother," are but a jarring parallel to what goes misperceived and, as in *Migrant Discourse*, veiled as Caribbean hospitality within the enclosure of the tourist resort.

In "Jamaica Farewell" Vega elaborates a brilliant account of political deliberation and its successful failure. From this vantage point, my reading of "Jamaica Farewell" unfolds along three lines of inquiry. First, I situate the story within the context of Ana Lydia Vega's explicitly pan-Caribbeanist narrative project, which harkens back to Caribbean intellectuals writing in the wake of both Latin American emancipation in nineteenth century and the decolonization of the British Caribbean in the twentieth century. Turning to theories of political deliberation, rhetoric, and persuasion, I describe this failure as "successful" because it betrays a strategy of sensorial redirection and misdirection, orchestrated under the aegis of the United States, to both secure its neoliberal domination over the Caribbean and disrupt the elaboration of an effective project of regional and national sovereignty by emphasizing a cultural politics of Caribbean unity.

Although "Jamaica Farewell" has gone unnoticed in the extensively critical commentary generated by the collection of which it forms a part, *Encancaranublado y otros cuentos de naufragio* (1983), it is paradigmatic of Ana Lydia Vega's oeuvre, which often thematizes intra-Caribbean relations. As the title, *Encancaranublado y otros cuentos de naufragio*, suggests, Vega is keenly interested in incongruous or, to use a common metaphor in her work, "shipwrecked" encounters between Caribbean subjects. One of Puerto Rico's master raconteurs, Vega infuses her prose with searing social and political commentary combined with dark humor in order to reflect more specifically on Puerto Rican national identity, which, as various scholars have noted, she deems "first and foremost Caribbean."[66] A leading figure of Puerto Rico's literary generation of the 1970s, a generation marked by genealogical rupture, a nationalist ethos, and a critical stance toward the island's neocolonial relationship to the United States, Vega finds in the plurivocality of the Caribbean an antithesis to what Ricardo Gutiérrez Mouat describes as the *"grand récit"* of "utopian . . . racial and sexual harmony" at a time when the lived experience of Puerto Ricans is one tainted by racialized and gendered "socioeconomic contradiction."[67]

A scholar of Francophone Caribbean literature who, as a professor of French at the University of Puerto Rico, also contributed to the formation of an entire generation of Puerto Rican cultural producers working across Francophone studies, Vega also betrays a particular affinity for the French Caribbean in her writing, as evidenced in "Jamaica Farewell."[68] This affinity is not accidental but rather informed by the kindred political status that Puerto Rico shares with Guadeloupe and Martinique to their respective metropolitan protectorates—the United States and France, respectively. The basis of this affinity is summarized by Sylvia Wynter, who notes what has been common to Caribbean people across the archipelago is their exclusion "from all autonomous processes of decision-making with respect to one's fate as a collectivity."[69] Making collective decisions about one's political fate is one of the key constitutive elements of citizenship in a democratic society. Likewise, in her reflection on "the sovereignty problem" and "the status question" specific to Puerto Rico, anthropologist Yarimar Bonilla captures the crux of the geopolitical affinities between Puerto Rico's redefinition as an Estado Libre Asociado (ELA) of the United States, or Free Associated State, in 1953 and the departmentalization of Guadeloupe and Martinique by France in 1946.[70] As Bonilla notes, for many Puerto Ricans, the debates over Puerto Rico's status constitute a "political impasse" rife with "uncertainties and contradictions," given that the benefits of U.S. citizenship belie the "unequal" economic and political "incorporation, marginalization, and exclusion of Puerto Ricans in the mainland."[71] Likewise, the collapse of the anticolonial struggle in

Martinique and Guadeloupe and their seemingly acquiescent surrender to French dependency has posed a bit of a conundrum and a sense of disappointment among decolonial thinkers. This historical reality notwithstanding, for Bonilla, Puerto Rico and the French Caribbean's nonsovereignty within the broader sovereign Caribbean should be seen not as exceptional but rather as a more glaring and naked representation of the fact that the "*majority* of Caribbean polities are non-sovereign," struggling to "assert control over their entanglements with foreign powers," while presenting to their subjects an illusion of sovereignty.[72]

Nowhere has the unmasking of this illusion been felt more viscerally than in postcolonial Jamaica, the setting of "Jamaica Farewell." A nod to the eponymous calypso song popularized by Jamaican crooner, actor, and activist Harry Belafonte, "Jamaica Farewell" might also be read as a lamentation of the failure of the progressive, anti-imperial politics heralded by Michael Manley's People's National Party (PNP), which brought hope and the promise of freedom to poor, disenfranchised Jamaicans—a politics that may be irrecoverable, like the enchanting Jamaican life serenaded by the singer as he says his goodbyes. Under Manley's first two terms as prime minister of Jamaica from 1972 to 1980, Jamaica appeared to adapt a democratic socialist ethos, notably defined by land reform, the nationalization of foreign-owned utility companies, free education, and an internationalist foreign policy that expressed support for African decolonization and Caribbean decolonial politics. It is this ethos that fueled the United States' intervention in Jamaica's economy and its alliance with the PNP's opposition, the conservative and neoliberal Jamaica Labour Party (JLP), ultimately forcing Manley to rescind a promise he made to his base to resist imperialism by succumbing to the "help" and influence of the International Monetary Fund (IMF) in 1977. What many Jamaicans viewed as internal contradictions between Manley's words and actions, coupled with an economic crisis of structural adjustment that brought about the devaluation of the Jamaican dollar and a wage freeze as a condition of the IMF's support, led the JLP, helmed by Jamaica's Reagan-friendly prime minister Edward Seaga, to victory in the elections of October 1980. More importantly, Seaga was instrumental in consolidating U.S. neoimperial influence in the postcolonial Caribbean in terms described as a "Mini-Marshall Plan."[73] Invoked as a passing mention in "Jamaica Farewell," Seaga's "triumph" elicits a toast among the gathering of delegates.[74] Yet the story's momentary gesture to Seaga's legacy sheds light on the economic desperation that produces the story's thief misrecognition of a bond with the Martinican delegate.

Set against the backdrop of a Caribbean still reeling from the lingering ephemera of this not-so-distant history, "Jamaica Farewell" seems to ask what exactly political deliberation means for Caribbean nations whose capacity to make decisions and to consent to such decisions concerning their functioning and well-being, the very meaning of sovereignty, is usurped. Vega allegorically emplots

DELIBERATIVE MISDIRECTION

the history of the postcolonial Caribbean's juridical stalemate into the narrative framework of "Jamaica Farewell," where key moments of contentious political deliberation between the Caribbean delegates are repeatedly misdirected, redirected, and eventually stalled, requiring the "aplazamiento definitivo de los trabajos del congreso hasta el año siguiente" (the indefinite postponement of the congress's assignments until the following year).[75] As Vega's story evolves, we glean how the senses of hospitality are mobilized to derail and neutralize whatever possible opposition this postponement, rendering void the delegates' responsibility to their constituents back home.

The Martinican delegate's inability to process that he is being robbed by a Jamaican subject who neither understands nor shares his appeal to a Caribbean brotherhood can be understood within the context of the story's subtle yet significant depictions of sensorial distortion. The tourist enclosure exists both within and beyond the literal physical enclosure. In "Jamaica Farewell," all of the five senses are activated for the purpose of thwarting debate and feeding the illusion of intraregional harmony. Let us consider and unpack some notable examples:

taste: from the opening line, Vega's text suggests that political thinking among representative Caribbean states will be subject to the influence of "el ron jamaicano en la cabeza" (Jamaican rum in the head);[76] or, further ahead, the daiquiris offered by the United States to prevent Martinique and Trinidad from coming to blows over disputes about the superiority of their respective national literary icons, Aimé Césaire and V. S. Naipaul;[77] or, in the final day of the gathering, when the "tamaña hartura" (colossal stuffing) of food puts them in a food coma[78]—effectively, a type of political brain death that places the political work of the gathering in abeyance until the following year.

touch: the sprinkle of ocean mist that reaches over the hotel's seawall to "baptize" their bodies every so often.[79]

sight: an "obstinately red" setting sun, a contradictory ill omen that serves to introduce, in the next line, the blinding hegemonic presence of the United States, who, as the presiding figure, conjures the illusory discourse of intra-Caribbean "democracy" and "welfare."[80]

smell: the pleasant smell of sugar molasses that dominates the "spicy" sessions.[81]

sound: the "arrullo turístico de calypso" (touristic murmur of calypso),[82] or the orchestra that intervenes "heroically" at opportune moments with a "unitary soka" (mobilized alongside the pacifying daiquiris) or a "medley of salsa, merengue, and reggae" to silence the Martinican delegate's politically incorrect jeremiad.[83]

The aforementioned elaboration of the sensorium at work in "Jamaica Farewell" suggests the failure of political deliberation that arises from the effects of political intoxication. In his brief and playful treatise *Intoxication*, Jean-Luc Nancy tells us that philosophy and poetry—along with reason and its polarity, passion—produce effects that are akin to the experience of physical intoxication.[84] To engage in rational or passionate discourse entails a dissolution of the self, the effects of being taken over by knowledge. But the Caribbean body, especially, as Guillermina De Ferrari has argued, is prone to a bodily vulnerability[85]—in its constitution and appropriation by Western discourses of reason, in such a fashion that this vulnerability may, in fact, resemble intoxication. However, in "Jamaica Farewell," intoxication occurs through an overwhelming of the senses not by discourses external to the Caribbean but rather by its very own cultural and natural ecology. Constituted within the enclosure of hospitality, metaphorized by the tourist resort, this cultural and natural ecology is turned against the Caribbean subject via the discourse of Caribbean unity, which renders them malleable to persuasive actions that are not in their best interest.

Turned against itself by a touristic appropriation of Caribbeanness, the Caribbean is placed at a deliberative impasse so that it cannot even decide whether it wants to decide. In order to understand how this deferral happens, it is important to comprehend the story's emphasis on the violence of this sensory experience. The postponement of the congress is but the culmination and the effect of a series of sensorial interruptions that take place throughout the text. In fact, the story tells us, politics is a touchy thing, referencing "el cosquilloso tema de la emigración Haitiana" (the touchy subject of Haitian immigration).[86] The literal translation of "cosquilloso" here would be "ticklish." Something that is touchy suggests sensitivity, thin-skinned. Caribbean politics, as seen in "Jamaica Farewell" itself, creates an affective alteration—a type of sensitivity or awkwardness when confronted by the realization that Caribbean brotherhood is conditional and illusory. Not incidentally, the text uses the same two words in different contexts: the blade against the Martinican's neck is "cosquillosa" (ticklish), the theme of Haitian immigration is also "cosquilloso" (touchy). Politics are prickly. The emotionally heightened nature of political deliberation in this gathering of Caribbean nations is *like* the experience of having a knife to your throat. There is, in fact, no room for negotiation, even if the rules of engagement state otherwise. The difference, however, is that the robber is direct about his needs, whereas political diplomacy calls for a more indirect touch. On the street, the threat level is intensified. Inside the tourist resort, the touchiness of the threat is more subtle yet much more destructive. But even as the story suggests parallels between these encounters, it is important not to lose sight of the power dynamics at play in the text.

Indeed, "Jamaica Farewell" makes evident the rather self-interested and strategic nature of international political deliberation in a scene where the United States promises to guide the Caribbean nations at hand "por la senda de la democracia y el bienestar económico, a cambio de algunos kilometrillos de cada uno de ellos para la instalación de discretas bases nucleares perfumadas al neutrón" (down the path of democracy and economic well-being in exchange for a few tiny kilometers from each for the installation of discrete nuclear bases perfumed with neutrons)—a sly gesture to the U.S. Navy's appropriation of the island of Vieques, a municipality of Puerto Rico, which it subsequently turned into a bomb testing site. The so-called "deliberative democracy" espoused by the United States is conditioned by the ever-present threat of war embedded within the equation of democratic exchange. The United States mobilizes the alchemy of "perfume" to misdirect the Caribbean delegates from perceiving extractive logic of neoliberalism. The faculty of smell, I contend, conditions the ability to make sound judgment. Thus, Vega's text corroborates that if consensus is to be achieved within a plural community or gathering, the content of the deliberation must, in fact, be compelling and persuasive. The Martinican delegate is so engulfed in his own delirium of cosmopolitan hospitality that he cannot discern and cannot see the threat of the war.

The threat of war is intensified by the loss of brotherly recognition between Caribbean subjects who encounter themselves as strangers. This encounter exposes the failed deliberation of intra-Caribbean discourse. The Martinican delegate's response to the demand for money—"Nou fwè we brothers, Caraïbes, Caribe, West Indies. . . . Understand?"—rehearses the elements of persuasive deliberation outlined by Aristotle in his *Rhetoric*. Aristotle famously enumerated three means by which the rhetorician can engage in persuasion through deliberative speech: *ethos*, which appeals to the moral character and trustworthiness of the listener; *pathos*, which is designed to change the disposition of the *listener* by working on their feelings; and *logos*, which emphasizes the strength of the speech itself.[87] In "Jamaica Farewell," the Martinican somewhat desperately evokes all three forms. He mobilizes *ethos* through the plurilingual invocation of Caribbean brotherhood in an attempt to make himself trustworthy to the Jamaican thief by removing the chasm of strangeness. Moreover, claiming brotherhood, he engages in a *pathos* appeal to the offender based on presumed affective kinship. And, as a last resort, he avails himself of *logos* in the solicitation of cognitive understanding. Yet, he fails on all three accounts. He does not succeed in echoing Aristotle to "discover the right and effective means of persuasion," for his appeal to brotherhood is modulated by a "broken voice" and textured by a "gaze clouded by fear" that would be expected of tourists and not of a so-called confrère. In the robber's eyes, this is, recalling Glissant, the manifestation of a verbal delirium—the art of saying nothing while speaking a lot. Rambling off senseless words in the hope of finding one that will stick and guide him to safety taints his speech with insincerity.

I would like to close my reading of "Jamaica Farewell" by bringing the Martinican's appeal into dialogue with more recent theories on political deliberation, particularly as they apply to hospitality. The meaning of political deliberation, as a process of arriving at decisive consensus, has been subject to exhaustive debate and disagreement.[88] Danielle Allen, however, offers a rather practical and illuminating definition of political deliberation as the art of "talking to strangers"—that is, making oneself heard, at times passionately, and listening to others, always attentively. Allen's usage of the word "strangers" is deliberate, as it is intended to highlight that, even in a plural democratic society like the United States, the object of her study, those who are united by their shared juridical status as citizens remain divided by a seemingly insurmountable sense of distrust—one rooted in racial difference—that they somehow must "overcome" in order to maintain the integrity of democracy.[89] Racialization, a process engendered by the West's conceptualization of universal Man, turns certain citizens into strangers. By contrast, Caribbean discourse envisions another form of political deliberation and political discourse premised on the removal of strangerhood from the category of being-in-common—for as Glissant has affirmed, "Relation is not made up of things that are foreign."[90] Talking to strangers may thus be understood as a rhetoric of hospitality.

Jacques Derrida's thinking is particularly instructive here, for he dedicates considerable thought to unpacking the rhetorical nature of hospitality as a means of talking to strangers. Indeed, he argues, "That is where the question of hospitality begins: we must ask the foreigner to understand us, to speak our language, in all the senses of this term, in all its possible extensions, before being able and so as to be able to welcome him into our country?"[91] The stranger who desires to entreat the host to their cause, to be welcomed, must, first and foremost, understand the host's language. But in order to know that one must understand the language to receive hospitality, one must first recognize one's strangeness. This is precisely what the Martinican delegate fails to remember. He is so swept up by the illusion that the Caribbean is but a "single homeland" that he is unable to perceive himself as a stranger before the Rastafarian robber. More specifically, he cannot perceive that this estrangement is fundamentally *economic*, rooted in the neoliberalization of the Caribbean. "Jamaica Farewell" suggests that, in the neoliberal era, the language of Caribbean kinship has neither literal currency nor cultural capital. Interestingly, it is the robber who betrays that he is, in fact, much more cognizant of what is at stake precisely because he uses the language not of brotherhood but rather of money, which is clearly the language that governs the relations of nations within the Caribbean Community.

In this light, "Jamaica Farewell" pushes readers to reorient their perspective of their encounter to perhaps consider the economic conditions that would drive the robber to reject the illusion of a harmonious Caribbean kinship. This is precisely the point Rodney drives home in *The Groundings with My Brothers*, which provides a blueprint for political deliberation in the Caribbean based on a shared experience that is established not through an illusory kinship but rather through a rethinking of hospitality. In his text, Rodney proposes his notion of "grounding" as an alternative framing of political deliberation. Addressing Black West Indian intellectuals and academics, who may not be in a position so different from the Martinican delegate, Rodney contends that they (we) must abandon the symbolic tourist resort—the ivory towers of academia—and instead go out to "the lumpen, the gully corners, the rubbish dumps," where those like the fictional Rastafarian robber in "Jamaica Farewell" might reside. Rodney explains, "I have sat on a little oil drum, rusty and in the midst of garbage and, and some black brothers and I have grounded together."[92] He then goes on to describe what grounding entails: "We spoke, we spoke about a lot of things, and it was just the talking that was important, the meeting of black people. I was trying to contribute something. I was trying to contribute my experience in travelling, in reading, my analysis; and I was also gaining."[93] In the picture he paints, the academically educated Rodney does not withhold his speech but rather reorients it through the language of the people.

The deliberative coalition building described by Rodney might explain why Caribbean intellectuals have not coalesced around CARICOM and the CSME, unlike its two short-lived but instrumental precursors: the Confederación Antillana (Antillean Confederation), which lasted from the 1860s until 1898, and the West Indian Federation, from 1958 to 1962, the latter of which CARICOM explicitly names as its precedent.[94] Two forms of multistate federation in the Spanish and Anglo Caribbean, respectively, both the Antillean Confederation and the West Indian Federation were conceived at pivotal moments in the formation of a post-emancipation Latin America and Caribbean. First, the Confederación is conceptualized both on the heels of the Haitian Revolution, to which some of its key thinkers gesture as a beacon, and in the wake of *criollo*-led Latin American independence projects. Six decades later, the West Indian Federation coalesces as a legal, self-governing body as British Caribbean colonies pursue greater autonomy from the Crown, and its dissolution coincides with Jamaica's withdrawal from the federation and subsequent independence from the United Kingdom in the summer of 1958.[95] In comparing these two projects, Yolanda Martínez-San Miguel and Katerina Gonzalez Seligmann note, "Although these con-federated forms included both imperial attachments and decolonizing dimensions, they both offer trans-Caribbean unity as a utopian reference for anti-imperial sovereignty and the decolonial achievement of racial equality."[96] Although nearly a century apart and marked by distinctive modalities of coloniality, these two visions of Caribbean confederation articulated in Spanish and English similarly sought to align the Caribbean beyond the illusory discourses of multiracial and cross-cultural harmony.

Yet what markedly distinguishes CARICOM from these earlier Caribbean federalist projects is the defining influence Caribbean intellectuals, writers, and artists had on the latter. The Confederación and, to a large extent, the federation were, more than anything, imagined communities. That is, they were more tentative than real as to the practical implementations of their ideal of Antillean unity. But the promise of this ideal not only "captured the imaginations of many artists, writers, and historians, and political theorists."[97] Through them, these federated forms came alive in the imaginations of ambivalent subjects isolated from one another across the Caribbean's fragmented, imperial geographies. Given the role Caribbean intellectuals and artists played as architects of the language of federation, these confederated forms cohere literary and aesthetic projects that gave meaning to the idea of a Caribbeanness in its various permutations, not only in the Caribbean but also globally.[98]

Curiously, CARICOM has not elicited the same creative and discursive engagement and alignment of intellectuals, writers, and artists. In fact, outside of political theory, there is scant mention (if any at all) of CARICOM within Caribbean narrative and aesthetic words. This is not to say, however, that there have been no aesthetic and discursive responses motivated by CARICOM. On the contrary, I do not think it a coincidence that in *Le Discours antillais*, which appears eight years after CARICOM's inception, Glissant mentions that "the dream of Antillanité is kept alive in a limited way in the *cultural sphere*," after mentioning the unrealized dream of the West Indian Federation.[99] His statement suggests that Caribbean intellectuals, like himself, have detached the cultural sphere not necessarily from the political but from state/regional politics. CARICOM, which has patently declared itself as an heir to the dream, appears as an absent presence that Glissant has, more than likely, relegated to the category of "non-history"—a term echoed throughout the *Discours* to describe, as Nick Nesbitt rightly shows, the absence of will and the postponement of critical decisions that could transform the Caribbean politically.[100] It is for this reason that Davis's *Migrant Discourse* and Vega's "Jamaica Farewell" resonate quite loudly—their chronology in the twenty-first and late twentieth centuries, respectively, bookends the unspoken nonalignment of contemporary Caribbean artists and writers and with the regional integration projects in their extant permutations.

CHAPTER 2

Disoriented Citizenship

MISREADING PUERTO RICO IN THE
UNCOSMOPOLITAN ELSEWHERE

The live telecast of Puerto Rican reggaeton artist Bad Bunny's performance at the 2023 Grammy Awards powerfully indexed the meaning of Puerto Rico's legal status. The meteoric rise and unprecedented international acclaim of the artist born as Benito Antonio Martínez Ocasio signaled the undeniable globality of Puerto Rican culture and, broadly, Latinidad, marking the shattering of whatever barrier remained between the all-encompassing Latin Pop genre and non-Spanish-language audiences. Bad Bunny's universal success as a "crossover" artist who, nevertheless, sings and raps in Spanish would be consolidated in his historic performance as the opening act of the Grammys, considered by many to be the highest and most prestigious honor in the U.S. recording industry.[1] As he appeared onstage mobilizing an enthralling pan-Caribbean panegyric to the Black roots of Puerto Rican music, dance, and literature, the Grammys' TV broadcaster, CBS, initially captioned Bad Bunny's words as "SPEAKING NON-ENGLISH / SINGING NON-ENGLISH."[2] Understandably, these words moved the Grammy's Latinx viewership to social media, where they expressed overwhelming shock, ire, and disapproval at the broadcaster's nonsensical rendering of the lyrics of what is, arguably, the world's most captivating *reggaetoneros*. These reactions, however, stemmed not from the fact that Bad Bunny's words were left untranslated but, rather, that they were captioned essentially as untranslatable nonlanguage—and, therefore, that the singer's Puerto Rican Spanish had no linguistic equivalency in English. All in all, what the caption really indexed was the universal incommensurability of Puerto Rico both in the United States and on the world stage.

Writing a decade prior, in an essay titled "El Estado Libre Asociado y la glosolalia" (The Free Associated State and Glossolalia), the award-winning Puerto Rican writer and visual artist Eduardo Lalo expresses in similar terms Puerto Rico's universal unintelligibility. Lalo's essay suggests that Puerto Ricans' unintelligibility is the expected outcome of existing under a legal status that by design provokes "confusión" and amounts to a *sinsentido* or nonsense.[3] For Lalo, the Estado Libre Associado (Free Associated State) or ELA, the legal designation for Puerto Rico's status since 1952, operates as a pernicious onto-political grammar that structures and weaves the discourse of everyday life such that when Puerto Ricans communicate among themselves, they hear and understand each other's words differently. The catalyst for his essay is, ironically, a conversation he overhears between two priests: one asks the other, who has traveled and lived extensively in Europe and North America, how he explains to foreigners what exactly the ELA is. We are never privy to the priest's answer. Indeed, the essay's indefinite deferment of the priest's reply becomes a simulacrum of the answer itself. The failure to explain the meaning of ELA has an ecclesiastical resonance. Like glossolalia, the religious phenomenon otherwise known as "speaking in tongues"—vocal utterances that resemble language but do not cohere into the logical structure of communicative speech—the ELA amounts to juridical babel that lacks a commensurate meaning within the language of international law. How, in fact, can a people be simultaneously "sovereign" and "associated" with a metropolitan protectorate, as the ELA's phraseology designates? For although the ELA was instituted as a "compact" between the United States and Puerto Rico, the people of Puerto Rico lacked a full understanding of its meaning to give their formal consent to the status.[4] Thus, the religious setting of glossolalia parallels Puerto Rico, whose people adhere to the language of the status through a "blind faith" and depend on politicos who endlessly deliberate on and interpret its meaning with no resolution. Ultimately, Lalo argues, in the absence of *common sense* about the ELA, there can likewise be no agreement between Puerto Ricans about the lived experiences of their shared reality.

While Eduardo Lalo's reflections on the "nonsense" of the ELA and the responses to the failed captioning of Bad Bunny's Grammys performance pose distinctive perspectives on the common world Puerto Ricans are unable to inhabit as U.S. citizens, more pertinently, they each betray an inhospitality toward Puerto Rico and its artists, writers, and intellectuals in their consignment to a space that could be otherwise described as *uncosmopolitan*. These texts reveal the way Puerto Rican literary and cultural production becomes senselessness *in* the world in ways that belie, as the case of Bad Bunny shows, their popular positioning in the global culture industry. Furthermore, these texts suggest a correspondence between this inhospitable unworlding of Puerto Rican literature and culture and the island's juridical indeterminacy, giving the sense that one cannot properly inhabit the world without settling the local.

This chapter investigates Puerto Rican writers' preoccupation with the placelessness and illegibility of Puerto Rican literary production, both at home on the island and in world literary space in the wake of critical efforts spanning the past three decades or so, to emplot and recalibrate Latin American and Caribbean literature within the coordinates of globalization, world literature, and cosmopolitanism. The three case studies under consideration—Giannina Braschi's experimental novel *Yo-Yo Boing!*, alongside Eduard Lalo's travelogue *Los países invisibles* (The invisible countries) and novel *La inutilidad* (Uselessness)—suggest that the island's senseless juridical status conditions the unintelligibility of Puerto Rican literature and the practice of writing in Puerto Rico. Exposing literature's mobility within a geopolitics of legibility, Lalo and Braschi's texts track the inextricable correspondence between a nation and its citizens' juridical status, conceptualized as a language of belongingness, and a literary text's status not only at home but in the world literary canon. Theorizing Puerto Rican literature's "senselessness," this chapter bridges and expands the first chapter's analysis of the sensory misdirection of Caribbean citizens and subjects by analyzing the entwined condition of literary unreadability and juridical disorientation—what Lalo refers to as the *nonsense* or Braschi calls "whereness" of Puerto Rico and its literature.

This chapter understands *sense* and its corollary *senseless* in Braschi and Lalo's texts as literature's aesthetic-proprioceptive function—that is, its capacity to disorient the reader in time and space, away from or toward home. Along these lines, one aspect of this chapter queries Puerto Rican literature's geopoetic location and "residence" within, for example, the U.S., Latin American, and Caribbean literary canons given Puerto Rico's uneven and partial incorporation into the United States as its nonsovereign territory. At the same time, this chapter demonstrates how the aesthetic-proprioceptive power of literature shapes its capacity to *make sense*—to the reader. I show that making sense ensues not merely from the text's linguistic or grammatical intelligibility but also from its perceived axiological function—the value of both writing and reading—in society. The interrogation of Puerto Rican literature's "whereness" in Braschi and Lalo's narratives adjoins the demand to justify why they even bother writing. Delineating these interconnected forms of literature's sensemaking, I argue that the rhetorical form and aesthetic mode of Lalo and Braschi's narratives re-present the fundamentally *disorienting* impulse of Puerto Rican literature. Put differently, they elucidate how "Puerto Rican literature" as a category confounds readers such that it cannot be easily oriented within either the U.S. literary canon or the Latin American and Caribbean literary canons. And, by extension, it becomes disoriented from the canon of world literature.

Disoriented Reading

Tracing Puerto Rico's disorientation from local, national, continental, and global literary cartographies, *Yo-Yo Boing!*, *Los países invisibles*, and *La inutilidad* query the constitutive role of reading in the practice and exercise of citizenship and in the conceptualization of the nation-state as a political geography plotted in the imagination of its citizens through the act of reading.[5] Undoubtedly, reading remains constitutive to the practice of citizenship for the simple fact that the laws that codify the conditions of membership and belonging of a political community have been set forth in written documentation—for example, in constitutions, declarations, passports, and literary narratives. In another sense, however, reading can operate as a compass that brings citizens' mutual ties to the nation-state within view. This latter point informs Sara Ahmed's claim that a political phenomenology underwrites the Andersonian notion of an "imagined community" that comes into view through the quotidian practice of reading. According to Ahmed, reading symbolically orients citizens toward the nation as a shared object of belonging. "The very act of reading means that citizens are directing their attention toward a shared object, even if they have a different view upon that object, or even if that object brings different worlds to view," Ahmed asserts.[6] Yet Puerto Rico's multirelational geocultural, linguistic, and juridical coordinates—its Latin American and Caribbean cultural and raciolinguistic inheritance, coupled with its indeterminate inscription in the United States as its nonsovereign Other—disrupts what, as Ahmed argues, becomes the nation's demand that citizens orient themselves toward it along a "straight line . . . without any deviation."[7] This chapter partially takes up Ahmed's broader claim that disorientation as a queer method can productively disrupt a politics of hegemonic straightness, only to the extent that disorientation be embraced as a strategy of collective counterreading that altogether resists the seduction of nationhood and, as this book argues, sovereignty.[8]

What I call *disoriented reading* signals how Puerto Rico's multirelational, raciolinguist, geocultural, and juridical positions are instrumentalized to foreclose practices of counterreading on the island. In my estimation, Braschi and Lalo's narratives interrogate this foreclosure in terms that bring into view their implicit indebtedness to the legacy of Antonio Pedreira's 1934 essay *Insularismo* (Insularity). Considered one of the key founding texts of Puerto Rican national and cultural identity, *Insularismo* explicates the predicament of the Puerto Rican subject in shades of a Spenglerian Hispanism that reflects both the ideological currents of its time and a desire to conceive a universally Latin Americanist orientation.[9] Pedreira's notion of *insularismo* (insularity) captures the island's vicissitudes at the hands of multiple custodians, producing a "guerra civil biológica" (a biological civil war) between two incompatible races.[10] The island, he suggests, exists in a state of abeyance between the Hispanic Catholic and Anglo-American Protestant culture, on the one hand, and the Spanish and African races, on the other. Pedreira couches his argument in terms that foreground the sense of disorientation that would later be reconfigured in Braschi and Lalo's narratives. On the one hand, he asserts that the biological "*fusion*" of Spanish settlers and enslaved Black Africans had begotten a racial "*con-fusión*."[11] On the other hand, coupled with the island's passage in 1898 from a colony of Spain to an incorporated territory of the United States, Puerto Rico, he maintains, amounts to a *"no man's land."*[12] Caught as "una nave al garate" (an errant vessel) in an irreconcilable frontier between home and elsewhere, Puerto Rico lay adrift between incompatible identities: a *nation* marked by Spain's cultural legacy on the one hand and the Anglo-American construct of the *state* as the site of its juridical authority on the other.[13]

Notwithstanding this grim racial-juridical scenario, Pedreira believed that Puerto Rico had a chance to right its course by cultivating a reading culture. This reading culture would be cultivated by the press, whom he tasked with fulfilling its "misión orientacional" (*orientational* mission).[14] In Spanish, *orientar* (to orient) can have two meanings: on the one hand, it can denote the act of aligning someone on a specific course in a particular direction; on the other, it can signify the act of providing moral counsel or guidance. Conjuring these entwined dimensions of orientation, Pedreira, unlike many intellectuals and politicos of his time, provisionally sidestepped the question of Puerto Rico's juridical status. Instead, he considered the "aesthetic" revitalization of Puerto Rico's national culture a more urgent and expedient path toward the goal of reforming and transforming the Puerto Rican subject, in starkly Enlightenment terms, into a morally complete and sophisticated Man capable of politics.[15] As scholar Luis Felipe Díaz discusses, for Pedreira and other like-minded intellectuals of his generation, the greatest threat posed by the U.S. annexation of Puerto Rico was not a juridical takeover but rather a cultural occupation.[16] Thus, the task assigned to Puerto Rico's Spanish-language press, broadly defined as print and literary institutions, entailed cultivating literary works that defined Puerto Rico's aesthetic "sensibilidad" (sensibility) and "espíritu" (spirit) by mining the island's elite Spanish cultural legacy.[17] Indeed, Pedreira asserted, these literary guides would reorient Puerto Rican readers toward a universal, Spanish American "rhetoricism" and grammar over and above the juridical and cultural dictates emanating from the United States and, even, the Caribbean.[18]

This brief excursus into the central themes of Pedreira's *Insularismo* clarifies the essay's significant inheritance in Braschi and Lalo's narratives and helps frame how they each reconfigure the theme of disorientation by returning to the question of language as the symbolic grammar of the island's legal status that informs the mode of reading Puerto Rico. The establishment of the ELA complicated the real and symbolic language of Puerto Rican politics by redefining Puerto Rico vis-à-vis terms that were incompatible with the language of political theory. Backed by the United Nations, the ELA purportedly brought closure to Puerto Rico's colonial status and eliminated any ambiguity as to Puerto Rico's relationship with the United States. Yet, as Puerto Rican legal scholar Pedro Malavet asserts, the ELA rendered Puerto Rico a juridical "misnomer."[19] Braschi and Lalo's narratives consider how this juridical misnomer becomes reified in everyday communicative practices, such that Puerto Ricans emerged according to what social theorist Juan Flores calls "interlingual" subjects.[20] Owing to the mass transmigration of Puerto Ricans between the island and the U.S. mainland beginning in the 1950s, Puerto Ricans likewise move between Spanish and English such that they confound Spanish speakers in the Spanish-speaking world and English speakers in the United States. In this latter regard, unlike Pedreira's, Braschi's and Lalo's texts give primacy to the status as a grammar that, in turn, structures everyday speech and the ability to read and interpret such speech in the mode of literature. Here, too, is where Braschi's and Lalo's representations of disorientation bifurcate—for, as I further elucidate, whereas Braschi embraces the disorienting misreadings that inevitably result from encounters with the legal and quotidian grammar of Puerto Ricanness, Lalo's text decries Puerto Rico's disorientation in terms that suggest a murky affinity with and longing for the orienting Hispanism that Pedreira espoused.

Yet, I contend that Pedreira's desire to rectify Puerto Rico's confused language by way of a Hispanist aesthetic also belies the impulse of a cosmopolitan hospitality that is constitutive of world literature. Indeed, Pedreira's theorizing of the no-man's-land wherein Puerto Ricans find themselves shipwrecked brings to mind Kant's description of the uninhabitable parts of the earth that preclude the coming together of men in a "cosmopolitan constitution." It is important to remember that Kant premises his theory of cosmopolitan hospitality in his Third Article *To Perpetual Peace* in the context of the earth's shape and constitution as a globe whose differentiated surface delimits where humans can live. The earth's surface, argues Kant, compels strangers to live in "close proximity" as they occupy its habitable parts.[21] Conversely, Kant argues that the uninhabitable parts of the earth, made up of the "seas and the deserts," provoke humans to act inhospitably. Living on the uninhabitable edges of society, beyond the checks and balances of the political community, causes men to engage in piracy, plundering, and enslavement. To inhabit the uninhabitable precludes man from becoming Man.

Kant's reading of human relations within the differentiated parts of the earth has several implications for my reading of disorientation in Braschi's and Lalo's texts as they move from the island to the space of world literature. While the uninhabitable parts of the earth form part of the globe, they are not constitutive of the "world," in Kant's words, that is, composed of a "cosmopolitan constitution" of men. As I previously discussed, in Kant's lexicon, existing in the community of men necessarily preconditions membership in the cosmopolitan. The inhospitable is that zone where the human can be thrown off course, shipwrecked, and disoriented from the cosmopolitical world of men. Likewise, the inhospitable, uninhabitable part of the earth does not, therefore, enter what Kant elsewhere calls the *sensus communis* of men—a "shared sense" that defines the "aesthetic power of judgment" as a universal.[22] To inhabit the nonsense grammar of the ELA is to defy, to paraphrase Édouard Glissant, the monolingual sense of the world as a universal.

In what follows, I turn to Braschi's *Yo-Yo Boing!* and Lalo's *Los países invisibles* and *La inutilidad* to examine how these narratives upend the cartographic orientation of the literary as these texts move from Puerto Rico and, ultimately, fail to enter the sphere of world literary space. By "literary" I mean the production and circulation of literature, the practice of writing, the consecration of the author's status, and the habituation of reading. Marking the disorientation of the reader that is concomitant to the disorienting script of Puerto Rican literature and writers, these texts track the conceptual and practical entanglement of literary legibility and juridical legitimacy. I explore how Braschi's and Lalo's narratives interrogate the fundamental strangeness of the Puerto Rican writer in the absence of mutual recognition from a readership incapable of "placing" and orienting Puerto Rico and its writers, owing to the island's nonsovereign status.

The following sections develop a close reading of Braschi's and Lalo's narratives, as they disclose the entangled circuitries of local misrecognition on the island, national misunderstanding in the United States, and global untranslatability in the global political and literary communities. The second section of this chapter confronts earlier criticisms of Braschi's deployment of a bourgeois aesthetics that make the form and content of *Yo-Yo Boing!* ostensibly unreadable. I propose an alternative way of reading the illegible nonsense of *Yo-Yo Boing!*, by abandoning the search for hermeneutic clarity of meaning and, instead, inhabiting the experience of misunderstanding it provokes. Aligning rather than fighting with the text's senselessness enables us to understand it as a cipher or metapolitical allegory of the frustrated and senseless meaning of Puerto Rico's status. From here, I examine how *Yo-Yo Boing!* engages in a self-reflexive questioning of its placelessness in world literature as a function of its near impossible untranslatability. In astoundingly prescient terms, *Yo-Yo Boing!* invokes the case of Puerto Rico's nonsovereignty to articulate a prescient response to the consolidation of world literary discourse.

Amid the ascendancy of world literary discourse by German, Anglophone, and Francophone literary criticism in the Global North, there has been a push to wrest Latin American and Caribbean literary production from the provincialism of nationalist and national-popular categorization. Recent Latin Americanist literary criticism has betrayed a commitment to the idea of a "world" composed of a transnational or world-making canon whose universality extends to Latin American literature.[23] The overarching sentiment in Latin Americanist scholarly circles is that the marginalization of Latin American literature from world literary and, thus, universalist considerations replicates and parallels the region's uneven development, disenfranchisement, and differential alignment within the globe's politics.[24] Whereas the tenor of Latin Americanist criticism spanning the 1980s and 1990s gleaned in the *modernista* aesthetics of writers like José Martí a desire to mediate, as Julio Ramos argues, the "unfixed place of Latin American literature in a world ruled by modernization and progress," the Latin Americanist turn to world literary studies in the first two decades of the twenty-first century largely responded to the impulses of globalization and neoliberalism, and their effects on the book market.[25] It is not that the question of Latin America's and the Caribbean's positions on the scale of modernity had been settled once and for all. Rather, there has emerged a renewed understanding that to be modern means to be worldly and, importantly, to be read universally.

To different degrees, Braschi's and Lalo's texts evince a frustrated desire for a local, national, and global readership and understanding. But this desire is tempered by acceptance of and, at times, resignation to their inhospitable dislocation from the sense of the world. The second section connects Braschi's thematization of misunderstanding to the third section's analysis of literary invisibility in Lalo's travelogue, *Los países invisibles.* I demonstrate how Braschi and Lalo unsettle the principle of translatability that conditions their reading, circulation, and inclusion as national (sovereign) literatures in the world literary system. My aim is to expose how this principle of literary translation works in alignment with the unspoken principle of juridical translatability that conditions the recognition of state sovereignty in the international system that extends to Kant's theory of cosmopolitan right and cosmopolitan hospitality. This translational equation, I argue, distorts and disorients the cosmopolitan legibility, visibility, and even national canonicity of Puerto Rican literature and its authors as citizens of a nonsovereign state. Thus, I argue, "misreading" and "illegibility" constitute forms of senselessness that foreclose Puerto Rican literature's "location" in the world literary space, against the global conceit of recent currents in Latin American and Caribbean literary criticism.

The final analytic section of this chapter attends to Lalo's subaltern and Orientalist self-fashioning as an "invisible writer," notwithstanding his overwhelming acclaim in Latin America and his often overlooked heteropatriarchal situatedness as a white male writer on an island where the field of literary production remains largely inaccessible to racialized and gendered Others. My aim here is to complicate the meaning of the Puerto Rican citizen-writer and the Puerto Rican citizen who is presumed to be a *non*reader of the literary form, in their mutually constituted relation as subjects whose juridical senselessness renders them strangers to each other, the state, and the world.

Misreading Puerto Rico

Giannina Braschi's *Yo-Yo Boing!* debuted in 1998 as the second installment in a tryptic of experimental, hybrid works that contend with the three juridical options that have been presented to Puerto Ricans: sovereign nation, neocolony

(ELA), or U.S. statehood. Bookended by the epic prose poem *El imperio de los sueños* (Empire of dreams) and the dramatic novel *United States of Banana*, *Yo-Yo Boing!*, as Doris Sommer and Alexandra Vega-Marino have argued, replicates the island's indeterminate status as an "Either/And" in its rhetorical form and aesthetic mode.[26] An intermedial, "novelized" work that reads as a performance piece, memoir, and, in the narrator's words, *"poetry disguised as a novel,"* *Yo-Yo Boing!* is held loosely together by a Babelian chorus of nameless voices who code-switch between Spanish, English, and "Spanglish."[27] Set primarily in New York City, described in the text as "the capital of Puerto Rico," these voices constellate as one polarity of what Jorge Duany has called the "back and forth" movement of Puerto Ricans as a "nation on the move" between the two islands of Puerto Rico and Manhattan.[28] Without question, the fragmentation, polysemy, and polyphony emerging from this movement situate *Yo-Yo Boing!* within the contours of what has been called the "postmodern condition" and instantiate Puri's notion of the "Caribbean postcolonial." Absent of a discernible plot or narrative telos organized around a central story, *Yo-Yo Boing!* frustrates readers' propensity to search for sense as a precondition of interpretation.

Much of the scholarly commentary on *Yo-Yo Boing!* has weighed in on the narrative's "difficult" language and the "frustration" and "confusion" this language produces in readers. As Ellen Jones observes, "difficulty has been the overriding criticism of *Yo-Yo Boing!* by readers and reviewers," who have suggested that it is meant to be read by a specific (read "elite") circle of academic insiders committed to the labor of interpretation that a text of this nature would demand.[29] Other critiques of *Yo-Yo Boing!* signal the well-worn distinction between a politics of representation and the disclosure of a *praxis* that will yield actionable decisions. This opposition or gap between theory as representation and practical politics has been, in the first two decades of the twenty-first century, at the center of Latin Americanist and Caribbeanist debates about the stalemate of a postcolonial and cultural discourse that could not move beyond "the aesthetization of the political" and the appropriation of subaltern positions.[30] In *Permissible Narratives*, Christopher González observes that some of the negative criticism toward *Yo-Yo Boing!* has centered on how Braschi appears to prioritize the aesthetic, "both in content and at the level of form, in ways that neutralize the political valence of the narrative."[31] Notably, José L. Torres-Padilla, whom González cites, accuses Braschi's novel of supporting "the continuing colonial status of Puerto Rico and undermines any desire for self-determination that might effect real change" through its "decidedly elitist and bourgeois" performance of a quintessentially postmodernist (and postcolonial) form of hybridity typified by its linguistic register and referential apparatus.[32]

I read this critical commentary concerning the opacity of *Yo-Yo Boing!* as a paratext that works dialogically with the narrative's deeply self-reflexive exploration of its translingual deformation of narrative form.[33] This self-reflexivity appears as Braschi's relation to her readership in the novel's second section, titled "Blow-up." One of the voices reveals itself as "Giannina Braschi" in conversation with a second voice, possibly that of her lover-cum-editor/translator, who appears earlier in the section. This second voice expresses disapprovingly to the novelized Braschi, "You must realize you're limiting your audience by writing in both languages."[34] Throughout the text, this same voice, or possibly another, accuses the would-be Braschi of not making sense. In this first instance, the voice of would-be Braschi insists, "There's always an understanding in misunderstanding."[35] Later, the voice we now know to be Braschi's reiterates the same sentiment with different words: "Confusion is my statement of clarity." Confusion, as the text's discursive mode, becomes the interpretive device that clarifies the confusion it begets in readers. What do we gain by allowing confusion to orient our reading of the *Yo-Yo Boing!*? Confusion in *Yo-Yo Boing!* constitutes a mode of interpretation that unsettles the sovereignty of understanding as resolution and decision.

Criticisms of Braschi's ostensibly "bourgeois" and politically detached aesthetics put pressure upon the text to immediately translate as, and to produce, a clear political position on the island's neocolonial status. It goes unsaid that reading literature has inspired people to act, for better or worse, in defense of political ideals. However, one could argue that at the level of representation, the opacity of *Yo-Yo Boing!* does, as Torres-Padilla avers, knowingly or unknowingly "side" with the status quo of the ELA by only averting and redirecting the reader's ability to extract from the text a clear meaning that makes known its decision for or against Puerto Rican sovereignty. When confronted with the novel's polyphony of multilingual voices and indeterminate context, we find ourselves grasping, albeit unsuccessfully, for meaning.

Without completely disavowing literature's potential to act as and articulate a theory of the political, my analysis of *Yo-Yo Boing!*, however, takes a different approach that invites readers, as I believe the novel does, to sit with the discomfort it produces and query its senselessness as *a* meaning itself. I contend that Braschi's text proceeds from the understanding that both Puerto Ricans and non–Puerto Rican citizens in the United States have misunderstood not just Puerto Rico's status. In this regard, I find instructive Erin Graff Zivin's assertation that "when the act of interpretation . . . is transferred to the task of ethical and political thinking, classical political concepts such as sovereignty, will, decision, and responsibility are shown to be constitutively defective."[36] If *Yo-Yo Boing!* is to be charged with engaging in a disinterested aesthetics devoid of praxis and alienating "the people" as potential readers, we must also take into account its publication five years after a 1993 referendum in which nearly 49 percent of Puerto Ricans who turned out to vote elected to maintain the status quo. The year of its publication, 1998, another plebiscite on the island's status resulted in 50 percent of Puerto Rico's voters who turned out rejecting all three options—

sovereignty, the ELA, or statehood—opting instead for, as Frances Negrón-Muntaner calls it, "a dark-horse column dubbed *ninguna de las anteriores* or none of the above."[37] Under these political conditions, Braschi's narrative poses not as praxis but rather as a structure of feeling that reproduces and re-presents the stalemate of the ELA in the grammar of *nonsense.*

I propose instead that *Yo-Yo Boing!* performs the ELA as a misnomer that, in turn, produces a misreading of Puerto Rico in the aesthetic mode of literary performance. What Braschi's experimental novel does is formulate a theory of what remains unclassifiable both within the language of political thought and according to the rules of literary canon formation. To be clear, although these "rules" of canon formation have an ecclesiastical history, they are more elusive than clearly defined or outlined in any manual today. These rules are configured within the competition of institutional, cultural, political, and economic forces, which include higher education curricula, academic and scholarly criticism, the literary marketplace, and media. *Yo-Yo Boing!* functions as metapolitical allegory, to echo Graff Zivin, of its very resistance to classification, by performing the impossibility of a political-aesthetic narrative.[38] More concretely, Braschi's text performs Puerto Rico's juridical status as a legal misnomer that exceeds the grammar of the law, such that it resorts to figuration. In *The Ethics of Reading,* J. Hillis Miller explores the figurative workings of the law, proposing that narrative stands in place of the law when the language of the law fails to convey its intended meaning. "Narrative, like analogy," Miller affirms, "is inserted in the blank space where the presumed purely conceptual language of philosophy fails or is missing."[39] Analyzing the use of analogy in Kant's philosophy, Miller explains that when language reaches a dead end, such that it alone cannot account for the law he is attempting to describe, the philosopher must then resort to "analogies and figures of speech" through storytelling to make the law plainly understood. According to Miller, "Insofar as narrative takes place within the space of a perpetual deferral or direct confrontation with the law it can be said that narrative is the narration of the impossibility of narrative in the sense of a coherent, logical, perspicuous story."[40] Since the law is always already figurative, narration attempts to make logical sense of the law only to be confronted with its own failure. A narrative substitution of the law continuously postpones and frustrates our wish to make sense of the law in literal language. The ELA is a cipher whose meaning would be like reading *Yo-Yo Boing!*: it is unreadable or misreadable according to a hermeneutic prescription that texts possess a linear, coherent interpretation.

In this way, *Yo-Yo Boing!* abandons the work of deciphering the ELA as political allegory in favor of another self-reflexive meditation on the reader and the location of the writer. If reading *Yo-Yo Boing!* is like reading the ELA, misunderstanding occurs because of the method and disposition of reading that the text demands of the reader—a way of reading rooted in a stalled and frustrated interpretation of the law. I believe this experience would extend to all readers of the text, regardless of socioeconomic standing, worldliness, or cultural sophistication, although with varying levels of patience and resolve. I suggest that the ability to "place" the text, to understand its orientation, is key to the practice and experience of reading. If *Yo-Yo Boing!* elicits frustration, confusion, and exasperation in its readers, it is because the text *disorients* us cognitively and spatially.

If reading is an act of habitation, the performance of misreading in Braschi's text puts it and, by extension, Puerto Rico in that part of the earth that Kant calls the inhabitable. As one of the voices in the text professes, "I can understand Spanish but I can't understand Puerto Ricans . . . Scum of the earth. Destiérrenlos de la república."[41] Speaking from New York City, the voice expresses a common indictment of Puerto Ricans for their failure to speak "proper" Spanish—that is, a monolingual Spanish devoid of anglicisms. This perspective also conceals what Jonathan Rosa calls a "raciolinguistic enregisterment," whereby race and language are rendered mutually perceivable.[42] Puerto Rican Spanish inevitably becomes racialized as unintelligible, recalling Pedreira, owing to its contamination of Caribbean Blackness. The voice in this section of the novel expresses its disdain for Puerto Ricanness in either monolingual English or Spanish that do not contaminate one another. The call to "banish them from the republic" reinforces the non-sovereignty of Puerto Ricans and links citizenship and sovereignty to what Édouard Glissant calls "the totalitarianism of any monolingual intent" that conditions the demand for universal intelligibility.[43] But language also signifies place, and the very banishment of Puerto Ricans makes them unlocatable in the "hereness" of language. Thus, Braschi's text demands a mode of reading that denies the generalizing universal of the cosmopolitan and accepts the fundamental senselessness that is "the world."

Yo-Yo Boing! investigates this demand for a monolingual sensibility by way of Braschi's fictionalized conversation with her lover-cum-editor/translator, who opens a broader critique on the politics of translation. When one voice declares, "You must realize you're limiting your audience by writing in both languages," it is followed by the declaration that "to know a language is to know a culture."[44] A form of neoliberal deindividuation that turns the *reader* into an *audience*, this declarative statement also reinforces the notion of a lingual "hereness." Against the threat of alienating readers for choosing to write translingually—or, as the novel's title suggest, like a yo-yo between two languages, Braschi's self-referential voice posits defiantly: "Desde la torre de Babel las lenguas han sido siempre una forma de divorciarnos del resto del mundo . . . I'm not reducing my audience. On the contrary, I'm going to have a bigger audience with the common markets— in Europe—in America. And besides, all languages are dialects that are made to break new grounds. I feel like Dante, Petrarca and Boccaccio, and I even feel like Garcilaso forging a new language." In one sense, Braschi's logical optimism about her text's global reach is rooted in the reality of a globalized world where many nations in Europe and the Americas have banded together as a common market to facilitate the free movement of capital, services, and people—as I have considered in the previous chapter, in the case of the Caribbean Community (CARICOM). Yet Braschi intentionally invokes the common market only to show how it is held together by a principle of universal translatability.

In another sense, we can interpret the text's market-based appeal as an espousal of the world literary market. *Yo-Yo Boing!* already anticipates the possibilities of a space that Pascale Casanova would later famously denominate the "world republic of letters." Envisioned as a denationalized, universal, and ostensibly neutral literary space, the world republic of letters would wrest writers from the "destitution and invisibility" of national literary ghettos and grant them worldwide legitimacy through translation, "one of the principal means by which texts circulate in the literary world."[45] According to Casanova, literary capital accrues to national literatures precisely because they travel as translated texts through international literary space. Curiously, Casanova has drawn parallels between this world literary space and the international political community. Just as the international political community recognizes the sovereignty of the nation-state, the world republic of letters legitimizes the authors and texts produced within a particular national context.[46] In other words, world literary space demands that a writer belong (juridically) to somewhere. As Casanova shows, even in the world republic of letters, texts can never shake off their affiliation with a national point of origin. What her text suggests and what it overlooks is that authors who write from juridically indeterminate locations—to wit, from places not recognized as nation-states—may be construed as "untranslatable" within international literary space. In my view, then, Braschi's affirmation of her text's appeal to the "common markets" of world literary space does not necessarily aspire to reorient Puerto Rico toward the world so much as it seeks to reorient or alternatively disorient readers' approach to her text.

Yet *Yo-Yo Boing!* cannot quite shake off anxieties about the political consequences of being misread in its untranslatability. At the tail end of a critical section that interrogates the novel's choice of narrative structure, one of its nameless voices disputes the legitimacy of Puerto Rican Spanish and Spanglish. Furthermore, the voice, in conversation with the would-be Braschi, offers Puerto Ricans' language as a cause for calling into question their right to political membership in a nation-state. The would-be Braschi counters by taking up a cosmopolitan position, locating Puerto Rico in the world on the basis of its untranslatability:

—How do you sleep at night.
—I snuggle with the dead when I go to bed.
—You feel colonized.

—You don't feel cosmopolitan.

Totally cosmopolitan.

That's a contradiction in terms.[47]

The exchange betrays the contradictory entwinement of the colonial with the cosmopolitan on the basis of the unity of independent (colonial) languages that produce neocolonial confusion. Braschi's text locates Puerto Rico's disoriented being in the world as a contradiction in terms to the extent that the cosmopolitan both produces and evicts the colonial Other from its universal worlding. As Kant has shown us, the cosmopolitan "world" takes shape through the violent settling or exploitation of what is considered not "worldly" but, rather, terra nullius.

Yo-Yo Boing! revisits this issue in slightly different terms by forcing Puerto Rican voices in the text to clarify how the ELA defines them as U.S. citizens:

Quieres dejar de ser puertorriqueña. Americana es lo que tú quieres
llegar a ser.
No tengo que llegar a ser lo que soy.
¿Tú eres americana? Escúchenla. Dice que es americana.
¿Por qué voy a negar que nací aquí?
Pero de dónde. Déjate de trucos.[48]

(You no longer want to be Puerto Rican, American is what you
want to become.
I don't have to become what I am.
You're American? Listen to her. She says she's American.
Why would I deny that I was born *here*.
But *where*? Stop playing games.)

Presented entirely in Spanish, the dialogue represents one of many instances throughout the novel in which its Puerto Rican speakers are mistaken for foreigners not only by other U.S. citizens but also by other presumed "foreigners"— in this case, Spanish-speaking Latin American readers. Although the answer to the question is documented in the written law, the interrogation suggests not only that the language of the ELA is at odds with the discourse of U.S. citizenship. Moreover, the interrogation of Puerto Ricans' political identity gives way to a dialogue about where the "America" of which Puerto Rico constitutes a part is actually located—especially since in the Spanish American literary tradition "America" has encompassed a continental identity. The speaker's ambiguous "here" blurs the distinction between the "here" that is insular Puerto Rico (both the Caribbean island and the island of Manhattan) and the assumed "here" of the United States, which conditionally extends to Puerto Rico. Yet, the questioner's skepticism discloses, to echo Ahmed, a failed orientation not only between the Puerto Rican Island and the continental U.S. but also between Latin American readers and the Puerto Rican voices in the novel. This failed orientation casts doubt on the "hereness" of Puerto Ricans' citizenship before the Spanish-speaking Latin American reader, who perceives the Puerto Rican as an impostor (for claiming U.S. citizenship), a traitor (for legitimizing themselves through U.S. discourse and not Latin American and Caribbean discourses), and last a dilettante (for writing an incomprehensible text that dispenses with "good," uncontaminated Spanish).

This returns us to the question of translation and monolingualism. As Emily Apter shows, even with translation, the neocolonial geopolitical impulse of the world literary *market* (to which, in our neoliberal times, the world literary "republic" ultimately answers) "carves up" Caribbean literature into linguistic and national families—notwithstanding their deep historical and cultural affinities.[49] How, then, does one classify literature emerging from the island of Puerto Rico? Is it "American" (U.S.) literature? Latin American literature? Caribbean literature? Is it a combination of some or all of the above?

The fact that most nation-states, with notable exceptions, generally make use of one official or de facto national language in matters pertaining to government affairs—for example, in voting and naturalization ceremonies—certainly speaks to the ways in which monolingualism is immanent to the rhetoric and practice of citizenship. Yet the speaker's valuation of monolingualism in *Yo-Yo Boing!* discloses the ways in which citizenship, as a juridical language, functions as a universally recognizable or translatable contract. Jacques Derrida hints at this in his essay "Des tours de Babel," wherein he explores the political implications of multiple contracts between languages. "It is generally supposed that in order to be valid or to institute anything at all, every contract must take place in a single language of appeal (for example, in the case of diplomatic or commercial treaties), to a translatability that is already given and without remainder: in this case the multiplicity of tongues must be absolutely mastered," he avers.[50] As Derrida observes and later critiques, a "proper" translation between two languages, as it has traditionally been understood, would eliminate the trace of "foreignness" or "strangeness" from the original language so that the final text expresses a universal meaning. Take, for example, the 1969 Vienna Convention on the Law of Treatises, which mandates that legal treaties between two states must use language that, when translated, can render an "equally authoritative" or congruent interpretation for all parties.[51] In the absence of a universally authoritative translatability, the legitimacy of the contract becomes disputable. Derrida's assessment of the translational nature of politics parallels ongoing debates concerning the legitimacy of the terms of the ELA as a "compact" between the island and the U.S. mainland and on the novel's concerns about its (un)readability.

The political implications of Puerto Rico's marginalization from the republic of citizens owing to its "unreadability" also parallel the implications of the "banishment" of *Yo-Yo Boing!*—and, broadly, Puerto Rican literature—from the

66   CARIBBEAN INHOSPITALITY

literary canon. In the concluding pages of the novel, a voice—one of many that point back to Braschi herself—reflects, "Because Puerto Rico is not a country that has power in the world, I cannot establish myself as a great poet."[52] Here, Puerto Rico's powerlessness stems from its inability to legitimize itself vis-à-vis the universal, monolingual language of the "law." And yet this "law" entails not necessarily the juridical law but rather the law that regulates the legitimacy of literary works—broadly speaking, the canon. This concept of the canon as "law" will be discussed further in the context of Eduardo Lalo's work in the next section.

In *Yo-Yo Boing!*, Braschi both directly and indirectly invokes the narrative of Babel, the biblical origin myth in which humans attempted to create a universal language, only to be scattered and confounded in multiple directions across the earth. By doing so, she challenges readers to consider the possibility of a multi-relational reading. If we recall Ahmed's phenomenological notion of reading as a political orientation, facing the nation as citizens entails reading it along a straight line, to the abandonment of all errant paths. Hence, the difficulty we encounter in reading *Yo-Yo Boing!* might also be due to the fact that we tend to approach a text with the understanding that, through its language, it discloses a particular juridical orientation. Moreover, we want our "here" and the novel's "there" to be clear and unambiguous. Alternatively, I argue, *Yo-Yo Boing!* forces readers to assume a symbolically oblique position, such that we no longer read from our monolingual, political orientation. In doing so, it is we, as readers, who abandon our straightness—our literary citizenship as readers—such that we see ourselves as part of an uncommon world.

LITERATURA NULLIUS

Braschi's representation of Puerto Rico through a multirelational framework not only disavows the potency of the nation-state's monolingual discourse but, importantly, challenges readers on the U.S. mainland to disorient themselves in ways that defamiliarize their understanding of "home," as members of the U.S. republic of citizens. Moreover, *Yo-Yo Boing!* reorients readers' vision of Puerto Rico toward what I consider an uncommon world such that the island's juridical and literary itineraries come to constitute an avant-garde. Braschi's worldly reorientation of Puerto Rico anticipates Eduardo Lalo's exploration of Puerto Rican literature's effacement within the world in *Los países invisibles*.

A philosophical travelogue of his journey throughout Europe, *Los países invisibles* (The invisible countries), contrasts the hypervisibility of European cultural centers—notably, London, Madrid, and Barcelona—against the erasure of Puerto Rico as an "invisible" country from the literary canon. The travelogue's title situates the text in a thematic relation to Italo Calvino's whimsical novel *Invisible Cities*, a fictional dialogue between the Mongolian emperor Kublai Khan and the Venetian explorer Marco Polo. The explorer captivates Khan with his lucid accounts of travels to decadent cities at the threshold of the Mongolian Empire. Yet, as the narrator tells us, the emperor remains a "foreigner to each of his subjects," whom he does not see and who speak "languages incomprehensible" to him.[53] Calvino's *Invisible Cities* underscores the predicament of (neo) colonial territories that remain occluded and silenced by their metropolitan states. Signaling Calvino's text, *Los países invisibles* makes the case for Lalo's authorial marginality within the empire of world literary space by finding kinship with other peripheral places that have been subalternized within the coordinates of global neocoloniality.

Where *Yo-Yo Boing!* performs the senselessness of ELA, *Los países invisibles* rehearses the very translational act that Casanova claims is vital for the legitimation of writers from "literarily deprived" geographies. In particular, Lalo's travelogue coheres around two organizing concepts: invisibility and visibility. These concepts encapsulate the narrative's trajectory from San Juan to Europe precisely as "periplo de la invisibilidad a la visibilidad pero también de una invisibilidad a otra invisibilidad" (the voyage of invisibility to visibility but also from one invisibility to another invisibility).[54] On the one hand, *visibility* encompasses political and literary translation since translation renders what is veiled and incomprehensible—that is, foreign—into something transparent and legible. Thus, visibility designates the status of subjects whose political and literary identities are recognized in international space. On the other hand, *invisibility* in Lalo's narrative symbolizes not only what is unrepresentable but, more importantly, what fails to translate into the universal language of the law and the world republic of letters. Ironically, Lalo's juridical status eclipses what he describes as a journey toward visibility.

Lalo's text catalogs the inhospitable experience of traveling from a state that is not legally recognized to a continent that, historically, is the birthplace of modernity's ideals—individual liberty and human progress under the mantle of Western citizenship. Five years after the publication of *Los países invisibles*, in August 2013 speech given in Caracas, Venezuela, on the occasion of receiving the Premio Internacional Rómulo Gallegos, Lalo recalls this experience of arriving in the cradle that spawned the Declaration of the Rights of Man and Citizen. A French customs officer could not make sense of the "opaque" incongruities in the writer's U.S. passport.[55] Some background is necessary here: Eduardo Lalo was originally born in Cuba and as an infant migrated with his parents to Puerto Rico, which he considers his homeland. Issued, ironically, by Puerto Rico's State Department, the document identifies Lalo as a Cuban-born U.S. citizen. The passport begets confusion abroad for several reasons. It identifies Puerto Rico, a nonsovereign state, as having a state department. Furthermore, it ciphers an incomprehensible multirelationality between incommensurate political systems (socialist, Spanish-speaking Cuba and its antithesis, the United States) that renders Lalo untranslatable within an international political system that requires a self-evident filiation and linear orientation to a nation-state.

Los países invisibles connects the juridical untranslatability of Lalo's nonstatus with the reality of his (non)status in the world republic of letters. Lalo's authorial legitimacy is called into question in Europe, where, as he puts it, "mis páginas se ven ennegreciendo sobre un libro que relata las interioridades, tantas veces amargas y hasta impresentables, de la República de las Letras" (my pages are turning black in a book that narrates the, often bitter and even unpresentable, inner workings, the Republic of Letters).[56] While the world republic of letters ostensibly grants writers visibility, Lalo urges us to consider how it also occludes the visibility of writers who possess indeterminate political identities. Lalo drives this point home in a recollection of another failed European encounter, this time with a Spanish literary functionary whose friendly demeanor suddenly turns into undisguised bewilderment and disinterest upon learning of Lalo's provenance in Puerto Rico.[57]

As gatekeepers of juridical and authorial legitimacy, respectively, both the customs officer and the literary official represent two sides of the same system that conscripts citizens within what Édouard Glissant calls "l'universel généralisant" (the generalizing universal) that is sustained by a monolingual intent.[58] Universal categories, such as citizenship, make subjects transparent, knowable, and thus universally "translatable" within a world political (and literary) system. Furthermore, these same universal categories also dictate who has the right to be canonized as an "author." Undoubtedly, his critique of monolingualism concerns the officialization of national (and even global) languages under the guise of political unity; for in actuality, Glissant sees monolingualism as a means of economic and cultural colonization, where the metropolitan state uses language policy to enforce its values over a community from which it is geographically and culturally detached.[59] However, at a symbolic level, the notion of "monolingual intent" also suggests that there is only one way of belonging and expressing one's identity in a political or literary community; anyone who does not conform is erased or, as Lalo suggests, rendered an incomprehensible stranger.

Glissant's claims can illuminate Lalo's reflections on his own invisibility. While *Los países invisibles* is primarily concerned with Lalo's erasure in the world republic of letters, the text links this to Puerto Rico's neocolonial status. Lalo encapsulates the subject of his travelogue in the following terms: "Los países invisibles son aquellos que ha sido intervenidos por el discurso del Otro y *Éste* habla por ellos convirtiéndose en el experto de las máscaras mudas o apenas balbucientes. El ser invisible, incluso cuando habla y es escuchado, cuando logra mostrarse, recibe el silencio educado, la sonrisa cortés que lo ningunea" (Invisible countries are those that have been transformed through the intervention of the discourse of the Other, and *This One* speaks for them, turning them into mute or barely *stammering* masks. And even when the invisible being manages to

DISORIENTED CITIZENSHIP   69

speak and be heard when they manage to show themselves, they are greeted with well-mannered silence or a courteous smile that dismisses them [as a nothing]).[60]

Using synesthetic metaphors that highlight the relationship between visual representation and verbal expression, Lalo develops a nuanced critique of Puerto Rico's effacement within the political imaginary of the United States. Neocolonial politics occludes the voices of marginal communities through the ventriloquism of the metropolitan state. Like Kublai Khan's vast empire in Calvino's *Invisible Cities*, the metropolitan state today remains geographically distant from its former "protectorates," even as the former speaks on behalf of the latter. Beyond the jurisdiction of the neocolonial metropole, the neocolonial subject's voice becomes symbolically aphasic and, thus, untranslatable in international political/literary space. As Lalo's text shows us, this is evidenced by the fact that not many foreigners abroad—and not even U.S. citizens on the mainland—can either cogently articulate Puerto Rico's status or identify its writers.

Yet Lalo's description of the invisible subject's foray into visible countries strangely echoes Pedreira's lament of the "empobrecimiento de la lengua materna" (impoverishment of Puerto Rico's mother tongue)—Spanish—which has devolved into a "tartamudez gangosa" (nasal stammering), owing to the introduction of English on the island.[61] Although Pedreira and Lalo's writing emerges within distinctive juridical realities (Puerto Rico had not yet been incorporated as a Free Associated State in Pedreira's time), they agree that U.S. political and cultural hegemony over the island devalues Puerto Ricans' discursive authority in the world. However, whereas Pedreira felt this dilemma could be mitigated by returning to a Spanish monolingualism, Lalo's critique of his encounters with a world, even a Spanish-speaking one, that cannot comprehend Puerto Rico suggests that the Puerto Rican subject's unintelligibility in the world stems precisely from a "monolingual intent." By law, the United States arbitrates Puerto Rico's status abroad such that it brings about, to echo Apter's phrasing, Puerto Rico's "sundered" geopolitical filiations with Latin America and the Caribbean.[62]

Puerto Rico's sundered filiations bring into view the interconnectedness of juridical law and the law of literature that governs the literary canon. "Ley/leí," writes Lalo.[63] The oblique stroke (/) in the Spanish homonym that Lalo sets up diacritically marks the relation between law (ley) and the reading (leí) in the indicative preterite tense. Reading obliquely from the coordinates of the noncanonical, Lalo suggests, can nullify the force of law as canon. Conversely, Lalo argues, the canon mobilizes a "discurso visible" (visible discourse) that turns "el desvarío en normalidad" (nonsense [or deviation] into normality).[64] Lalo's definition of the canon does not seem much different from our understanding of the law as a regulatory mechanism that, evoking Sylvia Wynter, normalizes the practices and behaviors of a given community. The law makes visible those considered to be the legitimate representatives of the state. Conversely, the law "straightens" those who deviate from it by effacing and expunging them from the national narrative. Likewise, the literary canon establishes universal principles by which we can measure the aesthetic value of a text and the authorial legitimacy of a writer; it distinguishes "authentic" literary works from "impostors" that do not measure up. Still, even today, the guardians of the literary canon remain an elusive entity. While we can name the heads of nation-states who make the laws of their communities, we cannot really specify who governs the consecration of literary works in the world republic of letters.

Notwithstanding the "invisible" and diffuse character of the world republic of letters, Walter Mignolo argues that the canon is, in fact, the product of visible juridical power. Writing on the evolution of the contemporary Latin American literary canon, Mignolo explains that the region's early written expression represents the "histories of the 'visible,' . . . that is, histories based on the texts which had been blessed by colonial institutional powers."[65] These same institutions defined the law of the land, which, according to Mignolo, mandated "the official languages of the colonizing culture." But the authorized texts also positioned the colonized—the Indigenous and the enslaved Africans, and, to a large extent, white women—as invisible subjects insofar as their voices were translated and subsumed under the visible rhetoric of Spanish colonial power. Today, Mignolo suggests, the institutional legacy of colonial power persists, albeit reconfigured in the distinction between "canonical" and "noncanonical" literary expressions. However, at a time when translation patently grants readers universal access to even the most obscure texts, it seems as though the criteria for canonicity are no longer contingent on writing in a dominant language. Rather, an author's entry into the literary canon is contingent on whether the author can speak for a legitimate political community—to wit, the nation-state.

If canonical literary works project the nation-states from which they emerge, the noncanonical in *Los países invisibles* symbolizes an indeterminate or stateless space. As Lalo explains, there are "otros que permanecen condenados al sinsentido de pretender la práctica de la escritura en un *no canon's land*" (others who remain condemned to the senselessness of affirming the practice of writing in a *no canon's land*).[66] The use of *sinsentido* in the original Spanish text implies that Puerto Rican writing becomes both meaningless to and disoriented from the world republic of letters. Here, Lalo's text makes another gesture to Pedreira's reading of Puerto Rico. But Lalo's play on words shifts the focus from juridical status to authorial space by invoking the concept of the no-man's-land as a paradigm of the "no-canon's-land."

Legal and political historians have noted that the concept of terra nullius was invoked to justify the colonization and dispossession of lands based on the premise that they were uninhabited and unclaimed as property by a sovereign state. The concept of terra nullius derives from Roman antiquity but reemerged in the nineteenth century when it was anachronistically attributed to the modern legal

DISORIENTED CITIZENSHIP   71

tradition in order to help European states shore up their weakening imperial power.[67] Lands that were, in fact, inhabited and claimed by Indigenous peoples could be declared terra nullius, thereby dehumanizing their inhabitants and presenting them as nonexistent or "invisible" (non)occupants. Extrapolating terra nullius to the world literary space, Lalo's analogy shows how the no-canon's-land—what I call *literatura nullius*, so to speak—effaces Puerto Rican authors from the U.S. literary canon and, subsequently, from the world republic of letters; as Casanova has argued, the world republic of letters grants texts literary legitimacy on the condition that they possess a literary nationality. Nevertheless, Lalo's text does not clarify whether this no-canon's-land extends to Puerto Rican writers in the continental U.S. mainland and the diaspora.[68]

Still, for Lalo, the no-canon's-land represents a space of possibility. Indeed, its mere existence hints at the ascendancy of the noncanonical today and, subsequently, the descent of the world republic of letters as the arbiter of literariness in the terms proposed by Casanova. In a move that parallels the anachronistic fabrication of the terra nullius, Lalo frames his writing as an "anachronistic *un*avant-garde of the twenty-first century" and a narrative of "*contra*conquista."[69] Lalo situates his writing anachronistically in relation to the early twentieth-century avant-garde, a period credited with elevating Latin American and Caribbean writers to prominence following their sojourns in Europe. Yet unlike many of his literary forebears, Lalo decidedly rejects the translational power and the legitimizing gaze of Europe's republic of letters. By advancing a literary counterconquest Lalo interrogates the legitimacy of the canon as a measure for determining which texts merit "visibility" and legitimacy as "authentic" literary texts, since the contemporary Latin America and the Caribbean cannot be dissociated from the region's history of conquest and colonization. Lalo's no-canon's-land, then, is a decolonizing gesture.

LITERARY SHIPWRECKS

Like *Los países invisibles*, Lalo's first novel, *La inutilidad*, thematizes the invisibility of Puerto Rico and its intellectuals. Yet whereas *Los países invisibles* is predominantly focused on the nonstatus of Puerto Rican literature in the world, Lalo's novel tracks the writer's gaze from the world toward Puerto Rico itself. Divided into two sections titled "Paris" and "San Juan," *La inutilidad* chronicles the flight of a young, nameless writer in search of a home to anchor his identity in the world, followed by his defeated return to a native land from which he feels estranged.

Broadly, *La inutilidad* expresses a preoccupation with the diminished status of the Puerto Rican writer as a public intellectual and an authoritative or, recalling Pedreira, an orientational voice on social and political matters and the accompanying devaluation of the literary form as a medium of reading. Published in

2004, Lalo's novel appeared on the scene at a time marked by global pronouncements about the death of the literary form, the devaluation of the book, and the diminished appreciation for reading books owing to the ascendancy of social media. In Puerto Rico, the conversation around the supposed crisis of the literary form and the book emerged as anecdotal declarations that "la gente no lee" (people don't read). More specifically, they do not read *literature*. Lalo has, for better or for worse, been a representative voice in this conversation on the island, as reflected in fiction where his semiautobiographical characters assume the role of disregarded and marginal writers who are radically estranged and at odds with Puerto Rican society. For example, his second novel, *Simone*, opens with the ruminations of a clearly depressed writer who questions the value of writing—his raison d'être—in the absence of a readership.[70] The questions raised in *Simone*—along with the novel's thematization of its male protagonist's serendipitous discovery of an audience of (one), an Asian woman— can be read as a continuation of Lalo's desire for orientation in *La inutilidad*. One could argue that Lalo has made his illegibility into a successful trope, in ways that have trumped the identitarian themes of other Puerto Rican writers and have rehabilitated Pedreira's Hispanism.

Since the publication of several novels, countless essays, and an equally significant visual repertoire, Lalo has gone on to achieve considerable international acclaim, becoming one of Puerto Rico's most visible and legible literary figures known for his excoriating commentary on the island's status and Puerto Ricans' complacency with regard to their self-determination. César Salgado writes,

> Lalo ha logrado suscitar, por una parte, la aspiración por una genuina ciudadanía escindida de los espejismos de la norteamericana y constituida por puertorriqueños y, por otra parte, la manifestación abyecta de una *in*ciudadanía que rechaza ciega y visceralmente el mero vislumbre de otra posibilidad de *polis* con insultos banales, agresiones gratuitas y procacidades nerviosas e inseguras

> (Lalo has managed to stir up, on the one hand, the desire for genuine citizenship, excised from the mirages of the North American one and constituted by Puerto Ricans, and on the other hand, the abject manifestation of an *uncit*izenship that blindly and viscerally rejects the mere glimmer of another possibility of the *polis* with banal insults, gratuitous attacks, and anxious and insecure impertinence).[71]

One could argue Lalo's renown and his writing incite polarizing responses that stand in deep contrast to the apathetic resignation that characterizes and conceals the existential angst of his writer protagonists in both *La inutilidad* and *Simone*.

La inutilidad is of particular concern to this chapter because of how it thematizes the writer's failed attempt to anchor and orient himself toward vocabulary or language that will allow him to articulate this *other* possibility of a Puerto Rico. On the one hand, the novel depicts French as a foundational language in Western modernity that symbolizes political legitimacy, progress, and citizenship. On the other hand, (Puerto Rican) Spanish becomes a marker of juridical indeterminacy, political indecision, and complacency. In turning toward Paris and the French language, the novel's Puerto Rican protagonist, I argue, aims to legitimize himself as both a writer and a political subject.

In a 2008 interview, Lalo rehearses this viewpoint when he explains Paris's appeal as the setting for *La inutilidad*. "For a Latin American, Paris was the door to enter modernity," he states. "There was no means of getting there in one's language. . . . There [Paris], it was possible to believe that modern culture was of utmost relevance."[72] Lalo's invocation of Paris recapitulates a long-standing relationship cultivated by intellectuals in the first half of the twentieth century. In the wake of decolonization, as Latin American countries sought to hone their distinctive postcolonial, national identities, Paris offered intellectuals from these regions the vocabulary with which to articulate the ethos of their evolving nation-states. As Pascale Casanova corroborates, in Paris, writers hailing from Latin America "discovered their national identity."[73] Paradoxically, the capital of the world republic of letters proclaimed a "universal" language even as it required writers to "declare" their specific national origin as a mode of literary and aesthetic distinction. Lalo construes French as a political prosthesis— something that can be amended to both his indeterminate and incomprehensible juridical status as a U.S. citizen and his tenuous literary status in the world republic of letters as a Puerto Rican writer.

In *Cosmopolitan Desires*, Mariano Siskind makes the case for reading representative works of Latin American literature as strategic and forceful claims for consideration with the "realm of universality," even as they denounce their Eurocentric exclusion and "nationalist patterns of self-marginalization."[74] However, the crux of this rigorous reappraisal of Latin American literary modernity through the lens of cosmopolitan thought hinges on the claim that this literature betrays a "desire for the world." Siskind has since reconsidered his cosmopolitan vision of Latin American literary and cultural production, as the world increasingly reckons with its "unworlding" in the wake of loss, dislocation, and disaster.[75] Yet, there is a way in which his identification of Latin American cosmopolitan yearning resonates with *La inutilidad,* only to the extent that the worldy conceit Lalo's Puerto Rican protagonist is ultimately frustrated or, in his words, shipwrecked.

Given that Puerto Rico is not recognized as a legitimate and autonomous political community, Paris's redemptive mystique holds sway over the Puerto Rican intellectual. As the novel's nameless protagonist ruminates retrospectively from San Juan, "Lejos de este país, había siempre defendido mi pertenencia a éste. Pensaba y había pensado que podíamos ser algo: una historia, una cultura con la que sostenernos, con las que validar nuestra existencia" (Far from this country [Puerto Rico], I had always defended my belonging to *here*. I always believed we had a history, a culture upon which to stand firm, with which to validate our existence).[76] The novel's writer-intellectual protagonist articulates a defense of his Puerto Ricanness vis-à-vis the hope that Paris will equip him with the armature ("history" and "culture") to envision a self-legitimizing narrative that countervails the island's juridical invisibility within the United States' foundational narrative. Ironically, his self-definition through French posits a dubious distinction between Paris (and, by extension, Europe), on the one hand, and U.S. neocolonial power, on the other. And yet situating Puerto Rico at the intersection of divergent colonial histories—a move that evokes Latin American writers' strategic use of Paris to frame their ideological emancipation from Spain—enables him to disavow the United States' dominance over Puerto Rico.[77]

In Paris, the writer attempts to fashion himself by way of his postgraduate Orientalist studies, which focus on a French ethnographic novel about a warrior named Klok—the last surviving member of a vanquished Amazonian tribe. Rescued and brought to France by an anthropologist, Klok teaches his language to students at the Normale. His language, the text tells us, constituted a "missing link" in the genealogy of the Tupí-Guaraní.[78] An intermediary of the now-extinct Brazilian Tupí and their Guaraní kin, Klok embodies an unbroken, untainted kinship. In France, however, Klok leads a solitary existence, as he is unable to communicate with others, and his language has been archived in the bibliographic memory of a sole anthropologist. Yet, an auspicious friendship with a young student in the neighboring flat brings an end to his confinement. In the wake of the Klok's passing, the student—who has learned the warrior's customs and language—returns to the Amazon to bury his ashes and, subsequently, disappears. The narrative concludes with unverifiable rumors of a white *cacique*—the student assimilated into a native community as its chief.

The placement of Klok's story in *La inutilidad* discloses the Puerto Rican protagonist's desire for authentic community, culture, and an uninterrupted history, all of which Klok's language supposedly embodies. Indeed, suggests James Clifford, ethnographic texts allegorically disclose universal truths about human behavior. He argues that one such allegory is represented in the trope of the "vanishing primitive," emblematized by an ethnographer who acts as the guardian and inscriber of a traditional and "authentic" past (the native) that the forces of modernity have steadily destroyed.[79] At the same time, Clifford states, knowledge of the inevitability of loss accrues salvific authority to ethnographic writing—entrusted with preserving this irretrievable, "pure" past.

But the protagonist's affinity for Klok brings to mind the revalorization of Taíno identity in the Puerto Rican diaspora in the eighties and nineties. Juan Flores has argued that the postcolonial rehabilitation of a romanticized Taíno identity makes manifest a "culture of national resistance" against the incursion of European values.[80] Effectively, the reinvestment of Taíno symbols and vocabulary in the Puerto Rican diaspora disavows the nation's foundational histories of Indigenous extinction, colonization, and failed emancipation in favor of a triumphant, oppositional narrative. We glean something similar from the protagonist's assertion that his study of Indigenous cultures in Paris serves as "armas de resistencia" (weapons of resistance) to anchor his Puerto Rican identity. And yet the irony of Klok's passing belies such restitutionary efforts. Considering that the (French) ethnographic text effectively erases Klok (behind the white, French cacique) and silences his language in an archive, "history" and "culture" are available only through the French text's rehabilitation of Klok. His language is never translated and vitalized into something that has functional value in modern society—that is, into something that is spoken. Rather, it simply reflects back on the "civilizing" power of French.

But the writer protagonist's attempt to reorient his identity vis-à-vis Klok rehearses a troubling Orientalist gaze, recalling Edward Said's classic text, through which the West distinguishes itself as a civilizing authority.[81] Extrapolating Said's original work, Ahmed further explains that "to become oriental is both to be given an orientation and to be shaped by the orientation of that gift."[82] *La inutilidad* collapses the specificity of indigeneity into a universal Orient(al) without contending with the racialized structures of coloniality that would cause the Klok to "vanish" into whiteness—a whiteness that Lalo himself embodies and with which his writing has refused to contend even as he claims for himself the condition of subalterneity.[83] In order to imaginatively fashion himself as a "modern" subject who possesses a legitimate juridical and authorial identity, the protagonist must, paradoxically, become estranged or disoriented from himself (and Puerto Rico) and assume the gaze of the Orientalist. This, I claim, translates his encounters with fellow Puerto Rican as misrecognition.

Nevertheless, his interactions with Puerto Ricans on the island betray the incommensurability of the identity shaped in France with what he really is at home. The novel illustrates this pointedly in a letter the protagonist writes to his friend Pétrement—a French Orientalist and translator, to whom he describes his frustrated efforts to acclimate to his new life in San Juan. He explains that, when writing to Pétrement, he must "translate" his life, "alterándola para que pudiera comprenderla y aceptarla sin enfurecerse" (changing things in the narratives so that he could understand and accept them without getting furious).[84] Here, "translation" is clearly a euphemism for dissimulation or, simply put, lying. The protagonist "translates" that in Puerto Rico, he must hold mundane jobs to sustain his life as a writer and that the glamorous life of an intellectual is a privilege. Effectively, this passage represents an undoing of the fictive identity the protagonist cultivated in France.

These circumstances inform the broader axiological and existential questions posed in the novel's concluding pages. Recounting his research of Indigenous cultures to associates in Puerto Rico, he bemoans their dismissive tone: "Pronto descubrí que se expresaba un corrientemente un menosprecio atroz, del tipo 'para qué sirve' o 'a quién le importa' por lo que me interesaba" (I would quickly discover that my interest were met with nasty, belittling expressions of contempt, like "So what?" or "Who cares?" [toward the things that interested me]).[85] The protagonist's declaration betrays an anxiety that is characteristic of Lalo's work: that Puerto Ricans neither read nor can find value in literary culture, that they cannot comprehend the life of an intellectual. Arguably, there is an element of truth to this, given the preponderance of mass media and material consumption on the island. This aside, I find that the interpretive disjuncture between the protagonist and his Puerto Rican compatriots cannot be reduced to mere intellectual docility or disinterest on the part of the latter. Rather, I suggest that underlying their supposed disinterest is a valid critique of a text fashioned and translated by the world republic of letters—embodied by the protagonist, and which conforms to an image of Puerto Ricanness crafted abroad and, thus, does not necessarily reflect the community at home.

La inutilidad contrasts the unintelligibility of the protagonist's Frenchified "text" with that of the island's political discourse at the time of his return. Lalo investigates the political conditions that produce what the author suggests is a culture of nonreading in Puerto Rico through faint but critical gestures to the annexationist party of then-governor Carlos Romero Barceló, the Partido Nuevo Progresista (PNP). Coinciding with the PNP's political upheavals were actions taken by the island's dissenting political parties to legislate Puerto Rico's official language (as Spanish, English, or both)—whether as a means of protecting its (Spanish) national legacy and (Latin American) continental identities, on the one hand, or to cultivate a more definitive legal kinship with the U.S. mainland government, on the other. When, in 1993, the PNP instituted Spanish *and* English as Puerto Rico's official languages—reversing the previous pro-ELA or "status quo" government's (Partido Popular Democrático) officialization of Spanish as the *only* language—it represented a stronger cultural realignment of Puerto Rico with the United States. Arguably, English was perceived metonymically, not only as a linguistic practice but also as a conduit of Anglo-American cultural practices, which Puerto Rican intellectuals such as Pedreira had historically opposed. So, while the status had always been a source of contention, when the purity of Puerto Rico's monolingual national language (Spanish) had also been muddled, many Puerto Rican intellectuals perceived it as an abrogation of their authority as, according to Carlos Pabón, the (unofficial) "legislators" of Puerto Rican national identity.[86] In the face of their diminished status as legislators, Puerto Rican social theorist Arturo Torrecilla explains, many Puerto Rican intellectuals demonstrate overwhelming anxiety as they struggle to find their raison d'être among a public who misreads them as strangers at home.[87]

Referencing the tenure of the annexationist governor, Carlos Romero Barceló, the protagonist declares, "El gobierno de Romero . . . parecía hablar en un dialecto que le era propio, apenas comprensible, plagadas de pausas sorprendentes, de interjecciones, de bloques enteros de oraciones que constituían una serte de delirio al que, ante mi perplejidad, casi todos escuchaban sin estupor, con la resignación y el costumbre del que ve llover" (The Romero government . . . seemed to speak its own dialect, barely comprehensible to others. Its rhetoric was plagued by unexpected pauses, interjections, whole sections of orations that devolved into some sort of raving, which most people, totally uninterested, listened to with the routine resignation of watching the rain fall).[88] The rhetoric of U.S. statehood, personified in the figure of Romero Barceló, is camouflaged under a garbled, frenzied message designed to stupefy Puerto Ricans into political complacency. And yet the protagonist's bemusement at his compatriots' uncritical acceptance of Romero Barceló discloses the confrontation of two untranslatable discourses—statehood *versus* political autonomy. This encounter explains their indifference and bafflement toward his intellectual interests and his political identity. More than anything, however, the passage reveals the futility or the uselessness—recalling the novel's title—of his efforts. In *La inutilidad*, no other event typifies this failure than the shipwreck.

Early in the novel, the protagonist suggests that Puerto Rican identity is "más o menos náufraga" (more or less adrift).[89] The protagonist's invocation of the shipwreck places Lalo's writing, once again, in dialogue with Pedreira's description of Puerto Rico as an "errant ship" trapped between the North American and Hispanic cultures. Pedreira likened the Puerto Rican subject to a castaway, describing him as a "half-man" in reference to his cultural and political debasement.[90] And yet the armature of *Insularismo* follows that of the Spanish American colonial narrative, which often stages the shipwreck of its European protagonist on an island in the New World as a plot device to bring about his psychological transformation. Effectively, the shipwreck emblematizes the predicament of being caught in a no-man's-land, a space where, by definition, everything is untranslatable. The shipwreck reduces the European castaway to an almost bestial native—for his clothes, his language, and the instruments he brought with him from Europe are rendered useless in the foreign habitat of the island; effectively, the castaway is left with his ravaged body as the only instrument with which he can survive and translate (himself into) the New World.

Undoubtedly, *La inutilidad* can be read as the story of a disoriented castaway who attempts to circumvent the reality of his condition, only to return to the very shipwreck that constitutes contemporary Puerto Rico. At the same time, the (translational) failure emblematized by the shipwreck forebodes not the end but, rather, the starting point for envisioning the emancipation of the Puerto Rican intellectual from his estrangement and invisibility. *La inutilidad* spurns the possibility of a conciliatory, happy ending as we watch the protagonist ruminate on the "el esfuerzo, el dolor y el fracaso de generaciones" (the efforts, the pain, and the failure of generations) of Puerto Rican writers.[91] With its seemingly hopeless ending, Lalo's novel—like much of his work—begs the question, why write in the face of dwindling readers? For Lalo, the novel suggests, writing from and in the face of failure is, indeed, an affirmation of a Puerto Rican existence.

CHAPTER 3

Freelance Personhood

LIVING OFF THE BOOKS IN THE OUTER SPACES OF CUBAN WRITING

Cuba has been largely conceived in the Western imagination as a space sealed off and frozen, geopolitically and temporally, from the world and the progress of history. Yet the economic crisis known, officially, as the "Special Period in Times of Peace" brought Cuban society into contact with a foreignness that, for three decades, the state had worked to expunge and had relegated to an "outside." As is now well known, to mitigate the crisis occasioned by the dissolution of the Soviet Bloc, which subvented a significant share of the island's economy, the Cuban state opened the island to the world market in the early to mid-1990s and, selectively, to capitalism. This critical "confrontation between capitalism and socialism" has been explored in terms of the ethical and ideological disorientation it has provoked in citizens borne of the Cuban revolution;[1] for not only did the state fail to materialize a promised socialist future, but it also limited many Cuban citizens' ability to access this newly appeared capital. Much has been written about this moment—and the dislocation of Cuban society for the state's socialist project. Notably, Cuba's contact with its outside spawned critical work on the commodification and exportation of Cuban culture for consumption in the foreign market, even as Cubans on the island were significantly immured from this foreign experience of Cuba.[2]

Contemporary Cuban studies have been shaped by a rich body of cultural criticism that has sought to make meaning out of a period marked by ideological contradictions through an exploration of Cuban aesthetics. The Special Period, as scholars like Guillermina De Ferrari and James Buckwalter-Arias have shown, occasions a "search for new aesthetic paradigms" in which Cuban writers, artists, and intellectuals reorient their frustrated relationship with the revolution through a reclamation of the personal and "liberal notion of individual freedom" and a reimagination of community.[3] While the aesthetic approach to these topics varies, in my view, these narratives cohere discernibly in their focus on the problem of personal and public representation.

In the sense that aesthetics, as I discussed in the previous chapter, concerns a politics of representation as the right of the citizen-subject to appear, I contend that the encounter between two seemingly antithetical political systems in Cuba—the qualified accommodation of the "inside" (socialism) to an "outside" (neoliberal capitalism)—likewise produces an encounter of the Cuban citizen with personhood. That is, as Charles W. Mills argues, personhood is defined as a political economy of socially recognized difference.[4] This chapter revisits this critical parenthesis in Cuba's postsocialist transition because the state's dalliance with and welcoming of international markets have not been fully appraised in terms of the qualified forms of personhood and abeyant citizenship that it engendered on the island.

Cuban literature emerging during and shaped by the Special Period has, thus far, provided the most incisive commentary on the meaning of belonging and membership in contemporary Cuba and the conditions that shape one's legal status as a person and citizen. Yet, as Cuban literary and cultural theorist Désirée Díaz has noted, there is a paucity of analyses on the question of citizenship in Cuba owing to how the socialist state resemanticized that very concept and, in particular, nearly eliminated its usage as a descriptor of belonging and membership from its juridical vocabulary.[5] Criticism on the literary production of Cuban writers born in the decade after the Revolution has rightly underscored their transgressive and dystopian postmodern aesthetics—disclosed through representations of personal and societal perversion, evil, and degradation, which signal the Revolution's "ideological collapse" and the ethical crisis it provoked in citizens.[6] But these texts also generate new readings and meaning if we consider that the ethical appeals they make arise out of their characters' direct confrontation of the law, the *nomos* of citizenship, and the way it engenders unnamed states of civic exclusion. The method of analysis that I advance throughout this book, and especially in this chapter, insists on placing cultural texts in conversation with legal discourse as fiction in order to expose and interrogate the contradictions between the official grammar of law and the lived, juridical experience of citizens.

This chapter contributes to the emergent work on citizenship in postsocialist Cuban in view of literary fiction and prose writing that interrogates how Cuba's reopening to the global market unexpectedly enabled citizens to work "off-the-books" through extra-juridical entanglements with foreigners. Two bodies of narratives are at the heart of this chapter: *Se alquila un planeta* (*A Planet for Rent*), a collection of science-fictional stories authored by Yoss, the nom de plume of José Miguel Sánchez Gómez, and selections of writings from the dissident social media collective that became known as the Blogósfera Cubana Alternativa (Alternative Cuban Blogosphere). Depicting a salable Earth invaded by aliens in a dystopian future, *Se alquila un planeta* allegorizes how Cubans negotiated their survival and livelihood during the Special Period through exploitative alliances with foreign tourists whose presence on the island exploded numerically in the nineties, as a result of the reforms that reopened the country to the international market and capitalism. Another expression of this was the Alternative Cuban Blogosphere, which emerged during the Special Period. Censored from publishing in the state-controlled publishing outlets, writers like Yoani Sánchez and Claudia Cadelo—two representative figures of the Alternative Cuban Blogosphere—liken themselves to stateless subjects as they document their inhospitable displacement from Cuban publishing outlets and are plunged into the virtual space of foreign host servers that house their posts through the assistance of a network of allies outside of Cuba. Because of the shared theme of authorially alienated Cuban subjects who must remake themselves in terrestrial, extraterrestrial, and virtual spaces reserved exclusively for foreign occupancy, the Alternative Cuban Blogosphere is a fitting nonfictional example of the systemic problems presented in *Se alquila un planeta*. The two also share a common protagonist: the more-or-less self-employed and "self-made" or remade Cuban subject, the freelancer who labors in spaces deliberately placed outside the legal purview of Cuba's socialist state. This chapter thus concludes with an account of how Cuban authors found themselves in real-world analogies of the depersonalizing conditions presented in *Se alquila un planeta*, demonstrating with full clarity the complexity of the spatiality-personhood juxtaposition that arose during the Special Period.

The now well-documented deprivation—visceral hunger, poverty, and widespread material scarcity—Cubans experienced during the early part of the Special Period, coupled with the state's abandonment of its fiduciary duties to its citizenry, immediately compelled citizens to develop newfound strategies of inventiveness and self-sufficiency to survive. Yet, as Ariana Hernandez-Reguant underscores, the subsequent "arrival of foreign stakeholders—companies, entrepreneurs, tourists—had extended the horizons of possibility for many people" by creating an informal and oftentimes illegal economy that allowed many Cubans to further improve their material conditions through "freelance work as self-employed workers."[7] I agree with Hernandez-Reguant's assertion that the ability of self-employed Cuban citizens to secure their livelihood through off-the-books, nonstate work with foreign stakeholders shifted their understanding of "work, property, profit, and community."[8] I depart from this reading of the freelancer as a semi-independent laboring class, however, focusing instead on their self-making as singular persons individuated from Cuba's socialist state.

The freelance sex worker in *Se alquila un planeta* and the displaced amateur writer of the Alternative Cuban Blogosphere represent (neo)liberal forms of self-proprietorship or what I call "freelance personhood" that is articulated simultaneously to Cuba's legally sanctioned contact with its outside while contravening

Cuban socialist legality's emphasis on an impersonal collectivity as one of its guiding principles of citizenship. While this freelance personhood, imagined through the act of writing, offsets an aesthetics of disenchantment, I am cautious to assert its emancipatory potential, which may be implied when narratives of survivalist self-making are filtered through the lens of "grit" and resilience or when dissident acts of postsocialist self-possession, as inevitably happens with Cuba, become the fodder of ideological one-upmanship. Instead, *Se alquila un planeta* and the Alternative Cuban Blogosphere suggest that the very attachments to and "asylum" offered by foreign entities that enable Cuban citizens to articulate this sense of freelance personhood from within the state also become subject to capture, possession, and occupation.

Denationalizing Self-Proprietorship

Before it came to define the occupational status of a person whose labor is not bound to a particular person or organization, the term "freelance" denoted the status of someone who worked as a mercenary without allegiance to a given nation. According to Merriam-Webster, the term "freelancer" in its original usage designated a person "who would fight for whichever nation or person paid them the most,"—that is, a mercenary with a "free lance" as their weapon.[9] Originally, then, the freelancer could be said to be dispossessed of their personhood. They become *no one* because to be someone (a person) would be to specify a geopolitical allegiance.

Paradoxically, in its more contemporary meaning, freelancing, the state of being self-employed, also recalls the association between personhood and self-proprietorship that is foundational to classic liberal thought and its complex relationship between shifting categories of personhood and the capacity to own one's labor. As scholarly consensus demonstrates, it is John Locke who delineates this relation in his classic pronouncement that "man has a *property* in his own *person*."[10] It is important to note that, in this work, Locke defines not so much what a person is as much as the relation of proprietorship that Man establishes with himself in the form of a person.[11] Because personhood is Man's first property, he also owns as property the labor produced by his body; likewise, his capacity for self-ownership conditions his ability to own *other* property that he has cultivated through his labor. Scholars have long debated Locke's syllogistic association of self-proprietorship with property ownership and the extent to which this lays the groundwork for capitalist accumulation.[12]

This chain of associations between freelancing, statelessness, and self-possession is recapitulated both in Yoss's short story "Trabajadora social" (Social worker) and in the dissident blog writings of the Alternative Cuban Blogosphere. In these texts, freelancing acquires its original denationalized meaning while also specifying a personalism that strives to be self-possessed but, ultimately, falls short. When citizens in these texts announce or re-present themselves as *persons*, as an act of individuation through their labor, the texts suggest that their personhood is essentially "freelanced." That is, since Cuban socialist legality does not allow for such acts of singular individuation within its *nomos*, personhood must be enacted, expressed, and contained within foreign networks and spaces that, although located within Cuba, are segmented and separated from Cuban civil society and adhere to the political economy of the island's hospitality industry, which is governed by the global market. The person, as both a property relation and a self-identity, must be "freelanced" through foreign networks precisely because it is a concept that was eschewed from the country's juridical grammar following the Cuban revolution. Cuban sociologist Velia Cecilia Bobes explains that the idea of citizenship was resemanticized in the constitution after 1959 such that the notion of "the people" replaced the citizen "elector" of representative democracies. In doing so, Bobes elaborates, "se refuerza el vínculo colectivista y se desdibuja el principio de individualidad (característico de la ciudadanía)" (the collectivist bond is emphasized and the individualist principle [characteristic of citizenship] is blurred).[13] With its emphasis on equity, justice, collectivity, and social uniformity, the idea of a revolutionary Cuban citizenry appealed to a nation previously divided along racial, class, and gender lines. Effectively, however, it subsumed and concealed identitarian difference and rendered personhood impersonal under an egalitarian sociality marked by uniformity and sameness.

The emphasis on collective uniformity delinks personhood from labor as an accumulative property relation. Since the Cuban revolution socialized and nationalized property, Cuban citizens could not derive any sense of personhood from the possession of property outside themselves or from their laboring of it.[14] By undoing the property relation between (self-)proprietorship and labor, the Cuban state redefined Cuban citizens as *workers* and elevated and "liberated" work from the exploitation of the market.[15] Work is simultaneously liberated and nationalized as a collective project such that the idea of freelancing, in both its original denotative and its contemporary connotative meanings, seems unimaginable.

In the wake of the fall of the Soviet Union, the Cuban state introduced a series of reforms that reopened the island to the global market. Notable among these reforms was the 1996 passage of the Foreign Investment Act, which, as Ricardo Pérez explains, "created the legal framework for joint ventures between transnational corporations and the Cuban government."[16] More specifically, the Foreign Investment Act denationalized land and allowed foreign business investors to purchase commercial real estate that would become the infrastructure for foreign tourism. Fidel Castro justified the revolutionary government's policy reversal as a temporary fix to the island's impending financial ruin, but Cuban citizens encountered even greater territorial, economic, and cultural disenfranchisement than before since land denationalization almost exclusively benefitted foreign investors and visitors.[17] For instance, foreign investment created a new foreign-oriented infrastructure—including grocers, clothing stores, restaurants, transportation services, and hotels—that operated solely via convertible currency, another reform introduced to boost the influx of hard currency to the island. As Aaron Kamugisha reminds us, even prior to their arrival, these local spaces are already configured to anticipate and respond to the desires of tourists who "occupy a space we might term 'extraterritorial citizens.'"[18] These local spaces extend to tourists the rights and entitlements of membership without naturalization and are, in turn, made foreign to naturalized citizens.

In the first volume of his *Hospitalité* seminar, Jacques Derrida tells us that the question of hospitality, which is itself a twofold question—of who has the right to be received and welcomed as a guest/stranger in a given space and who can act in the capacity of the host who welcomes—that requires that we unmoor our thinking of space from the terrestrial. In light of modern technological achievements that made possible "the political and techno-political appropriation of non-terrestrial spaces and places"—among them, the moon landing and the development of the internet—Derrida shows that it is necessary to extend the spatial geographies of hospitality beyond the terrestrial domain through which Kant posited his idea of cosmopolitan right.[19] Derrida's insights about nonterrestrial space will be vital to my reading of bodily, extraterrestrial, and virtual spaces as extensions of tourist host spaces in "Trabajadora social" and the Alternative Cuban Blogosphere, respectively.

Space delimits the "proper" of the "I" (of what is "mine") from the "improper" of the stranger.[20] In other words, how space is appropriated distinguishes the ownership of the property by the self—and the family and the state—versus the nonownership of the stranger. Therefore, Derrida shows, to the extent that the *host* would be defined as the *proper/proprietor* of a given space, there is a correlation between the *host* and the juridical person as the property of the self.[21] This raises the question of what happens to Cuban personhood when it cannot be expressed in the body of the citizen and must, instead, be freelanced and take asylum in nonterrestrial spaces that are sealed off by the state for use by foreign tourists.

Thinking through this question unfortunately discloses a not-so-bright side to these expressions of personal sovereignty. The person is (self-)possessed within spaces accessible only to foreigners—whether a hotel, an airport, or cyberspace, which act like asylums. Although to be clear, I am not suggesting that Cuban subjects can see themselves as persons only through some type of salvific relationship with the foreign entities who give asylum to the being. Instead, my reading elaborates on how the person is possessed by the very thing that allows them to become a person to the extent that they lose that sense of autonomy.

NEOLIBERAL PALIMPSESTS

"Se alquila un planeta" (A Planet for Rent), the titular opening of Yoss's collection, is scripted as a promotional advertisement that announces the Earth's vacancy and invites *xenoids*, the overarching term for nonhuman aliens, to bid on the parts of the planet they would like to rent. In the dystopian future of *Se alquila un planeta*, the Earth is a *Protectorado Galáctico* (Galactic Protectorate) whose political economy is underwritten by the Planetary Tourism Agency, a UN-like body of two hundred human members who govern under the façade of a participatory democracy while, ultimately, yielding to the influence of xenoids, "los verdaderos amos del planeta" (the true masters of the planet).[22] The bustling economy fueled by xenoid tourism has sent the Earth's marketing campaign into overdrive, churning out slogans like "La hospitalidad es nuestra segunda naturaleza" (Hospitality is our middle name).[23] In actuality, xenoids have taken over the Earth in the wake of a failed nuclear assault against them. Although humans' resistance to their colonization has been abated, for the most part, by the unfulfilled promise of galactic citizenship and its attendant rights, *Se alquila un planeta* betrays terrestrials' disaffection with their alien overlords and their political indeterminacy as quasi-stateless subjects in the planet they call home. Humans, the opening story suggests, not only are excluded from owning terrestrial property but also are leased with the Earth as a package deal.

Segueing into the collection's second story, "Trabajadora social," the above marketing campaign has proven successful: a terrestrial astroport is teeming with all manner of xenoid tourists arriving to experience Earth's adventures or, having had their fill of earthly hospitality, departing to their galactic homes. This, in turn, has given way to a dominant form of planetary wage labor that almost exclusively employs and compensates humans in the capacity of "hosts" to xenoids. Immersed in the belly of a neoliberal, neocolonial beast, however, "Trabajadora social" unmasks hospitality as a euphemism, revealing the actual stakes of interplanetary and interspecies contact between xenoids and humans.

Delving deeper into the personal and ontological implications of being bound to land as stateless property, "Trabajadora social" narrates how humans negotiate—to varying degrees of agency, flexibility, and skill—their occupational status as hosts in Earth's political economy. In Yoss's text, the term "host" describes a broad labor category under the aegis of the Planetary Tourism Agency and covers various types of employment where humans are tasked with entertaining and acclimating xenoids to Earth. Although employment options are severely limited for humans, those who strategically leverage their host relationship with xenoids can survive and thrive as independent contractors outside the system, as is the case with "freelance social workers." In this light, "Trabajadora social" investigates what it means for humans to be "occupied," in one sense, as freelance hosts with no terrestrial property rights or a home of their own to offer hospitality and, in another, as an extension of terrestrial property that xenoids inhabit as renters-cum-owners of the Earth.

As a whole, *Se alquila un planeta* betrays the representational aesthetics of an assiduous reader and student of science fiction. In particular, Yoss's text signals to earlier, popular alien invasion fictions—among them H. G. Wells's novel *The War of the Worlds* (1898) and cinematic adaptations of literary works such as *The Invasion of the Body Snatchers* (1956) and the *Alien* film franchise. Critics have noted that the conceptual and representational framework of these foundational alien invasion narratives, on the one hand, constitutes critical commentary about colonialism and, on the other, depicts the West's angst about its constitution and integrity as an agent of techno-scientific progress and the arbiter of a global political economy in light of the perceived infiltration of racial and political Others.[24] The indelible traces of this past are glimpsed in the rich referential apparatus of *Se alquila un planeta*, which translates and resemanticizes the language and contextual histories of its fictional predecessors within a neoliberal economy that overlays and coexists with Cuba's postsocialist present. Thus, for example, in "Trabajadora social," the Wellsian "war of the worlds" is reconfigured as a soft yet no less dystopian "commercial warfare" waged by xenoids against terrestrial humans "por nuevas tecnologías, por mercados, por clientes, por mano de obra barata" (for new technologies, for markets, for clients, for cheap labor).[25] Furthermore, the "body snatching" novelized by Jack Finney and subsequently canonized in film, is reimagined in the figure of the "host-human" tourist worker who is willingly inhabited and possessed by certain xenoids as a technology that both facilitates their mobility and sightseeing on Earth but also ensures the continuity of their species.

Bringing the collection closer to home, Yoss also pays homage to his Cuban literary forebears, as is the case in the collection's opening, eponymous story, "Se alquila un planeta," which mimics the magisterial prologue of Guillermo Cabrera Infante's *Tres tristes tigres*. Like the promotional call for tourists that unleashes Yoss's alien invasion, Cabrera Infante's novel begins by drawing back the curtains of prerevolutionary Havana's legendary Tropicana nightclub, where the spotlight shines on an MC who welcomes the club's "international clientele" with "esa misma hospitalidad de siempre" (that same hospitality as always).[26] In her attentive reading of this scene, Jeanine Murray-Román observes that this typical hospitality "articulates the Cuban audience's training as colonized subjects under the purview of the United States' Good Neighbor Policy."[27] By contrast, Yoss's dystopian recapitulation of Cabrera Infante's masterpiece does not necessarily trace an unbroken yet dislocated temporal line—"as always"—between a (neo)colonial past and a postsocialist present. Rather, it indicates that the Cuban state's accommodation of a neoliberal political economy during the Special Period birthed a form of coloniality that, like the xenoids, was alien to those born in the wake of the Cuban revolution. Thus, it is not European colonial and imperial expansion that strictly provides the source material for Yoss's depictions of alien invasion but, rather, Special Period Cuba and a future world absorbed by globalism. According to Yoss, in an interview with David Shook, *Se alquila un planeta* narrates the Special Period as a "real-life dystopia" during which the author witnessed friends leave the island by illegal and dangerous means and be driven to sex work as a means to survive.[28] During this time, the author himself was plunged into desperation by hunger, subsisting on a barebones diet of rice and, at one of his lowest points, cat meat.[29] Of course, these personal accounts of human deprivation occur parallel to the now well-documented "new boom" in post-Soviet Cuban tourism, which injected the island's economy with new capital, new commerce, and a new mass of tourists whose experienced Cuba in a manner that was in stark contrast to Cuban citizens' lived experience of hardship.[30]

In one sense, the human toll of the Special Period may be described as dystopian insofar as it reveals the Cuban state's failure to make good on the utopian promise of the revolution. In another sense, what also characterized the particularly dystopian quality of the Special Period was the state's insistence that Cuban people remain steadfast to an "irrevocable" socialist ethos even as it arguably consented to the island's peaceful invasion and occupation by global capitalism.[31] This follows Gregory Claeys's reading of dystopia as a group's coerced adherence to an "extreme ethos of sociability" and personal sacrifice.[32] Depicting humans as Cubans and xenoids as tourists, Yoss's "Trabajadora social" tells the story of how many Cuban citizens navigated this contradictory, dystopian terrain through freelance work that allowed them to survive off a neoliberal economy from which they were technically barred access.

Jacqueline Loss offers an acute take on the situation, asserting that, in the absence of Soviet subsidies, "Cuban creators had to enter into distinct networks of obligation that obliged them to perform not only their national allegories but also their intimate histories for new suitors."[33] Extrapolating Loss's comment, it suggests Cubans' performance of socialist hospitality as dependency on foreign (previously Soviet) assistance—or, in Loss's words, "a satellite status," which, nevertheless, had to be reattuned for new, neoliberal "guests." In similar terms, the Earth in *Se alquila un planeta* may be regarded as a satellite of the galactic, planetary system on which it subsists.

John Rieder, in his definitive text on the genre, *Colonialism and the Emergence of Science Fiction*, reminds us that the history of colonialism provides the context for early science fiction.[34] But *Se alquila un planeta* aligns with what Rieder states happened next; in later foundational science fiction, coloniality is transmuted into a "new, postcolonial form of hegemony" that secures the West's global economic dominance and cultural influence.[35] In other words, canonical works of modern European and North American science fiction elucidate colonialism's afterlife in the postcolonial nation-state, that is, the neoliberal influence that Yoss's book thematizes. If, as Rieder argues, science fiction is "a kind of palimpsest," a genre whose texture discloses inscriptions of "displaced references to history," *Se alquila un planeta* might be more accurately described as a science-fictional Cuban palimpsest, to rephrase José Quiroga's concept.[36] Quiroga conceives Cuba as palimpsestic—a textual "site" "that multiple temporalities were coexisting in the same space—a space that could not fashion the future except as a return of the most odious forms of the past that the state had always tried to eliminate."[37]

In *Postcolonialism and Postsocialism in Fiction and Art: Resistance and Reexistence*, Madina Tlostanova also brings clarity to the colonial resonances of neoliberalism's encounter with socialism in her analysis of post-Soviet European aesthetics. Drawing on Foucault's idea of the heterotopia, Tlostanova argues that the postsocialist world is constituted as a spatial palimpsest through an overlapping and intersecting of "multiple spaces . . . permeated by and broached with multiple histories."[38] In the case of Cuba, this is exemplified in the act of reconfiguring previously nationalized spaces and land that were supposed to be the purview of Cuba's citizenry and setting them apart for foreign tourists and those Cuban citizens who have legal access to foreign currency through their foreign familial networks. For Tlostanova, this palimpsestic rewriting of landscape begets in citizens a "peculiar" yet anachronistic "postcolonial complex"—a sense of alterity, difference, and placelessness within a neoliberal modernity that they were being called to inhabit as post-Soviet countries.[39] Tlostanova's point, and one that applies (with qualifications) to Cuba, is that neoliberalism produces a spatialized differentiation of human life that adheres to a colonial logic, even in postsocialist spaces that broke with the colonial telos of the racialized, postcolonial state.[40]

From this standpoint, the palimpsestic intertext of *Se alquila un planeta* calls for a reading of planetary hospitality not as a temporal "as always" or even colonialism's "post" but rather as a spatial ontology that indexes the relation between the property of the self and the appropriation of space. How does a "host" offer hospitality when they don't have a home proper into which they can welcome the guest? I consider this question by turning to "Trabajadora social," which suggests that the host's offer of hospitality, the act of welcoming someone into a space that is not one's own, requires that another space within an occupied space—that is, the body—stand in for the nonproper.

Occupied Hosts

The spatial ecology of a terrestrial astroport organizes the plot of "Trabajadora social," which follows the passage of Buca, the story's eponymous social worker, from the astroport's entrance to the shuttle on which she will leave Earth. Divided into three rings, the astroport segregates and differentiates levels of contact between humans and xenoid tourists, with humans' presence dwindling as the story advances to the departure gate. The terrestrial astroport serves as a small but resonant instantiation—a "micromundo" (microworld)—of xenoid-human relations on Earth.[41] As it were, the astroport sets terms and conditions for how humans relate to xenoids as their hosts in advance of their exit into both terrestrial and planetary communities on either side of the doorway.

Buca's promenade through each of the astroport's classed and speciated spheres discloses the different categories of labor occupied by humans in the hospitality economy that governs the Earth. An intricately layered story whose schema parallels the social partitioning of the astroport, "Trabajadora social" is about the hospitality work that sustains planetary tourism and how humans are spatialized and plugged into the Earth's hospitality system as xenoids' hosts. The astroport's wage labor is segmented, on the one hand, between those who maintain the integrity and continuity of the Earth's hospitality economy, such as the agents of Seguridad Planetaria (Planetary Security), and, on the other, authorized workers who directly provide hospitality services to xenoids. This latter group includes the "social workers" who provide personal entertainment to xenoids and the infamous sistema de Recambio Corporal (Body Spares system), in which xenoids can rent human bodies to facilitate their mobility and enjoyment of the Earth's tourist paradises.

Yoss's attentiveness to how the human body is mobilized to re-create tourist space is evocative of what Mimi Sheller and John Urry call "tourist mobilities," the way tourist places are constituted and shaped through the interactive, performative mobilities of local hosts and foreign guests.[42] Sheller and Urry note that tourist places—places where people "play"—are always places "put *into* play."[43] That is, tourism is performed in places shaped by a mass chain of global mobilities—systems, peoples, transportation, objects, and images—in order to make such places possible. In "Demobilizing and Remobilizing Caribbean Paradise," Sheller traces the "mobilization of plants, people, ships, material resources" in the constitution of the New World Caribbean to the region's contemporary tourism mobilities.[44] At the same time, Sheller writes, Caribbean tourism mobilities are constituted dialectically by "demobilizations of local people, who are barred access to resort areas except in so far as they perform service work: cooking, cleaning, providing entertainment, selling local crafts, offering local knowledge as guides and drivers, and selling bodies for sport and sex."[45] Demobilization, Sheller clarifies, works doubly: tourist spaces are fortified to simultaneously keep local people in (their) place and "remobilize them to perform various services." As I consider further on, Yoss's text complicates this dynamic of embodied spatial mobilities by exploring how even when local people are given access to these tourists as hospitality workers some aspect of their *person* must be demobilized and left behind.

In another sense, tourist mobilities are also facilitated through the decentralized and unsanctioned labor of unofficial "hosts" whose work begins and takes place outside of authorized tourist spaces. Tracking Buca's spatial movement through the astroport, "Trabajadora social" is particularly attentive to the undocumented labor of those broadly categorized as "negociantes por cuenta propia" (self-employed businesspeople). Confined to the "Corte de los Milagros" (Court of Miracles), these self-employed include businessmen, hawkers, money changers, beggars, and freelance social workers, among other questionable characters who make their living in Earth's illegal, black market economy. Not incidentally, the Court of Miracles was also the name given to the community of social outcasts confined to the Parisian slums that proliferated under the reign of Louis XIV. In Yoss's dystopian analogue, this community of the self-employed is the detritus of planetary tourism. However, the text tells us, they appeal to "turistas ávidos de emociones fuertes" (thrill-seeking tourists) by providing a more adventurous, "alternativa riesgosa" (risky alternative) to the safer, authorized hospitality on offer.[46] Notwithstanding the illegal labor status of the self-employed, Planetary Security turns a blind eye to their activities, for the most part, so long as it does not cause a major disruption to the seemingly effortless flow of planetary tourism.

Among this liminal group of delinquent workers, however, Buca figures as a kind of exception. A freelance social worker, Buca strategically works the system, exerting varying degrees of personal agency, flexibility, and skill to ensure her livelihood and acquire a semblance of freedom on her own terms. Unlike her self-employed counterparts, who are confined to the astroport's first ring, and other humans for whom off-planet travel is restricted to approved government travel, Buca is one of a lucky few who has managed to secure her permanent exit from Earth owing to the sponsorship of a xenoid Grodo patron who goes by the pseudonym Selshaliman.

Nevertheless, when Buca arrives at the astroport's third and final ring, "Trabajadora social" reveals that her asylum status in outer space comes at a heavy price—one that she, admittedly, is willing to pay in exchange for the material security and luxurious lifestyle promised to her by Selshaliman. Her contract with Selshaliman stipulates that her womb will serve as an incubator for eggs deposited inside her by his ovipositor since the hermaphroditic, arachnid-like Grodos are incapable of carrying and birthing their offspring. Chosen among all the other social workers for her superior health, Buca's body will nourish the larvae of hatched eggs until she is fully consumed. When Buca passes through the astroport's final gate and boards the shuttle to the galactic hypership, it is understood that the principle of hospitality that demarcates the host-human relation to xenoids extends beyond Earth into the extraterrestrial planetary system: even when humans are technically guests and cannot make claim to a home proper in outer space, they remain bound to xenoids as hosts. Specifically, in

Buca's case, her body becomes the parasitic "home" in which xenoids are received and given hospitality.

Through another euphemism, planetary "hospitality," names and titles in "Trabajadora social" disguise and forget the complicated, uneven, and conflictive nature of interspecies, interplanetary contact between xenoids and humans. Thus, only when the story further details *who* does "social work" (mostly women) and *what* the risky and, at times, fatal responsibilities of the social worker entail does it become clear that "social work" is, in fact, a euphemism for sex work. More specifically, when the narration briefly dovetails from Buca's journey through the astroport to reflect on her harrowing origins, born and baptized as "María Elena" in a short-lived utopia "en la pequeña isla cuyo nombre prefería olvidar" (on a small island whose name she would rather forget), "Trabajadora social" allegorically links freelance social work to *jineterismo*, a particular type of sex work formed within the marketplace of sexual tourism in Cuba at the end of the 1980s and intensified during the Special Period.[47]

By making this linkage, Yoss lets Buca perform two social commentaries about the sociality of work in postsocialist Cuba. First, by euphemistically classifying Buca as a freelance social worker, Yoss's text legitimizes sex work as an *occupation* that provides care and welfare, whether formally or informally, to foreigners within Caribbean economies like Cuba's, which have been largely subsidized by the hospitality industry. Second, and on the other hand, by letting Buca act as a host or a "home" for the Grodo parasites, Yoss turns the importance of revolutionary "sociality" in Cuba on its head. According to De Ferrari, Cuba's revolutionary government ensured its survival in an economy that was deeply unfavorable and hostile to its citizens by upholding an ethos of sociality that organized citizens' loyalty to the state around the shared principles of community, friendship, and solidarity.[48] Insofar as Cuban sociality becomes codified as a consuetudinary practice, the ideals of Cuban socialist citizenship disqualify those deemed "parasites." The term "parasite" has been historically invoked as a pejorative by the Cuban state against those perceived to engage in unproductive behavior that does not advance the revolution's communitarian ethos. It extends even to those who work: notably, those who work only for personal gain and "antisocials" who, for example, make a living on the black market.[49] "Trabajadora social" comically troubles Cuban sociality in its titular reinscription of sex work as "freelance social work" provided not to another human (citizen) but, instead, to a xenoid foreigner—who, rephrasing Kamugisha's description of tourists as "extraterritorial citizens," may well be considered an "extraterrestrial citizen." Since Buca is the one being parasitized by a xenoid, she inverts the parasitic, antisocial dynamic articulated in Cuban socialist discourse. In my view, Yoss's depiction of her bodily labor as a host to xenoid parasites draws attention to how *jineterismo*, by being a form of hospitality that extends beyond terrestrial space proper, engages the very principles of companionship that are foundational to Cuba's socialist state in order to cultivate a sense of agency and personhood interdicted by the state.

The concept of *jineterismo* entangles "body work" and care work within the marketplace of sexual tourism. Unlike other forms of sex work, it entails the cultivation of nuanced and sustained forms of intimacy and romance with a client, but it does not always involve sexual intercourse. Sex work was not new or unique to Cuba's Special Period; rather, it accompanied the development of tourism in the late nineteenth century on the island.[50] But it was with the collapse of Cuba's economy at the end of the 1980s and the inauguration of the Special Period that *jineterismo* evolved within the island's black market economy, spurred by the necessity of survival. Amalia Cabezas notes that *jineterismo* is consistent with informal labor constitutive of tourist economies.[51] In particular, *jineterismo* is marked by the hustle—the capacity of the *jinetera* (or *jinetero*) to cultivate the illusion of intimacy and friendship with the tourist in order to sustain the flow of material resources beyond the initial encounters, which, in many cases, can give the *jinetera* a new life abroad if the relation evolves into a long-term partnership. The nature of the hustle is understood in the word itself: *jineterismo* is a neologism derived from the Spanish word *jinete*—jockey or horse rider.

In my estimation, "Trabajadora social" offers a unique and nuanced take on *jineterismo* as a mode of sexual citizenship in its depiction of humans' embodied, spatial mobilities as hosts to xenoids.[52] Implied in the terminology of *jineterismo* is a sense of agency ascribed to and experienced by the female sex worker, the *horse rider*. Framing the *jinetera* as the one who rides the horse—that is, the client—the terminology of *jineterismo* challenges the denial of (sexual) agency, as Kamala Kempadoo has observed, in representations of Black and Brown sex workers who are reduced to "sexual objects."[53] Presumably, the *jinetera* exists in a position of domination and power relative to the tourist client, the *horse* she mounts. Steered by the rider, the horse facilitates a politics of spatial mobility, whereby the *jinetera* can access tourist places that, as I previously noted, are spatially sealed off from citizens for the exclusive use of foreigners. For example, *jineteras* regularly accompany their clients into hotels, restaurants, cafés, and other tourist establishments. Alongside their clients, they occupy these spaces publicly and visibly, while authorities and authorized workers often turn a blind eye to their generally unwelcome presence.

It could be argued that the *jinetera*'s agency is embodied in her capacity to circumvent and move across the boundaries of tourist spaces. Drawing on Merleau-Ponty's phenomenology of the body, Brenda Farnell asserts that the body of the self that moves is a body that is in "command" of the actions of the self.[54] Extending Farnell's argument, it could be claimed that the body that moves *across* and through interdicted, symbolically foreign space—as does the *jinetera*, embodied by Buca in her movement across the astroport—asserts a command not only of the self as a stateless subject but of the space as an asylum. As hospitality service providers, however, *jineteras* enter these tourist spaces neither as authorized employees nor as "guests" proper of the tourist but rather as a type of "guest worker" and companion vouched for and sponsored by the tourist-guest. A guest worker, by definition, is a migrant who is authorized to work in another country, which, for all intents and purposes, is how the tourist spaces appeared to many Cuban citizens under the Special Period. As a guest worker, the *jinetera* occupies these spaces extra-juridically, absent the labor protections afforded to an authorized worker. The *jinetera*'s extra-juridical presence in such spaces is typified in "Trabajadora social" when, upon arriving at the astroport's third and final sphere, where the human population has completely thinned out, Buca is violently detained by a Planetary Security agent who is unaware of her protected status as Selshaliman's "host," the xenoid patron.

Further deepening its exploration of the host/guest dichotomy, Yoss's text considers whether Buca's agential capacity leads to a sense of personhood. Derrida, as I have previously noted, tells us that hospitality shores up the property of the (juridical) person. It delimits what is *mine* by virtue of my being able to receive someone as the host-proprietor of a given space. Put differently, the host commands the authority of receivership. This receivership, however, presumes a physical separation and boundary between the space of hospitality and the bodily "I" of the host. If, as in Buca's case, the geopolitical space of hospitality converges with and extends to the human body as a host, the host must either share or relinquish their self-proprietorship.

Although Buca doesn't have control over her body, she manages to exercise control over her person—or at least she thinks so. This distinction between an agential personhood and a possessed body performs, as Zakiyyah Iman Jackson argues, the "self-defeating" nature of the liberal humanist notion of self-determination, where "claims to self-ownership are paradoxical in that they reject the master's authority but not the property relation" of the "Self as 'Proprietor of his own Person.'"[55] Yoss's narrative attempts to work around this paradox in its representation of *jineterismo*—and sex tourism broadly—as a practice that metonymizes personhood. Buca knows, "Trabajadora social" tells us, that her success in leaving the planet as a freelance social worker hinges on being able to "fingir que sus relaciones no eran mercenarias" (pretend their relationships are not mercenary).[56] Yoss's description of Buca as a freelance social worker signals a self-proprietorship that recasts the original usage of the term "freelancer," which, as I previously noted, is a mercenary by definition. The sex worker who pretends that sex tourism is not mercenary exercises a disinterest with regard to her renumeration by feigning that money is being exchanged for sex. Furthermore, it is to presume that the worker is *loyal* to the client. But it also necessitates the taking on of a persona, which the mercenary generally discards in order to become a *no one* whose only allegiance is the task for which they are being compensated. A *persona*, Mauss tells us, is related to, yet can also be different from, the (legal) *person*. Historically, the Latin *persona* described "an artificial 'character'" and "a mask."[57] These masks could take the form of a pseudonym, a sacred name, or bodily adornment.[58] In signaling the relationship between the idea of the *persona* and function of the mask, I am indebted to Angela Naimou's reading of the legal person as a fiction (mask) whose configuration cannot be disentangled from its invention within histories of colonialism and imperialism in the New World.[59] However, my reading of what I have called freelance personhood takes an approach that slightly deviates from Naimou's in that I see the *persona* of the sex worker as the affectation of a personhood that is disavowed by the Cuban state and, therefore, can only be engendered and articulated through fictive emotional attachments to foreign guests.

This fictive persona is a central feature of what in sex work is called the "girlfriend experience." Gezinski and colleagues note that sex workers in the context of sex tourism are rarely called "sex workers" or even "prostitutes" but rather are referred to by other euphemistic names that convey that sex workers are *ordinary people voluntarily* having sex with strangers."[60] From the perspective of the client, usually male, "whore" or "prostitute" is impersonal and thus not a *person*. However, when sex workers feign the persona of a girlfriend, it is "implied that clients are paying for time with an everyday *person* who will fawn over them rather than a sex worker engaging in sex simply for money."[61] In these terms, it is not only the body that is being "sold" for sex. The sex worker also freelances, so to speak, a fictive persona to the client.

In this latter regard, "Trabajadora social" explores how the success of the hustle is contingent on the social worker's ability to both convincingly feign desire, love, and intimacy and get the xenoid (tourist) patron to believe the human's performance of intimacy. Yoss's narrative tells us that, as Buca passes through the astroport, she feels a sense of unease with her performance given that Grodos are telepaths, which means that Selshaliman may read Buca's mind only to discover that she is not in love with him, as he may be given to believe. Consequently, Buca must actively conceal her thoughts by humming "un pegajoso tecnohit de moda" (a catchy current technohit).[62] Given that the conscious, thinking mind is, as the philosophy of Western reason suggests, the emanation of the person, Buca must temporarily kill her "natural" person so that the fictive persona might emerge.

Although Buca celebrates her ability to take on a fictive persona by concealing her thoughts and justifies her future possession as host-incubator, Yoss's text evinces skepticism toward the agential possibilities of freelance social work—and, by extension, *jineterismo*. In her promenade across the astroport's outer ring, Buca's gaze falls on a booth from which a human body with a vacant stare surfaces. Scattered throughout the astroport, booths like these contain Body Spares, human bodies that can be rented and inhabited by xenoid tourists to facilitate their mobility and enjoyment of Earth's tourist paradises. The Body

Spare System, the story explains, was the invention of the Auyars, a powerful xenoid race among several that are "biológicamente incompatibles con la biosfera Terrestre" (biologically incompatible with the terrestrial biosphere).[63] The Auyars are, as explained in the collection's fourth story, "El performance de la Muerte" (Performing Death), the wealthiest and most powerful xenoid race in the galaxy.[64] However, there is no indication that other xenoids with bodies capable of enduring Earth's environment cannot also acquire their own Body Spare. Held in the booths in a state of "suspended animation," a process that involves slowing down or halting the body's vital, biological functions to a state of near death, just enough to keep it alive, the spare's brain is temporarily reprogrammed and encoded with the xenoid's faculty, identity, and physiological "parámetros del 'cliente' (memoria, personalidad, coeficiente de inteligencia, habilidades motoras)" (parameters of the "client" [memory, personality, intelligence quotient, motor skills]) while simultaneously retaining the "movilidad y acceso a todas las habilidades y recuerdos" (mobility and access to all the skills and memories) of a "humano hospedero" (host human)."[65] Although the Body Spares appear as a minor detail within the major storyline of "Trabajadora social," their strategic placement early in the story serves as a key interpretive parallel to Buca's narrative arc as a sex worker. The Body Spares enter Buca's gaze right after the story discloses that she cannot yet be at ease with her thoughts until she has boarded the ship that will take her off the planet. This is reminiscent of Sheller and Urry's "tourist mobilities" in two ways. First, the Body Spares are analogous to service workers who are barred from entering tourist areas unless their purpose is to perform work duties. The Body Spares' bodies are present in the astroport, but their minds are mostly absent, as they would have to be for the Grodos to possess the bodies. Second, as she passes through the astroport, Buca becomes a link in the mass chain of global mobility that constitutes the astroport as a "place of play."

Buca is in denial about this state of agentic disenfranchisement, which she will not escape until she reaches her off-Earth destination. That Buca's survival and extraterrestrial life with Selshaliman will require a vigilant closure of her mind, as the story intimates, shades her visions of how she sees herself differently from other social workers. It exposes the self-deception that she, or any freelance social worker for that matter, can make agential choices in her role as host for the Grodos. By the time she gets to the final ring, forbidden to unauthorized humans, she feels she has "triunfado" (triumphed) both over the fate to which most humans are destined and over the former life she had as "una vez fuera casi esclava" (once nearly a slave).[66] This triumphant feeling is cemented when Selshaliman comes to her rescue against Planetary Security agents who detain and harass her after they mistakenly assume she has entered the final ring illegally. With the protection, care, and lavish material goods that Buca receives as a freelance social worker, it may be tempting to believe, as the text suggests she does, that she is somehow better off than a "spare" human body programmed and dispossessed of agency and instead possessed by a xenoid to do its bidding. Still, after Selshaliman orders the security agents to release her, they remind her of the cruel fate that awaits her as a human incubator or host.

While "Trabajadora social" does not completely escape Yoss's own moral anxieties about selling sex, intimacy, and companionship for survival under the duress of material and economic deprivation, it does invite a rethinking of the complex relationship between labor and bodily intimacy as a waged occupation that produces a corporeal occupation. To be clear, read within the totality of *Se alquila un planeta*, where other kinds of workers also find themselves occupied and possessed by the tourist system, "Trabajadora social" does not appear to be an indictment or moralization of sex work or *jineterismo*. As an allegorical meditation on both the necessarily desperate choices Cuban citizens were forced to make to live and survive the Special Period and the future that awaits the island under neoliberal globalism, "Trabajadora social" juxtaposes Buca and the Body Spare's decisions about their bodies, knowing the fate that awaits them, with Earth's acquiescence to xenoid occupation. It asks whether a person can act agentially, under duress, when the options are few and the capacity to choose as a person has been wrested by the state. Similar questions might also be raised about whether Cuba's socialist state had much of a choice in selectively consenting and accommodating to the global market, given both the toll of U.S. sanctions on Cuba and the inevitability of neoliberal capitalism as a global colonizing force. Tlostanova weighs, in rather decided terms, on the ethical dilemmas of the postsocialist, post-Soviet state confronted with neoliberal capitalism, arguing that they represent "a case of *voluntary self-colonization* by the rhetoric of Western modernity."[67] Whether Cuba's self-colonization can be deemed "voluntary," given the way neoliberalism functions as a colonizing, dispossessive force, remains in question.

What is clear, however, is that in Cuba this self-colonization manifested in the denationalization and partitioning of social space, laying bare how the tourist economy dispossesses those working on its margins of their personhood all the same, regardless of their occupation or their skill set. Indeed, "Trabajadora social" betrays the workings of what Rocío Zambrana has called "neoliberal coloniality," which amplifies the race/gender dimensions of Quijano's "coloniality of power" concept to show how "territories, economies, and bodies" are inscribed in "apparatuses of capitalist capture, predation, and land extraction" in ways that ensure prolongation of colonial life under the guise of the "postcolonial."[68] Although Zambrana conceptualizes neoliberal coloniality within the context of Puerto Rico's neocolonial subjection to the United States, it underscores this book's broader claim that postcolonial Caribbean nation-state sovereignty alone cannot safeguard citizens from the logic of capture, dispossession, and occupation, insofar as nation-state sovereignty remains beholden to the neoliberal mode

FREELANCE PERSONHOOD

of hospitality. It is through Yoss's textual transposition of Buca's narrative with that of the Body Spares that the stakes of this dispossessive occupation are made clear.

"Trabajadora social" draws the most clear and obvious parallel between the Body Spare System and *jineterismo* in a passage that likens the process of humans having their bodies possessed by xenoids to "ser un 'caballo' (un término tomado del vudú)" (being a "horse" [a term derived from Voodoo]) for xenoid "riders."[69] The text's likening of the Body Spares to horses inverts and subverts the discursive logic of *jineterismo*, which, as I have previously noted, maintains the *jinetera* in an agential position as the *rider* who dominates and manipulates the client (the *horse*) to her advantage. As the passage tells us, being a horse "era voluntario" (was voluntary). Using terms derived from voudun, however, allows the text to do a different type of critical work, revealing how tourism justifies the exploitation and possession of human bodies through a perversion of local culture and spiritual practices that are marketed to tourists for the consumption of authenticity.

As Colin Dayan has elucidated, there is a cultural parallel in how Haitian voudun practitioners give themselves over to be inhabited and mounted as *horses* by the *lwa*, the gods or spirits. In these rituals of spiritual intimacy, the human becomes a host for the *lwa* to make its presence known *and* to expand the practitioner's sense of self. Notably, Dayan underscores that the act of being mounted and inhabited by *lwa* contrasts with the domination of women under slavery: "This history of slavery is given substance through time by a spirit that originated in an experience of domination. That domination was most often experienced by women under another name, something called 'love.' In that unnatural situation where a human became property, love became coordinate with a task of feeling that depended to a large extent on the experience of servitude," she argues.[70] Likewise, the performative act of love that Buca engages in may thus be seen through the lens of racial domination.

In this latter regard, the racialization of hospitality is the untold story of "Trabajadora social," and this goes beyond the narrative's references to voudun terms like "horse" and "rider." The narrative's treatment of racial difference may be overlooked in the pursuit of a strictly allegorical reading of the text that consolidates, as a single category, humans (as a metaphor for Cuban citizens) against the personification of tourists as xenoids. Such a reading collapses the text's subtle gestures to human difference in the face of the physically diverse races of xenoids, who, as a whole, have dominion over humans, both on and off the Earth. Yoss signals the ontological distinction between xenoids and humans by translating the materiality of the body into a differentiation of their location and status in space and who has access to these differentiated spaces within the mobilities of tourism. The narrative maps racial difference in its emplotment of Buca's movement through the astroport's rings. While Buca's race is never clearly specified, she is described as having skin that is "*casi* lo bastante pálida" (*almost* pallid enough) to allow her to be mistaken for a Centaurian.[71] As further explained in the collection's subsequent story, "Mestizos," Centaurians are a hybrid species, the product of interbreeding between xenoids and humans.[72] When Buca compares her skin color to that of Centaurians, she does so in order to distinguish herself from other freelance social workers, who serve as an amusing and repulsive reminder of a past from which she believes she has ascended socially and which she will soon ascend spatially from the Earth. Her being almost white enough to pass as not fully human, the lowest on the scale of beings, seems to countervail her being almost but not quite a slave prior to being rescued by her client-guest Selshaliman. The *almost* as a descriptor of racial proximity suggests that Buca embodies enough positive difference to attain the sponsorship of Selshaliman and receive minimally better treatment from him, unlike other, less fortunate freelance social workers she is leaving behind. Still, the figure of the slave and, thus, Blackness itself haunt the text so that, by way of an analogy with voudun, the text conjures the inescapable racialization of sex work in Cuba as dispossessive capture and occupation.

Thus, although Yoss's narrative evades specifying the racial/gendered positioning of the Body Spares in the planetary tourism system, I suggest that the voudun analogy tacitly bespeaks the racial mythification of *jineterismo* as a practice performed mainly by Black and mixed-raced Cuban women. Moreover, when "Trabajadora social" ("Trabajadora social") likens the possession of human Body Spares to voudun, it signals the sinister ways in which the (dis)possession of the will from the body is resemanticized under neoliberal cultural tourism. The Planetary Tourism Agency justifies the Body Spare system by arguing that the humans give their bodies over to be possessed voluntarily, like the human horses of voudun. But the text also makes an interesting note of the fact that "solo había un 'pequeño detalle' . . . el individuo cuyo cuerpo y cerebro eran *ocupados* por el extraterrestre, *continuaba consciente*" (there was just one minor detail . . . the individual whose body and brain were *occupied* by the extraterrestrial *remained conscious*).[73] The Body Spare system distinguishes the personhood of the body's individual human owner from the will that is co-opted by the xenoids. Most importantly, the text attributes personhood to the Body Spares since personhood—as Locke noted—is a "forensic term," which derives from the ability to give an account of your actions and thus is tied to consciousness.[74] This internal partitioning of human bodies is essential to the functioning of Earth's tourist economy. It resembles the individuation of the citizen as a person found in neoliberalism. As Emily Martin argues, in neoliberalism, persons are regarded as "mini-corporations" who "'shapeshift' in their changing environments."[75] Of course, most formal corporations are structured to limit the liability for the humans involved, thereby separating the acts of "the body" from "the person." If "Trabajadora social" is an allegory of the Special Period, then we see this process of individuation when neoliberalism overlaps with socialism. The illegal labor economy, where people find freelance occupations, enables an individuation of the person that is not emancipatory. To have an occupation is also to be occupied—possessed, inhabited. The body becomes something rentable that can be occupied. The person is the host but the body is the host space.

"Trabajadora social" emphasizes how the human body itself surfaces as a space that is mobilized or placed in play to facilitate the xenoid's entry into tourist spaces from which nonworking humans would otherwise be forbidden. To be a host is not only to be made into a body but also to be made into bodily space. In the context of slavery, for example, the enslaved Black's function as instruments of their masters or as appendages. But the Body Spare, seen as an enslaved person in the overlap of neoliberalism with socialism, is a space of bodily habituation. In a way, when the tourist relies on the worker to habituate them to the tourist environment, to help them experience the tourist environment the way the worker does, the tourist inhabits the worker's body. The body enters a tourist space as a guest under the persona of the xenoid.

"Trabajadora social" raises the question about the person who remains behind. The Body Spare contains the consciousness of the person, along with that of the xenoid. The text tells us that many who gave up their bodies as Body Spares often "lost their minds," their bodies having been attuned to the space of another body in a way that is not familiar to them. Auyars, having invented the Body Spare system, were also reputed to abuse the spare bodies, running them to the ground until all that was left was a barely sentient human gone mad, with nothing but a body. The threat of fines for abusing host bodies and failing to return them to their human owner in good condition did nothing to curtail the exploits of the Auyars. In fact, the story tells us many overworked human Body Spares became schizophrenic and lost their already indeterminate membership in Earth's political community, for a nebulous law required that humans demonstrate sound mental health in order to enjoy their full civil rights. Importantly, once human Body Spares have lost their mind, xenoids are no longer obliged to "devolver el uso de un cuerpo a su legítimo dueño" (return the use of a body to its legitimate owner).[76] As a way of describing the loss of cognitive and mental function, and the loss of reason, the term "to lose one's mind" also suggests that the body ceases to house thought and consciousness. The mind has gone missing—where, is anyone's guess—from the person.

It bears noting that this passage in Yoss's text is likely an allusion to a section of Cuba's Criminal Code, known as Ley No. 62, which allows for the psychiatric detention of persons declared "en estado peligroso" (state of dangerousness).[77] This same law, notes Amalia Cabezas, was strategically used in Cuba to criminalize women involved in sex work, which, although not illegal, contradicted "socialist morality."[78] Among others considered to be in a "state of dangerousness" are "enajenados mentales y . . . personas de desarrollo mental retardado si, por esta causa, no *poseen la facultad de comprender el alcance de sus acciones*" (mentally deranged and . . . persons of retarded mental development if, for this reason, they do not *possess the faculty to understand the scope of their actions*).[79] Personhood, recalling Locke, is the ability to give an account of oneself and be held accountable for oneself. Within the Cuban criminal code, the body is given asylum by the state, who, in the absence of a metaphysically missing person, now becomes the host-master of the body. In the planetary tourism system imagined in "Trabajadora social," Earth's planetary (state) system has been absorbed by the market, which reduces depersonalized bodies—bodies dispossessed of personhood—to goods. Here, Yoss's narrative moves from the Special Period to an imagined future, where under a fully corporatized state that, nevertheless, selectively holds steadfast to an irrevocable socialist ethos, deems those incapacitated by work as antisocial.

I propose that "Trabajadora social" positions the Body Spares' madness as a parallel to Buca's intentional effacement of her thoughts with music, a process that she repeats in the narrative's closing, to both challenge the integrity of the self-possessed person and, in particular, to show that hospitality also entails a dispossession and occupation of the mind. Buca does not lose her mind in the manner of the Body Spare, but she occupies it with something else—another persona that inhabits a shared space with her "true," muted self. With the Body Spares having receded far into the background, the story's ending leaves us to speculate how and whether Buca's mind will be able to give space to these competing personas—and whether, in the ceding of that space, her fate will inevitably follow that of the spares.

Making her way onto the hypership, Buca muses on the future that awaits her: the many entitlements she has negotiated with Selshaliman in exchange for her womb and, notably, the possibility of Selshaliman discarding his Arabic pseudonym and adopting another, more fashionable, modern one—a Japanese name. In a system governed by hospitality, the story suggests, guests and hosts equally perform variegated personas. If the world conceived by Yoss in *Se alquila un planeta* oscillates between an unmaterialized utopian future that is now present and a future world system to come, in substituting the xenoid Grodo's national personas "Trabajadora social" performs the movement of the freelance sex worker-cum-*jinetera* across different national geographies under the patronage of a nationally diverse clientele. Regardless of where and with whom the freelance sex worker obtains asylum abroad, she will, "Trabajadora social" intimates, remain a host-human.

Virtual Asylums

This system of transnational, global hospitality that interpellates Cuban citizens is also on display outside of the fictional, dystopian futurescape Yoss unveils in

"Trabajadora social." In the narratives of what become known as the Alternative Cuban Blogosphere, there is a similar dislocation of the Cuban writers' bodies, grounded in Cuba, from a personhood cultivated in cyberspace. Writers like Orlando Luis Pardo Lazo, Yoani Sánchez, and Claudia Cadelo described situations in which they, like Yoss's protagonist Buca, constructed what I have called a "freelance personhood"—a writerly identity "off-the-books" that enabled them to not only work and survive but also embody a sense of personhood repudiated by the Cuban state. Not unlike Buca's situation, their work as self-identified writers was, and remains, unauthorized and unrecognized by Cuba's state-run cultural institutions, which, in some cases, led to the confiscation or revocation of the documents that officially tie them to the Cuban state.

Preempting the emergence of the Alternative Cuban Blogosphere, Cuban writer Iván de la Nuez envisioned Cuban citizens' capacity for self-making from "outside" in a 2001 prefatory essay titled "El Hombre Nuevo ante el otro futuro" (The New Man before another future). Here, de la Nuez invites fellow intellectuals of his generation to rethink how they might inhabit a utopian future that does not look like the one promised to them and for which they were "programdos para vivir el comunismo" (programmed to live communism) as the first-born children of the Cuban revolution.[80] In that now-present future, well into a period defined no longer by hopeful anticipation but instead by the economic, moral, and ideological devastation that followed the dissolution of the Soviet Bloc, de la Nuez declares, alternatively, that the now-adult children of the revolution write by taking on "una especie de extranjería—un carácter forastero y extraño" (a sort of alien status—a foreign and strange character) in "un espacio que está fuera de lugar" (a space that is out of place).[81] Reconfiguring spatiotemporal metaphors that have defined Cuban revolutionary discourse, the essay reads as a rejoinder to Fidel Castro's historic 1961 speech to Cuba's intellectuals, wherein he demarcated the limits of their creative liberties "within the revolution" while affirming the sovereign right of the revolution against its "outside."[82] De la Nuez describes the "non-bourgeois" concept of the "self-made man," born from the ideological ruins of the revolution, who refuses the cognitive and intellectual stagnation that inevitably stems from disenchantment.[83] Instead, the self-made man emboldens the Cuban intellectual to "pensar el día después" (think the day after) as a "hacker" who develops a deinstitutionalized aesthetics through the virtual and physical infrastructure configured by the related expansion of both the internet in Cuba and neoliberal tourism.[84] Thus, the essayist betrays, rather ironically, the predicament of utopia, whose denotative meaning refers to a nonplace: to inhabit in advance a future that did not come as it was imaginatively conceived is precisely to live in a space that has no place.

In a belated rejoinder, titled "Cuba, los intelectuales ante un futuro que ya es presente" (Cuba, the intellectuals in the face of a future that is already present), Cuban writer and cultural critic Arturo Arango suggests that both de la Nuez's essay and the collection it prefaces, *Cuba y el día después*, are inextricable from the "disenchantment" context that became the affective blueprint of Cuban literature of this period and which, according to Arango, is "ya hoy superado" (already overcome today).[85] Against the critical posture taken by de la Nuez's peers toward these fields, Arango affirms both the relevance and the capacity of Cuba's cultural institutions to adapt to emergent digital technologies, which derive their legitimacy and "permissibility" from the state.[86] In the hacker aesthetics of de la Nuez's self-made beings, I see a corollary to the freelance worker and artist that figure centrally in *Se alquila un planeta* and the Alternative Cuban Blogosphere. Conversely, Arango's affirmation of Cuba's cultural institutions is indicative of the environment against which the freelance worker and artist must struggle.

In this section, I explore how writers in the Alternative Cuban Blogosphere enact and express a sense of personhood that bypasses Cuba's state-run publishing infrastructure and instead taps into the virtual infrastructure of the new and improved hospitality industry generated by the economic reforms of the Special Period. In the incisive critical commentary on how alternative Cuban blogging forged alternative notions of citizenship through the constitution of an online public sphere, little to no attention has been paid to the role of Cuba's foreign-oriented infrastructure played in making these blogs possible in spite of the state's efforts, and in catapulting these writers from amateur status to renown abroad. By considering how Orlando Pardo Lazo, Yoani Sánchez, and Claudia Cadelo specifically gesture to and make use of the foreign spaces that exist within the island, my reading of the Alternative Cuban Blogosphere excavates hospitality and the dual nature of "hosting" and being hosted in nonterrestrial, international space. In turn, I track how the virtual "outer space" that is the internet emerges as a host space not only for their writing but also for their *person* in light of the state's suppression of their legal personality as citizens and writers.

One such interpellation of the *person* that is conjured in foreign space is evinced by Orlando Luis Pardo Lazo in "Reportaje al pie de la horda" (Report at the foot of the horde), where he describes the event of naming himself as a singular person in response to an older Cuban woman who questions whether he is a foreigner, owing to the nervous stutter with which he hesitantly addresses her request to put away his camera. Later, Pardo Lazo identifies himself through the grammar of the personal, declaring, "Como ciudadano, me represento solo a mí mismo" (As a citizen, I represent only myself). The final paragraphs of Pardo Lazo's essay read as a manifesto on liberal self-authorship: rejecting the state's massification of the people, he elevates the power of writing as the preferred medium that can fully account for his life in Cuba and make manifest a new "*Realpersona*" unbound from the "*Realpolitik*" of the state.[87] In a rhetorical move that brings his initial encounter with the older Cuban woman full circle, Pardo

FREELANCE PERSONHOOD   103

Lazo likens documenting his life through the power of the written word to an act of exorcism in which the *real person* is expelled into Cuban society as a *foreigner*.

Yet the personal ethos that unfolds from Pardo Lazo's personal, virtual essay is not singular in its expression but rather reflects the discourse of *Voces Cubanas*, the first dissident blog platform on which cohered more than a dozen Cuban writers. In the mid-to-late aughts, *Voces Cubanas* coalesced into what came to be known unofficially as the "Alternative Cuban Blogosphere," of which other dissident platforms with varying agendas formed a part. I focus on *Voces Cubanas* because it is here where Pardo Lazo's personal blog, *Lunes de Post-Revolución*, Yoani Sánchez's *Generación Y*, and Claudia Cadelo's *Octavo Cerco* were hosted. As a result of their posts, these writers were barred from publishing in print because their work did not meet the approval of Cuban state censors. More than simply a rebellious circumvention of state-enforced limitations, their work redefined a sense of personhood, typified by Pardo Lazo's *Realpersona*, in light of their grammatical and spatial exclusion from publishing in print. As I further elaborate, the discourse of *paperlessness* or *undocumentation* is central to the blogosphere's construction of stateless personhood in virtual space.

Voces Cubanas featured critical, creative, and personal pieces by a diverse group of Cuban writers—young and old, "amateurs" and established writers. As Cuban blog scholar Beatriz Calvo Peña explains, the Alternative Cuban Blogosphere is notable for its inclusion of everyday "common folk"—amateurs who have no formal training or recognition as cultural critics, established authors, or journalists.[88] Thinking with Judith Butler, I suggest the Alternative Cuban Blogosphere came into view as an "assembly" of bodies gathered in a virtual, public space to exercise "a plural and performative right to appear," not just for the sake of appearing but, rather, to demand a "more livable set of economic, social, and political conditions."[89] The demands made by the Alternative Cuban Blogosphere, censored and blocked by the Cuban state, seemed personal, given the state's ad hominem attacks that trivialized their vocation as writers and rendered them "undocumented" in some cases. In a bold move, some alternative Cuban bloggers responded to this state-driven depersonalization by exhibiting their personal information on their blogs. Yoani Sánchez and Claudia Cadelo, for example, posted their national identity cards on the frontispiece header of their blogs. In an earlier version of *Lunes de Post-Revolución*, Pardo Lazo's telephone number appeared on his blog's sidebar in a taunting repetition, inviting anyone to call him.

The Alternative Cuban Blogosphere cohered around a radical disengagement from Cuba's intellectual and cultural institutions and from Cuban civil society writ large—not unlike "the horde." Indeed, the Alternative Cuban Blogosphere was the product of what may be deemed as the "uncivil" exclusion of Yoani Sánchez—considered to be the pioneer of alternative blogging in Cuba—from Cuba's intellectual spheres. According to Sánchez, she was spurred to create her blog, *Generación Y*, in 2007 after she was repeatedly excluded from a series of meetings convened by the island's intelligentsia in January of the same year. Absent from these meetings, Sánchez has noted, were "amateur" writers and intellectuals like herself. Ostensibly, Sánchez was unofficially excluded from this meeting because she had not been recognized as a legitimate writer, critic, and intellectual by the Cuban state and within the country's intellectual circles. Sánchez's account underscores how written and cultural expression and access to literary and cultural spaces in Cuba are moderated and gatekept by Cuba's socialist state.

In excluding alternative Cuban bloggers, the Cuban state mobilizes inhospitality toward citizens as consuetudinary practice. As intellectual historian Rafael Rojas confirms, Cuba's socialist state occupies a dual role as both sovereign and editor-in-chief.[90] Thus, the writers cannot express their personhood on paper, which, in a sense, leaves them *without papers*. Both the literal and the extended meanings of this phrase become reality for some of the writers. Paloma Duong recounts a July 2009 incident in which blogger Claudia Cadelo suddenly found herself denied admission to an event at a museum because she had been among the spectator participants in an art performance earlier that year: "She was now *persona non grata* in public cultural events. The blogger was informed that her intervention had not been a performance but a 'sabotage,' and as such, she was barred from future cultural events."[91] A persona non grata is a person who is unwelcome in all spaces governed by the state, including the online sphere. Duong, for example, cites a government description of bloggers in the alternative blogosphere as "people outside of culture" (*ajenas a la cultura*). As Duong writes, "The language is revealing, since the phrase 'ajenas a la cultura' can be translated as either outside of, or foreign to culture, simultaneously denoting people who are not associated with cultural institutions, and, more telling, people who have no relationship to culture or are somewhat beyond its bounds."[92] The *person*, as an expression of that which refuses social uniformity with the people, is the foreigner.

In light of this exclusion, one of the most interesting facets of alternative blogging in Cuba has been the workarounds and the coalitions the bloggers have constructed to enable their activities. Their original "host," the Cuban state, refuses to extend any hospitality to and host the writers because of their expressions of their dissident personas. In this sense, Cuba has become *inhospitable* to them, and they must instead seek a form of digital emancipation of their writer personas by shedding their legal and juridical personhood through illegal engagements with alternative forms of hospitality and other hosts. One such example, in yet another parallel to Buca's passage through the astroport in *Se alquila un planeta*, is how bloggers were forced to enter spaces reserved for foreigners and tourists to do their work and enact their "freelance" personhood. As *Voces Cubanas* blogger Yoani Sánchez has explained, she disguised herself

FREELANCE PERSONHOOD

as a tourist, which allowed her access to hotels and cafés in Havana, from where she emailed her blog posts to friends outside the island.[93] Then, from their respective international locations, Sánchez's allies posted her blog entries onto *Generación Y*. The physical displacement of the alternative Cuban blogger from the real, international locations where the blog posts are published complicates our ability to distinguish the local from the foreign and the citizen from the noncitizen. Moreover, by furtively embodying foreignness, the blogger plays "host" to non-Cuban values and sentiments, further manifesting their personhood as separate from Cuban state-promoted, collectivist notions such as "the culture" mentioned above.

The practice of sending posts to allies abroad challenges what it means to write *from* Cuba today. The material conditions under which alternative Cuban bloggers write require that we interrogate the very notion of "writing from Cuba"— for the Cuban state has erected firewalls to ensure that no unauthorized blogger, and citizen, can post from the island. This is further complicated by the material-physical structure of the internet. As of the time of writing, Cuba is connected to the internet in the rest of the world through a single fiberoptic cable, ALBA-1, that connects the island to Venezuela and which also is connected to Jamaica. Any traditional high-speed internet connections from Cuba to internet servers around the world go through these two other nations.[94] There are two other fiberoptic cable connections connecting Cuba to Florida and Puerto Rico, but as the names of the cables (GTMO-1 and GTMO-PR, respectively) indicate these are reserved for internet traffic flowing to and from the U.S. naval base at Guantánamo. In other words, when bloggers access the internet from hotels by posing as tourists, not only does the hotel—involuntarily—become the host venue for their activities, but there are several host *countries* involved in moving the blog posts to their destination. In this sense, the content that expresses a blogger's personhood as a dissident must rely on the digital hospitality of other nations to come to full fruition through publication on a blog, thus strengthening the notion behind the rejection of the Cuban self in favor of Pardo Lazo's concept of the "citizen" without a national qualifier.

There is more to be gained by following this path of inquiry. When the emails containing Yoani Sánchez's blog posts land in her allies' email inboxes, these allies download them from an email server located in the region where they live. If, for example, this region happens to be Spain, Yoani Sánchez's work is stored on a Spanish email server before an ally takes it and posts it to the *Generación Y* blog. Thus, in addition to the countries whose hospitality Sánchez's blog posts enjoyed on their light-speed, fiberoptic journey to their destination, Spain also plays host to Sánchez's work and, by extension, the unfolding of her personhood. In reality, Sánchez's blog was a subsection on the Desdecuba.com website, which appears to have been registered and run from Spain through a subsidiary of the German cloud service company Cronon. Technically, that also involves Germany as another host nation for Sánchez's work. Like Buca in *Se alquila un planeta*, Sánchez must transcend the constraints of her own home and her Cuban origins and travel far to emerge as a "freelance" worker and host. But because Sánchez's personhood emerges not through embodiment and her physical location but through aesthetic expression, her body does not need to travel physically. She can instead leave the traveling to digital bits. These entanglements gain yet another dimension when considering the technical terminology used in internet contexts. Since the days of the internet's predecessor, ARPANET, computers that store data and information that others can retrieve by connecting to the computer through the network have been known as "hosts." The language of hospitality is inextricable from even current internet parlance. Colloquially, a website is "hosted" on a "server," terms that are traditionally associated with lodging and food. Like its hospitality equivalent, the practice of offering a "service" that makes digital things accessible to the public via the internet is known as "hosting." The computers or apps that connect to a "host server" are known as "clients." Though "guest" is the most typical term for a person in a similar position within hospitality language, "client" usually refers to a customer in a longer (as opposed to a onetime or ad hoc) relationship with a "host" or service vendor. Not incidentally, the use of the term "client" is not uncommon in the wellness industry, an extension of the hospitality industry, in which spas and other treatment facilities welcome "guests" as "clients." When Sánchez emails her blog posts to her allies, she might be using what is technically known as an "email client," such as Outlook, Apple Mail, or the Gmail app. Hence, while Buca seeks personhood by transcending the constraints of her home planet using the infrastructure of interplanetary travel, Sánchez achieves something similar through the infrastructure of the internet and the international hospitality that is a core function of the network, even down to its associated terminology.

The fact that no single nation owns or has dominion over the internet was touted as one of its main strengths in the early days of the network. It should be mentioned, though, that private companies based in the United States and in most of the former colonizer nations in Europe control and own most of its infrastructure. Early prophets of the online sphere saw the coming, internet-connected era as emancipatory, as a place where the voiceless could gain a voice, a credo that echoed far into the so-called Web 2.0 era with the emergence of blogging, as mentioned above. One of these early prophets was John Perry Barlow, the lyrist of the Grateful Dead, poet, and cyberactivist who in 1996 authored "A Declaration of the Independence of Cyberspace."[95] Barlow's declaration proposes a postnational, poststate vision of the internet as "disembodied and stateless," which, as Daniel Kreiss writes, is "premised on a myth of independence."[96] It is a myth in the sense that it "leads us to misdiagnose all the ways that media spaces are *always* entangled in economic relations, governmental and regulatory structures, and the workings of institutions."[97] Blogs are hosted in a cyberspace that, although existing in nonterrestrial form, contra Barlow, is far from being denationalized but, as Derrida emphasizes in *Hospitalité*, are under the jurisdiction of the state.

While this state-independent condition underpins Pardo Lazo's notion of the "citizen," a less optimistic reading is that something that exists purely on the internet is also stateless and perhaps even homeless, two conditions that decidedly challenge the concept of personhood. Sánchez's work and personhood as a blogger may be hosted by both human and technological entities across the planet, but none of them can offer Sánchez the person a home. In an essay republished from her blog in *Voces*, Claudia Cadelo thus describes the alternative Cuban bloggers as being consigned to a state of "sin tierra" (landlessness), a term that portrays alternative bloggers as territorially displaced in a manner similar to refugees.[98] Similarly, given their lack of access to print media and, specifically, paper, alternative Cuban bloggers have been keen to highlight the correlation between their relegation to the online sphere through textual disenfranchisement and their precarious juridical status. Likewise, the rhetoric of political "undocumentation" pervades Yoani Sánchez's writing—although in a less celebratory manner than Cadelo's rebellious affirmation of landlessness. In one instance, she equates alternative Cuban blogging to a narrative "apartheid," given that bloggers are excluded from Cuba's literary space.[99] "We Cubans," she explains, "continue to exist as undocumented internauts, since our incursions into the territory of the Internet are defined by illegality."[100] The alternative Cuban blogger, suggests Sánchez, embodies a double illegality. In addition to being banned from both the Cuban online sphere and the country's print media, their banishment to the internet and now their forced reliance on the hospitality of humans, cables, and computers in a range of foreign nations position the bloggers, symbolically, as "illegal" immigrants—euphemistically described as "undocumented subjects."

Sánchez further elaborates on the complexity of her "undocumentation" in a 2011 blog post, in which she discusses very real threats against her Cuban citizenship status. Not only did Cuba's Office of Immigration revoke her passport in 2008, when she won Spanish newspaper *El País*'s prestigious Ortega y Gasset Prize in recognition of her blog, but in January 2012, the Cuban state denied Sánchez an exit permit after the government of Brazil granted her an entry visa and an invitation to attend the premiere of a documentary, ironically about freedom of expression in Cuba.[101] In light of these incidents, Sánchez reasonably asks, "Have I become undocumented?"[102] Clearly, she remains a citizen under the law. Yet her question encapsulates the seemingly indissoluble relationship between the loss of literary and intellectual capital that accompanies the loss of paper and the loss of juridical capital.

In 2010, Sánchez diversified her authorial status when she released an anthologized edition of her blog in a printed book under the title *Cuba libre: Vivir y escribir en La Habana.* The English-language edition followed a year later. The Spanish-language book was published by the Mexican press Debate, a subsidiary of the Barcelona-based Random House–Mondadori—itself a joint venture of Random House Books, which is based in New York City. These transnational, transterritorial, and translinguistic significations of *Cuba libre* reenact a virtuality that, once again, dislocates the book—and particularly the hand/body of the person who authors the book—from Cuba's publishing structure. I interpret the print publication and translation of Sánchez's anthology as a form of "textual asylum" in international literary space to the extent that it moves from its "undocumented" status in both Cuba's blogosphere and its publishing houses to the symbolic refugee camp offered by international publishing houses.

The Guest's Hostages

The book form alone could not and has not offered permanent sanctuary to a younger, emerging generation of Cuban artists, writers, and intellectuals, empowered by their predecessors and emboldened by the inevitability of the internet's expansion in Cuba. Indeed, Cuban cultural production and aesthetic practices have been marked by a diminishment of the traditional narrative form of literary fiction, the renewal of poetic expression, and the ascendancy of performance and visual art since the unofficial end of the Special Period sometime before the second decade of the twenty-first century. With new reforms that continued to loosen restrictions on commercial property and infrastructure came greater access to the internet and, thus, to an ever-increasing number of social media platforms and new modes of audiovisual expression. Realizing the potential "dangers" of the internet's expanded forms, beginning in 2018, the Cuban state, once again, changed the rules of art. I close this chapter by considering how these rules, which culminated with the protests of July 11, 2020, have enabled the state to "rehome" Cuban writers, artists, and intellectuals in ways that introduce hostage taking into the logic of inhospitality.

These new rules of art were introduced in January 2018 by the Ministry of Culture and the Ministry of Justice as the Decreto-Ley No. 349 (or Decreto 349), which delimits the meaning of "art" and prohibits conduct, language, and practices deemed *not* art.[103] What is most interesting about the Decreto 349 is how it shifts the terms of the aesthetic and the popular. Invoking as its antecedent Decreto-Ley No. 226, which regulated and curtailed the proliferation of unauthorized freelance artistic services in the wake of Cuba's opening to foreign investment, the 2018 decree specifically addresses the diffusion and circulation of art in audiovisual formats. Since the foundation of the state-run Instituto Cubano del Arte e Industria Cinematográficos (ICAIC) in 1959, which radically transformed the nation's cinema landscape, the state has defined the role and sociopolitical orientation of cinema on the island.[104] Thus, one can surmise that the audiovisual formats signaled by the decree refer to the organic production of social media content, which unlike film under the ICAIC escapes the state's censorial apparatus. This unsanctioned social media content is not the cultural product of the unlettered, Gramscian organic intellectual that Castro imbued with revolutionary promise in his *Palabras a los intelectuales*. While Decreto 349 makes several goodwill and ethical proscriptions against hate speech/content that discriminates against protected groups, it defines what is *not* art in terms that recall the Kantian logic of good or universal taste—condemning audiovisual works deemed "vulgar" or "obscene." Eleven months after Decreto 349 was issued, *Granma*, the Cuban state's and communist party's official news outlet, published a Q&A clarifying that the decree's purpose is to prohibit not "auténticas expresiones de la cultura popular" (authentic expressions of popular culture) but rather works that reflect "chabacanería" (tackiness) and "mal gusto" (bad taste).[105] The audiovisual format of social media, it seems to suggest, lends itself more readily to the unaesthetic, to productions of bad taste, than the hegemonic narrative of the book insofar as it individuates its creator from the revolutionary will of "the people."

Decreto-Ley No. 35, the second normative delineation of the scope of artistic expression in Cuba, was handed down by the state in August 2021 in response to protests that ensued from Decreto 349. Decreto 35 heightened the stakes of social media usage and expression by conditioning the use of telecommunication technologies such as the internet and mobile phones. Outlining its objectives and the rights and obligations of telecoms users, the 136-page document that makes up the decree enumerates a list of acts that would be considered "incidentes de ciberseguridad" (incidents of cybersecurity) and their corresponding levels of danger. Ironically, the language of Decreto 35 seems to mimic Donald Trump's popularization of the "fake news" concept, turning it against itself. Notable among the incidents categorized as "high" and "very high" threats are the dissemination of "noticias falsas, mensajes ofensivo, difamación con impacto en el prestigio del país" (false news, offensive messages, and defamation that impact the prestige of the country) and the use of telecoms infrastructure and platforms to spread "contenidos que atentan contra las preceptos constitucionales, sociales y económicos del Estado, inciten a movilizaciones u otros actos que alteren el orden público" (content that threatens the constitutional, social, and economic precepts of the State, incites mobilizations or acts that alter the public order).[106] *Granma*, once again, provided clarity on this decree and justified its necessity by claiming Trump's White House was investing millions of dollars on "proyectos de subversión" (projects of subversion) designed to "fomentar líderes y estrategias anticubanas en el ciberespacio" (foment anti-Cuban leaders and strategies in cyberspace).[107] If, as Trump has averred, the mainstream media traffics in "fake news," the Cuban state appeared to join Trump in recriminating and, going further than the former U.S. president, incriminating artists, journalists, and intellectuals who, as conduits of fake news, shared a critical posture toward the state.

Consequently, the Cuban state's incrimination of artists and intellectuals through the promulgation of decrees sparked a series of protests that altered the meaning of "home" in ways I describe throughout this book. On April 21, 2021, a collective of more than three hundred Cuban artists, intellectuals, and journalists who called themselves 27N—in reference to the day (November 27, 2020) they initially gathered in protest in front of Cuba's Ministry of Culture—took their voices to Facebook, where they issued a manifesto demanding the state's recognition of their rights and condemning its violent repression.[108] Both the November 2020 protest and the April 2021 manifesto were motivated by the state's escalating threats, harassment, and imprisonment of Cuban artists and intellectuals who were critical of the state. The November 2020 protest was organized around the arrest and temporary disappearance of Cuban rapper and activist Denis Solís two weeks prior. Solís had been charged with the crime of "desacato"—disrespect or contempt—against an officer in the Policía Nacional whom Solís reproached for entering his home without authorization. Meanwhile, 27N states in their manifesto, "el detonante de esta manifestación fueron los hechos ocurridos en el barrio San Isidor la noche anterior" (the trigger for this demonstration was the incidents that occurred in [Havana's] San Isidro neighborhood the previous night). These "incidents" refer to the raids on the homes of musician Maykel "Osorbo" Castillo Pérez and performance artist Luis Manuel Otero Alcántara, who were subsequently arrested and condemned to prison—for five and nine years, respectively—following a closed trial from which international and local observers, diplomats, and journalists were barred. Both Castillo Pérez and Otero Alcántara cofounded the Movimiento San Isidro (San Isidro Movement), of which rapper Solís was also a member, to organize protests against the decrees issued by the state curtailing citizens' right to free expression on the island. They were certainly not the only artists and intellectuals who found themselves besieged by the Cuban state, but perhaps the most prominent for the fact that they gave a name to their experience through the consolidation of interconnected movements.

Reflecting on the experience of these artists and intellectuals, I keep coming back to the meaning of being "at home," when one's home can be transgressed by the state and when one's home can become, as Du Bois also considered, a prison-house. When the Cuban state did not incarcerate artists and intellectuals in official jails, it turned to house arrests, as was the case with artist Hamlet Lavastida and his partner, writer Katherine Bisquet. Upon his arrival in Cuba in June 2021 following a residency in Berlin, Lavastida was arrested and charged with "inciting a crime." The alleged crime, according to official government channels, was the proposed stamping of Cuban bills with "MSI" and "27N," the acronyms of the Movimiento San Isidro and the 27 de Noviembre collective.

The charges against Lavastida were later changed to "inciting rebellion" when mass citizen protests broke out in response to the government's handling of the COVID-19 pandemic on July 11, 2021. Although, as far as it is known, the timing of what became known as 11J appears completely unrelated to either Lavastida's private chat messages or his arrival in Cuba, the Cuban state placed Lavastida and fellow dissident artists at the strategic center of the protests. Following a mandatory six-day quarantine, Lavastida was transferred to Villa Marista prison. Only after three months was Lavastida granted release and, along with his partner, escorted to José Martí International Airport, from which they took a flight to Poland, where he holds residency, without the possibility of ever returning to the island, at least under the current governmental and ideological conditions.

Following this book's reading of the nation-state as "home," I have chosen to frame Lavastida's and other Cuban artists' and intellectuals' predicament as "house arrest" rather than mere imprisonment to underscore the sense of radical estrangement these artists and intellectuals experience at the hand of the state. This experience of being a stranger under house arrest would be akin to being taken hostage. Recalling Derrida's deconstruction of the etymological multiplicity of hospitality, Cuban artists' and intellectuals' usage of the Spanish word *hostigamiento* captures this sense of being a hostage at home. Although translated in English as "harassment," *hostigamiento*, as one can glean from the spelling of the word alone, shares with "host" and "hostility" an etymological kinship with the Latin *hostes* and *hostis*. Derrida has argued that an act of unconditional hospitality requires hosts to relinquish their sovereignty and mastery of the house by making themselves "almost the hostage" of the guest.[109] By exercising a right of free expression not authorized by the law, Lavastida and his dissident peers embody this logic in a strangely perverse way that reveals the state's position as a stranger to its citizens.

CHAPTER 4

Altered States

BORDERING THE INHUMAN IN RENÉ PHILOCTÈTE'S
LE PEUPLE DES TERRES MÊLÉES AND
PEDRO CABIYA'S *MALAS HIERBAS*

In *La isla al revés* (The island upside down), originally published in 1983, former Dominican head of state and writer Joaquín Balaguer describes the geographic contiguity of Hispaniola's neighboring countries as a barrier to the cohesion of a national Dominican identity and, ultimately, as a problem of classification: "La vecindad de Haití ha sido . . . y sigue siendo el problema principal de la República Dominicana" (The proximity of Haiti has been . . . and continues to be the principal problem of the Dominican Republic).[1] This "problem," as Balaguer's essay specifies, begins with the "denationalization" of the country's shared border owing to the strong moral and cultural influence exerted by Haitians upon Dominicans,[2] and, like a contagious malaise, threatens to move inward, resulting in the "denaturalization" of the Dominican nation.[3] In using the Spanish word *vecindad*, which translates as both "neighborhood" and "proximity," Balaguer's text reads Haiti and the Dominican Republic's geopolitical adjacency as not only a spatial problem but also a racial-juridical one (or one that has to do with racial-juridical taxonomies). Balaguer's repeated concerns about the need to maintain the integrity of the Dominican nation's "abolengo español" (Spanish lineage) appeal to a notion of *vecindad* rooted in an early modern Spanish notion of citizenship as membership in a community whose members demonstrate a genealogically pure, uncontaminated lineage.[4] Warning that Dominicans symbolically lose their citizenship (denaturalization) the closer they get to Haitians, Balaguer's essay foresees a zone of racial-juridical indistinction between Haitians and Dominicans, a site where the national ethos is tainted—or, in other words, blackened. Scholars such as Silvio Torres-Saillant have underscored Balaguer's critical role in consolidating Dominican state rhetoric with literary discourse.[5] But *La isla al revés* also foregrounds the *vecindad* of the Haitian neighbor for its capacity to unmoor citizenship from the legal fictions of *human* lineage and descent.

112

ALTERED STATES

This taxonomic rewriting of citizenship is the subject matter of Haitian writer René Philoctète's 1989 novel *Le Peuple des terres mêlées* (translated as *Massacre River*) and Puerto Rican–Dominican writer Pedro Cabiya's 2011 novel *Malas hierbas* (translated as *Wicked Weeds*). Philoctète and Cabiya's novels exist within a genealogy of literary fiction, from both sides of Hispaniola, that re-present the contentious if not traumatic history of internecine conflict between Haiti and the Dominican Republic. The Haitian-Dominican borderland has been at the center of this conflict between the Dominican Republic and Haiti since the official demarcation of the shared border in 1907 (although, unofficially, it extends back to Haiti's annexation and occupation of what was then Spanish Santo Domingo in the early to mid-nineteenth century).[6] Inhabited by Haitians and Dominicans who have for years coexisted and worked alongside one another as associates, friends, neighbors, and families, the Haitian-Dominican borderland instantiates a threatening hospitality that exceeds the law.

Geopolitical borders have always been contentious spaces where the very juridical and ontological principles of hospitality are put to the test. If, as Kant once argued, hospitality is the right of every *human* to peacefully present themselves as strangers in a foreign land without being greeted with enmity, arguably, the border of the nation-state exposes who or what can be considered a human before the law in said land. While it remains unclear in Kant's exposition of his hospitality principle whether the right of hospitality is itself a recognition and affirmation of a stranger's human beingness, Haitian-Dominican border narratives suggest that geopolitical borders hold strangers in a state of onto-juridical abeyance as they await passage or return.[7] We might consider Gloria Anzaldúa's reading of the borderland, writ large, in *Borderlands/La Frontera*, as a space that delimits the boundaries between the human and the nonhuman, the living and the dead in its capture of racialized Others.[8] Traversing both sides of a geopolitical border, the borderland is inhabited by those who can be regarded as living dead and marginally human. I complicate this reading, and the way it misrecognizes the spatiality of Black abjection, by considering the state's reconfiguration of Haitian-Dominican border spaces as zones of unfulfilled passage into the community of the living and the human.

This final chapter of *Caribbean Inhospitality* examines the onto-juridical self-estrangement of Haitian-Dominican border subjects by reading René Philoctète's *Le Peuple des terres mêlées* and Pedro Cabiya's *Malas hierbas* as texts that disrupt the passage—that is, the biopolitical process more commonly known as "naturalization"—of the human being into citizenship. I contend that Philoctète and Cabiya's novels unsettle philosophical, legal, and clinical-scientific discourses that regard self-consciousness and the possession of reason as the key attributes that condition this passage, insofar as Haitian-Dominican subjects' conscious perception of themselves as living, human beings is interrupted by the state's overwriting of the skin of the Dominican body politic in racial-juridical terms that contradict citizens' perception of the material reality of their bodies. In other words, they highlight a cognitive and affective disjuncture between what the Dominican citizen's body announces—both to itself and to the world outside itself—and what the state says about it. Undoubtedly, the notion that the human body has a material reality that has been systematically taxonomized such that it produces a racial text that can be near-universally read is itself the result of a historical, political, and economic imposition constitutive of what Quijano calls the coloniality of power.[9] That race is a fiction is, at this point, to state the obvious. Yet the material reality of race continues to have countless sociopolitical, juridical, and ontological implications—among them, the identification of a people racially marked as "Black" and the historical unity of said people based on their shared conditions of emergence as the Others of modernity. By allowing the material reality of the Haitian-Dominican body to speak in resoundingly louder terms that countervail the state's fictive dermal-juridical narrative, Philoctète's and Cabiya's novels not only suggest the transhistorical entwinement of Haitians and Dominicans in the flesh of history but also, importantly, demonstrate that there is a universal border checkpoint—an international political, anthropological, and economic systems of inhospitality that both conjoin and exceed the Dominican state's racial-juridical narrative—that adjudicates the recognition and passage of the racially marked Haitian-Dominican subject into the universal community of the living and the human. Philoctète's and Cabiya's narratives elucidate how the borders and surface of the Haitian-Dominican subject's body become a contested site through which the Dominican Republic affirms its legitimacy as a sovereign state in the terms set out by global political and economic systems.

In analyzing the self-estrangement of the Haitian-Dominican subject, this chapter ties together the book's analysis of the hospitality/inhospitality dynamic and extends the previous chapter's reading of personhood by exploring its antithesis—the depersonalization of the Haitian-Dominican subject as a consequence of a racial-juridical narrative that produces a disembodied perception of the self as nominally human and nominally alive. Although descriptive psychology and psychiatry generally ascribe a clinical etiology to the phenomenon of depersonalization, the speculative aesthetics of *Le Peuple des terres mêlées* and *Malas hierbas* reframe the depersonalization of the Haitian-Dominican subject vis-à-vis the encounter between otherwise disparate and incompatible discourses: on the one hand, the legal, clinical-scientific, and philosophical discourses about the meaning of being human and human aliveness and, on the other, supernatural fictions of otherworld.

THE UNPASSABLE

Originally used to describe the introduction and acclimation of foreign plant and animal species into a new ecosystem that is not indigenous to them, the concept of naturalization is appropriated in Western political discourse as a legal fiction that describes the biopolitical wedding of human beingness to citizenship. In *Homo Sacer*, Giorgio Agamben excavates the legal-philosophical bridge that conjoins the human being and the citizen, noting that citizenship entails the "passage" of the human from "bare," unprotected life into a protected "sovereign subject" of the nation, a concept whose etymological origins connote the site of a fictive, second "birth." Extrapolating Hannah Arendt's damning judgment that statelessness expels citizens not only from a political community but, more importantly, from humanity itself, Agamben argues that documents such as the 1789 Declaration of the Rights of Man and of the Citizen disclose that the humanity of "Man" can be preserved only through his association with the nation-state as a citizen.[10] Put another way, the nation-state grants unconditional hospitality to humans on the condition that they are citizens.

Writing in the interval between Arendt and Agamben's philosophical archaeology of the human, Frantz Fanon theorized the Black subject's derailment from the political equation linking the human being to the citizen. In *Peau noire, masques blancs* (*Black Skin, White Masks*), he argues that this estrangement derives from anti-Black language encoded in dominant Western narratives— "details, anecdotes, and stories" that construe whiteness as the default of the human and Blackness as its negative and aberration.[11] Concealing themselves behind the mask of this anti-Black language, Black Antilleans mistakenly believed they could "amputate" their Blackness so as to exist on equal footing with (white) humans qua citizens. To the contrary, Fanon explains, for Black Antilleans unable to reconcile the material reality of their Black bodies in a white world, "le connaissance du corps est un activité uniquement négatrice" (consciousness of the body is only a negating activity).[12] To be clear, Fanon held to a phenomenological understanding of consciousness, meaning that he understood humans developed their consciousness—"the absolute certainty of my existence for myself" as defined by one of Fanon's key interlocutors, Maurice Merleau-Ponty—from being in the world, in contact with other humans.[13] For Fanon, then, the mask of an anti-Black Western world places in abeyance Black Antilleans' certainty of their existence as human beings. Fanon was thinking about the effects of coloniality under the conditions of nonsovereign citizenship, in which Black Antilleans were being conscripted into a system where whiteness was the default. Arguably, both the Dominican Republic and Haiti differ from Martinique as sovereign nations that, ostensibly, were able to decide on the terms of their self-determination.

Given Haiti's immediate proximity to the Dominican Republic, the Western international community feared Haiti's Black revolutionary ideology would contaminate eastern Hispaniola. In fact, this very fear prompted the U.S. occupation of the Dominican Republic from 1916 to 1924. Social historian Michael Baud suggests this occupation consolidated Dominican intellectuals' desire to demonstrate their country was more than capable of governing itself as any true (white) nation-state.[14] To this end, these intellectuals cultivated a narrative that would radically distinguish the Dominican Republic from Haiti based on race and effectively conceal their country's legacy of Blackness and Black enslavement. This dubious racial-juridical narrative, as sociologist Ernesto Sagás details, bore two "national prototypes": on the one hand, Blackness came to constitute a signifier of Haitianness, such that only Haitians could ever be Black; on the other, Dominican national identity became rendered, in the words of renowned Dominican nationalist Francisco Moscoso Puello, as "Constitutionally white."[15] Moscoso Puello's constitutional definition of Dominican whiteness suggests that he may have also had in mind the racial taxonomy of Haiti's postrevolutionary constitutions—namely, Jean-Jacques Dessalines's constitution of 1805 and the subsequent ones in 1843 and 1868. These juridical documents, literary scholar Sybille Fischer explains, pronounced all Haitians as Black and the foreigner (*étranger*) as white, a move that reflected a "radical resignification" and inversion of the language of the European colonizer.[16] Undoubtedly, that Haiti's postrevolutionary leaders framed Haitian citizenship as constitutionally Black made it all the more convenient for Dominican intellectuals to impute a symbolic, racial-juridical whiteness to the country's predominantly mixed-race and Black population and thus assert a racial-juridical distinction between Dominican sovereignty and Haiti's tenable statehood.

Dominican intellectuals' actions seem to reflect a keen awareness that the nation-state is, as scholars David Theo Goldberg and Charles Wade Mills contend, fundamentally racialized. On the one hand, in *The Racial State*, Goldberg contends that all nation-states are, by default, "racial states" insofar as they govern and regulate access to spaces and means in ways that fundamentally include certain racial groups while excluding others.[17] By contrast, Mills pointedly asserts that the whiteness of the nation-state bespeaks a "racial contract" that subtends the traditional social contract. In the overarching racial contract, the (white) state recognizes whites, and only whites, as full persons (human beings and citizens) while demarcating "the permanently prepolitical or, perhaps better, *non*political state . . . of nonwhite men."[18] The fundamental whiteness of the nation-state form derives from its legitimation, as per Trouillot, as a North Atlantic universal within the international political community.

Le Peuple des terres mêlées and *Malas hierbas*, however, trouble this standard discourse by exposing the incongruities underlying Dominican intellectuals' anti-Black assertions about their country's purported juridical whiteness. In addition to the novels' speculative framework, the authors' juridical status helps make these incongruities visible. On the one hand, Philoctète's authorial gaze proceeds from the vantage point of his native Haiti, where, but for two brief periods of exile in 1966 and 1992, he lived and died. And yet Philoctète's Haitianness—his assertion that the borderland constitutes, as the novel's title

ALTERED STATES

denotes, a *terre mêlée* (mixed/conflicted land)—suggests that the imposition of anti-Haitian ideology in the borderland severs the Haitian lifeline from which Dominican citizens patently derive their humanity. On the other, hailing from Puerto Rico, Cabiya has resided in Santo Domingo for over a decade; his own affective ties to Dominican society are notable in view of his public, albeit critical, allegiance to Dominican sociopolitical matters.[19] Still, one could argue that Cabiya's Puerto Ricanness has purchase on the interpretation of *Malas hierbas* because of the liminal status many Haitian and Dominican migrants have occupied in Puerto Rico, where both are prejudicially marked as Black, making them subject to discrimination and, in some instances, forms of de facto segregation.[20] In this regard, both Philoctète and Cabiya, through their works, can be said to enact a discursive exposure of Dominican citizens' racial-juridical concealment. Turning now to my extended close readings of *Le Peuple des terres mêlées* and *Malas hierbas*, I hold these two interconnected views of the human in tension, alongside other theories of affect, consciousness, and the inhuman.

"Flesh of My Flesh"

Set in the Dominican province of Elías Piña, *Le Peuple des terres mêlées* retells the story of the 1937 massacre of Haitians residing in the borderlands separating Hispaniola's neighboring nations. Unfolding across the first week of October 1937, the genocidal operation was the apotheosis of so-called *programas de dominicanización* (Dominicanization programs), state-sponsored ethnic and social cleansing initiatives ordered by president and dictator Rafael Trujillo and tasked with restoring the Dominican side of the borderlands to its supposed authentic racial and cultural character. Remembered under various names in Spanish (El Corte) and Kreyòl (Kout Kouto) that reference the dismemberment of Haitian bodies, the event is most famously known as the "Parsley Massacre" (*Masacre del Perejil*) because Dominican soldiers required border people to pronounce the Spanish word for "parsley," *perejil*, a shibboleth to detect suspected Haitians. While recalling the horror of the Haitian genocide, *Le Peuple des terres mêlées* suggests that national fictions of lineage and descent, like shibboleths, are prone to the error of misrecognition, as many Dominicans are caught up in the terror "by mistake" alongside their Haitian loved ones.

Although the novel has been translated in English as *Massacre River*, which functions dually as a reference to the Dajabón River that forms the international border between Haiti and Dominican and to the massacre of Haitians—many as they were crossing the Dajabón—the original title *Le Peuple des terres mêlées* captures much more poignantly the contradictory sense of unity and strife that defines the Haitian-Dominican borderland.[21] The title's literal translation exploits the polysemic sense of the participial adjective *mêlées*, which could refer to a skirmish (as connoted by adaptation of the word "melee" into the

English language) or could denote mixture, confusion, muddling. Thus, a literal translation of the novel's original French title could be "The People of Mixed Lands" or "The People of Conflicted Lands." I believe that Philoctète purposely inflects his fictional remembrance of the 1937 massacre with representational and discursive polysemy in order to show how the racial-juridical indistinction that characterizes the Haitian-Dominican borderland fuels the conflict. But, as I will show, *mêlée* as mixture does not necessarily connote a racial mixture that may be detected at the epidermal level. Rather, I contend, *Le Peuple des terres mêlées* concerns the mixtures of the flesh that entwines Haitians and Dominicans, beyond national prototypes, in the shared history of coloniality.

The *mêlée* as a skirmish, a minor incident of a bigger war, conveys the sense in which the massacre entails a laceration of the flesh. In this regard, *Le Peuple des terres mêlées* resonates with Dominican literary critic and writer Basilio Belliard's assertation that Haitian-Dominican writing bespeaks "una reapertura de las heridas del ominoso pretérito, que las conciencias de ambas sociedad" (a reopening of *wounds* of an ominous past, which *lacerated* the consciousness of both societies).[22] Belliard summarizes the history of Hispaniola as an injurious saga—beginning with Haiti's occupation of the Dominican Republic from 1822 until its independence in 1844 and culminating in 1937 with the Dominican state-sponsored massacre of Haitians occupying its side of the border. Yet what I find most striking about Belliard's assertion is that, in framing literary responses to these countries' divergent ethos, he mobilizes language that brings to mind the skin and flesh. On the one hand, he brings into view the ascendancy of skin as a fictional text mobilized by the Dominican state to mark the juridical identity of its citizens and to justify its wounding of Haitians, marked universally as Black and, therefore, foreign; this unintelligible and dubious skin betrayed their foreignness. More importantly, the wounding of this fictive skin produces a laceration of consciousness. Belliard's dermatological discourse on Haitian-Dominican history foregrounds my reading of how the Dominican state's rewriting of bodies that Dominican citizens share with their Haitian neighbors conditions their derealization and depersonalization as inhuman. On the other, I claim, the state's laceration of skin—a deep, traumatic wound that reaches below the dermis—also positions exposed flesh as an alternative form of belonging that sidesteps the supremacy of skin in Dominican political rhetoric.

Le Peuple des terres mêlées is a novel about the disruption of neighborly proximity, embodied by the inviolable love of the novel's protagonists, Pedro Alvarez Brito, a *mulato* Dominican citizen, and his Black Haitian wife, Adèle Benjamin. The novel represents Pedro and Adèle's marriage through a political theology of the *chair* (flesh) as the biblical "flesh of my flesh," which emblematizes the larger social and cultural intertwining and relationality that founds this Haitian-Dominican border community. The plot's motor is driven by Pedro's attempts to protect Adèle and rally Elías Piña's residents to remain unified—as

ALTERED STATES

husbands, wives, lovers, friends, and neighbors—against the Dominican state's violent and deceptive efforts to differentiate Haitians from Dominicans and turn the latter against the former by invoking a racial-juridical fiction of skin color. Not unlike the historic Trujillo's racial schematization of Dominican society, Philoctète's Trujillo anachronistically calls on Dominicans to reimagine themselves as *blancos de la tierra* (whites of the land), a concept that emerged in the nineteenth century and, according to Anne Eller, was used across a number of Spanish American rural colonies.[23] Meanwhile, Pedro's rallying cries echo the novel's refrain that this border community is neither Haitian nor Dominican but instead "un people unique" (a single people) who form part "d'une même terre" (of the same land).[24] In these terms, Philoctète's novel highlights two contradictory ways of relating to the land—one that connects national lineage to soil and another that sees the land as an expression of the people who inhabit it.

The inhuman is foregrounded already in the opening chapter of *Le Peuple des terres mêlées*: a menacing specter of a bestial bird looms large and lifeless over the Dominican border town of Elías Piñas, longer than the fictive boundary that would divide its inhabitants into citizens of two countries. The bestial bird is reminiscent of the biblical angel of death; by extension, *Le Peuple des terres mêlées* reads like an Exodus story, which is confirmed in the closing chapter called "Exodus." In between warning and flight, this Haitian-Dominican border is plagued with the undoing of its own humanity. It is said that massacres dehumanize its victims. Here, however, human becomes denaturalized—and conversely, the inhuman is naturalized.

Readers of *Le Peuple des terres mêlées* can appreciate a prime example of Dominican anthropodenial in a comically speculative scene depicting Trujillo conspiring and theorizing with eugenicists to develop a new biopolitical vocabulary that would distinguish Dominican citizens from Haitians. In the scene, we find a series of experts convened to weigh in on the status of Dominicans, first with respect to Black Africans and then with respect to the broader human race:

> On fit venir des ethnographes, des ethnologues, des sociologues, des historiens, des linguistes, même des statisticiens. On délibéra. D'aucuns, imbus de la question, avancèrent tout de go: "La nation dominicaine est un produit de race africaine et de race rouge ou américaine." Hors du sujet. "Propositions simplistes," considéra l'autorité. On réenquêta. On apporta des ouvrages de sémantique, de thématique, de sémiotique, de dermatologie, de philosophie. Des Études de conjoncture, un Traité de l'éducation des peuples. On fouilla laborieusement. On sua sang et eu. On découvrit: "La race humaine est dominicaine!" Une minorité quelque peu timide proposa: "Elle est à la fois dominicaine et humaine!" Qui? On ne suit qui. Ni quoi.

> (They called in ethnographers, ethnologists, sociologists, historians, linguists, even statisticians. They deliberated. Some, experts on the question, spoke right

up: "The Dominican nation is a product of the black African and red American races." Quite beside the point. "Simplistic propositions," declared the voice of authority. They reopened the inquiry. Brought in works on semantics, semiotics, dermatology, philosophy. Studies of the overall situation, a *Treatise on the Education of Nations*. They beavered away. Sweated like pigs. And discovered: "The human race is Dominican!" A rather timid majority proposed: "It's both human and Dominican!" Who? Who knows who. Or what.)[25]

This scene of specialists and academics rearticulates, as I discussed in chapter 1, the meaning and nature of political deliberation. Yet it is no coincidence that this field of experts come from disciplines that emerged from colonial science. Ann Stoler has shown how the development of anthropology and the constitution of its original ethnographic subject—the colonized—were means by which colonialism could classify the Other of Europe.[26] To wit, anthropology, sociology, history, statistics, and linguistics are neighboring discourses that, according to George Steinmetz, allowed the colonial project to "insinuate itself into . . . broader formations of social thought."[27] One could argue that they delineate and delimit the sociality of thought and knowledge itself. Although appearing as an outlier in these disciplines, dermatology can be understood as an extension of what Stoler describes as European colonialism's obsession with and investment in gleaning knowledge about the carnal and "carnal relations" to delimit the possibilities of sense, sensibility, and intimacy.[28] In *The Caribbean and the Medical Imagination*, Emily Senior tracks how dermatology emerged both in the wake of and as a continuation of Europe's taxonomic ordering of the world. Dermatology, she clarifies, becomes a new method of classifying human difference, in the place of, religion and clothing.[29] In Philoctète's novel, political deliberation about what it means to be Dominican is filtered through the episteme of these interconnected disciplines. The scene of specialists recapitulates what Étienne Balibar describes, as I briefly discussed in the introduction of *Caribbean Inhospitality*, the anthropological dimensions of citizenship, such that Dominican citizenship comes to represent the human who is differentiated from the universal.

The historical record also provides an interpretive framework for this scene. According to Dominican historian Bernardo Vega, Trujillo's racial-juridical reconfiguration of Dominican identity drew from Nazi, Falangist, and Fascist ideologies. In fact, Vega notes, the Dominican dictator went so far as to consort with the Nazi Party's top officials and scientists, whom he invited to Santo Domingo to inaugurate the Instituto Científico Domínico-Alemán (the German-Dominican Scientific Institute).[30] Returning to the text, however, it appears that while Trujillo purportedly based his reclassification of Dominicans on a dubious Nazi science, the gathering of semioticians and semanticists—masters of the word—consolidates the fictive nature of his endeavor. If citizenship is a

ALTERED STATES

fiction, for Trujillo so too can human physiology be subject to narrative reinvention. But the fiction devolves into a joke. Notwithstanding experts' attempts to elevate Dominicans to the highest echelon of humanity vis-à-vis anti-Black discourse, Dominican space seems to have an inhuman effect on them—as evidenced by the passage's ironic invocation of animal metaphors (they "beavered away" and "sweated like pigs"), which nullifies the subsequent attempt to situate Dominicans evolutionarily as an exemplary form of humanity. Here, the act of political deliberation does not result from the faculty of reason that conditions the human in their passage into the community of men (citizenship). Instead, Trujillo's qualification of Dominican proximity to Haitianness constitutes, in terms that recall Sylvia Wynter, a genre of the inhuman.

Among all the expert fields crucial to the reimaging of the Dominican body politic, I want to hesitate on the mention of dermatology—the science of skin—for, above all else, the Dominican state mobilizes a dermatological discourse to render Dominicans insentient to (Haitian) touch. Indeed, the dermatological permeates the visual repertoire of Philoctète's novel, gesturing toward the significance of skin as a metaphor both for the border and for proximity to Haitianness in Dominican political discourse. If the Hobbesian concept of the body politic functions as a metaphor for the nation-state, in a parallel manner, the skin—the body's largest protective organ—represents the nation-state's borders. Thus, as cultural historian Robin (Lauren) Derby elaborates, early twentieth-century Dominican state and popular discourse reproduce this notion of the Haitian-Dominican border as the skin of the body politic to distinguish Dominicans from Haitians based on bodily practice. In these terms, Haitian bodies are deemed open, extended, and porous such that they "seep onto whatever they touch."[31] Interestingly, Derby explains, Dominicans came to believe in—and fear—the mystical "power of Haitian touch" to alter Dominicanness at the border.[32]

In revisiting the history of Elías Piña's constitution as a factory town, *Le Peuple des terres mêlées* discloses the nature of this affective denaturalization. Reverting its gaze to a less ominous time before the massacre, the novel reminds readers of the province's significance as a major artery for Dominicans leaving the country to sell goods to Haitians and for Haitians entering the country to labor in the sugar factories or *bateyes*. The familiarity of Haitian and Dominican faces who make the same trajectory, day after day, causes the Dominican border agents to, in a manner of speaking, let down the emotional guard that forms the basis of anti-Haitian sentiment: "On s'embrasse . . . sans qu'on se le demande surtout! . . . On va, on vient, des deux côtés. Le gardes ne regardent plus aux passeports. Toutes les chaleurs sont aboutées" (Strangers embrace . . . and without asking permission too! . . . People going back and forth, from both sides. The border guards waving away passports. All hard feelings are forgotten).[33] Here, resentment, hostility, and especially patriotic contempt—affective estrangement embodied by the hard feelings of skin-as-passports—dissipate under the embrace of hospitality. At the same time, this pivotal scene of mutual recognition between strangers brings into view the multifarious and often conflicting dimensions of memory as it pertains to the configuration of the Haitian-Dominican borderland. Notably, I hesitate on the novel's equation of the embrace that blunts the hardened skin of the border with a form of forgetting.

In *Memory, History, Forgetting*, Paul Ricoeur proposes a way to understand the forgetting that unites Haitian and Dominican strangers as the consequence of being touched by the hands of time, which wears down the surface of an object—in this case, skin—on which the past has been recorded. Forgetting, Ricoeur argues, entails the "effacement of traces"—the lifting of an imprint from an image.[34] It follows, then, that to forget an experience, one must first remove the emotional traces impressed upon the psyche by said experience. For this very reason, Ricoeur underscores that forgetting is not always an involuntary endeavor but, often, the outcome of a deliberate work of repetition.[35] Hence, one must repeatedly work to forget with as much determination as one works to remember. Given that the narrative of Dominican citizenship is coded in highly affective terms, the narrative of forgetfulness in *Le Peuple des terres mêlées*—effectively, a border love—suggests that the repeated embrace of Haitian-Dominican strangers passing through the borderland eventually wears down not only skin but, importantly, the traces of contempt.

Yet it is this wearing down of skin that prompts Trujillo's dubious re-creation of the nation-state's white origins. Dissatisfied with the Nazi, Falangist, and Fascist scientists' inability to deliberate conclusively on Dominicans' placement on the spectrum of humanity, Trujillo makes an alternative pronouncement: Dominicans are "*blancos de la tierra*" (whites of the land). More specifically, the narrator affirms, "Leonidas Rafael Trujillo y Molina [*sic*], chef d'État domincain, définit la nation dominicaine non par sa vie commune ni par son project collectif, mais à sa couleur de peau" (Rafael Leónidas Trujillo y Molina, the Dominican head of state, defined his nation neither by its daily life nor by its collective aspirations, but by the color of its skin).[36] Given the effacement of the geopolitical border, Trujillo erects a new, fictive border. But in this movement from defining what it means to be human to imputing whiteness to the Dominican body politic, the Dominican state discards the human. It matters not that citizens are human but rather that they are white, for, as Trujillo very well recognizes, whiteness is what grants legitimacy on the global stage. However, as later passages make clear, Dominicans remain unconvinced by Trujillo's mandate: "Matin, midi, soir, on se regardait dans les miroir. Mais, au fond, on ne leur faisait pas confiance. Celui, qui un quart d'heure plus tôt se contemplait hermine, une heure plus tard se détectait café-crème. On doutait totalement de soi, de sa spécificité, de ses roots" (Morning, noon, and night people looked at themselves in mirrors, but deep down, they didn't trust them. Someone who had seen himself as snow-white fifteen minutes earlier would detect a café-au-lait tint an hour afterward . . . and lost all faith in themselves in the specificity of their roots).[37] That Dominicans fail to buy into the racial-juridical mandate is unsurprising, for although Haitians are seen as Black and only Black and Dominicans as mixed-race and white, the fact is—and this fact will become even clearer in my reading of *Malas hierbas*—they are often indistinguishable from one another; in the borderland, this would incite laughter, which is what the text precisely invokes. Instead, I believe the text invites a reading of Dominican whiteness as an onto-affective disposition, with a twist: for Dominicans to claim whiteness, they must feel contempt not only for Haitian Blackness but also for their skin (or, in the text's words, the specificity of their [Black] roots). This contempt of (Haitian) Blackness—and thus for the Dominican self—initiates a disturbance in Dominicans' consciousness: they question the certainty of their very existence.

The novel allegorizes this loss of Dominicans' human consciousness vis-à-vis the specter of a bestial bird, whose hybrid features incite terror in those who deign to look defiantly upon its countenance. The narrator's gaze descends from the bird's aerial position, which casts its shadow over Elías Piña, to the supranational unity of Elías Piña, now under threat as the image of the bestial bird quickly vanishes into the image of Trujillo. Through the bestial bird, I argue, the text captures the meaning of Dominicans' affective concealment under fictive white skin. It is the Dominican Pedro Brito—married to Haitian Adèle—who anticipates the affective implications of this prophetic bird in his warning to fellow Dominican laborers against colluding with the state: "Nous tendons à lui ressembler. Nos enfants sur leurs ardoises dessinent son profil en louant son autorité. Il est dit que la chose participera de nous jusqu'a ce que nous nous perdions pour nous retrouver totalement transformés. Pattes, griffes, en lieu et place de notre cœur, de notre conscience" (We measure ourselves against the horror of the beast: we begin to resemble it. Praising its authority, our children draw its profile on their slates. People say the thing will be part of us until, losing ourselves, we find ourselves completely changed. Paws, hoofs, claws, instead of our consciousness and our hearts).[38] The novel atomizes the beast's profile down to its paws, hoofs, and claws—terms used to describe animal appendages, in distinction from human hands. From a bioevolutionary standpoint, both sets of appendages fulfill analogous functions insofar as they enable both nonhuman animals and humans to grasp, touch, and feel. And yet, as the passage intimates, not all touch elicits the same type of conscious and affective experience. In describing the bestialization of Dominican citizens, Brito establishes a boundary between the affective violence wrought by the beast's desensitized touch and the loving touch that engenders human consciousness. The appearance of the bird serves as a warning that no one is spared from Trujillo's hand. The massacre wages war on the humanity of Dominicans and Haitians alike: the former find their consciousness inhumed under a bestial skin, while the machete reduces the latter to dismembered flesh.

Still, amid the carnage that overflows the text's visual rhetoric, *Le Peuple des terres mêlées* accounts for the human. Ultimately, the effacement of the trace of hard feelings exposes the flesh to a subdermal ethos. Philoctète's novel holds this voluntary, amicable exposure of Haitian-Dominican flesh in tension with the carnage wrought by the machete, the instrument of choice mobilized by agents of the Dominican state to violently dismember the flesh of Haitian bodies. To be sure, even Dominicans who disavow Haitians do not remain unscathed by this persecutory gaze of the state. It becomes clear to them that they simply cannot afford to remain indifferent to the carnage, for the dismemberment of Haitians from Elías Piña will certainly fragment the community's economic life force: the Dominican *bateyes* or sugar factories, described by Moya Pons as a "prolongación modificada" (modified prolongation) of the colonial plantation system.[39] The awareness that both Haitian and Dominican bodies labor side by side in the *bateyes*, yet another denaturalizing space that further dissolves their respective natural allegiances, precipitates a powerful reflection about their shared condition as flesh: "And the workers had gathered together. The flesh of workers is common flesh. It gleans red in the light of dawn. Closes up shop at night. Always faithful to what it firmly believes, it cannot believe that night should lay down the law. The flesh of workers is both a political statement and the rattle of chains. It has the force of law when the law has foundered."[40] Broadly, this scene of enfleshment emblematizes what Kaiama Glover describes as Philoctète's "spiralist aesthetic," whereby the Haitian author draws attention to the continuities between Hispaniola's colonial past and its postcolonial present by creating temporal discontinuities in the storyline.[41] Alternatively, I argue, the passage brings into view what we might call the coloniality of flesh. In these terms, the enchainment of flesh constitutes a transhistoric signifier that links Haitian and Dominican workers' mutual exploitation in the contemporary Dominican *batey* to the enslavement of ancestral Black bodies in the plantations of colonial Saint-Domingue.

At the same time, I argue, this flesh can also be understood as a material representation of what Édouard Glissant calls the abyss. In *Poétique de la Relation*, Glissant contends that the Caribbean originates in "le gouffre-matrice" (the womb-abyss), a metaphor both for the slave ships carrying living and dead Black bodies side by side across the Atlantic and for the plantations where enslaved Blacks labored in a state of social and political death. Later, Glissant asserts that the experience of death touching and engendering life in the abyss constitutes "connaissance partagée" (a shared knowledge)—indeed, I suggest, what Philoctète calls a "common flesh."[42] Putting Glissant's abyssal ethos in the context of *Le Peuple des terres mêlées*, Haitians and Dominicans laboring together gives rise to a postcolonial, abyssal remembering that impedes Dominicans from colluding with the law against their Haitian counterparts.

While there has been a tendency in posthumanist criticism to theorize the flesh in terms that suggest a movement toward the postracial, common flesh in *Le Peuple des terres mêlées* disavows the utopian horizon with which racial mixture has been invested in the consolidation of globality.[43] Philoctète has spent the greater part of his novel telling us that the political instrumentalization of racial mixture can produce only death, wiping out the very bodies that it envelopes. Alternatively, I contend, Philoctète's common flesh constitutes an ethos that binds Haitians and Dominicans to the history of Black enslavement that founds Hispaniola and that cannot be effaced by the juridical fiction of skin-as-border. Hortense Spillers's theorization of the flesh in "Mama's Baby, Papa's Maybe" continues to be instructive. In her essay, Spillers interprets flesh in relation to the captivity of Black people and their reduction to bodies that have been stripped of their humanity by the marks of chains and the wounding of whips. "Before the 'body,'" she pronounces, "there is the 'flesh,' that zero degree of social conceptualization that does not escape concealment under the brush of discourse."[44] Enslaved Black people are reduced to bodies of flesh, which precedes and escapes the discursive constitution of the human as Man (political subject, citizen, person) with a conscious body. Expanding Spillers's reading vis-à-vis Maurice Merleau-Ponty's phenomenology of the flesh, Alexander Weheliye locates in the flesh the condition of possibility for an "alternate instantiation of humanity."[45] Merleau-Ponty posits flesh (*chair*) as the invisible or, stated differently, the immaterial material substrate of the body; he goes on to associate the subdermal invisibility of flesh with consciousness, which does not reside solely in the mind but rather arises from the sense of touching and being touched by another.[46] A phenomenology of the flesh would, therefore, make possible the articulation of the human otherwise for Black people's bodies that are seen as housing neither consciousness nor will. Indeed, Weheliye asserts, this phenomenological vindication of the flesh constitutes a "modality of relation"—that is, the very sense of relation through which persons become conscious of their humanity. This modality of relation restores the human from their burial under what Frantz Fanon has called a racial-epidermal schema—or, in Weheliye's words, the "armor" of Western Man.[47]

Le Peuple des terres mêlées, however, articulates a common humanity of the flesh through a return to Haiti as a site of radical hospitality. The novel concludes with an exodus story that mirrors the liberation of ancient Israel from Egyptian captivity in the biblical narrative of Exodus. In this Haitian-Dominican exodus, Philoctète—with no pretense of impartiality—vindicates Haiti, the first Black republic and the first independent nation-state in Latin America and the Caribbean, as a refugee promised land. Even so, Philoctète maintains the neutrality of the refugees without imputing on them the political agenda of the

Haitian nation-state. Given the temporal displacements fundamental to *Le Peuple des terres mêlées*, it would not be far-fetched to imagine that Philoctète sees in the love and hope of these early Haitian-Dominican refugees a paradigm for a future Haiti that, at the time of the authorship of his novel (1989), finds itself wrecked, in a state of political turmoil as the kleptocracy of Haitian dictator Jean-Claude "Baby Doc" Duvalier is replaced by a series of unstable and inefficacious governments.

PASSING LIFE

The continuities that bind the legacies of Trujillo and the Duvalier regimes are at the center of Pedro Cabiya's 2011 zombie novel *Malas hierbas*. Framed as an "album" or "scrapbook," the novel's four seemingly disconnected intertexts oscillate between the Dominican Republic and Haiti from the mid-eighties to the mid-aughts.[48] The main narrative thread of *Malas hierbas* revolves around a man of unknown parentage and dubious origins who suffers from Cotard's delusion—a psychotic disorder in which the affected person believes they are dead or decaying. Convinced he is a zombie, he spends his waking hours searching for a cure that will free him from the curse of zombification. To be clear, both the protagonist's mental disorder and his name remain concealed until the novel's conclusion, in which the Dominican police betray his psychiatric diagnosis and his identity as Dionisio. His name is a clever gesture to the myth of Dionysus, wherein the Greek god of wine, associated with ritual madness, is brought back to life after descending into hell, somewhat like zombies.

Notwithstanding these important revelations, *Malas hierbas* passes as a speculative text—namely, a science horror-fantasy. Thus, for most of the novel, readers labor under the illusion that Dionisio is really, as he says, a zombie. As corpses resurrected from the dead, zombies lack the ability to feel and think, yet they move, walk, and faintly gesture in ways that give them a semblance of life. In Cabiya's brilliant postcolonial zombie narrative, however, readers encounter a protagonist whose features and disposition depart from those of the archetypal zombie in not insignificant ways. Quite unlike the senseless, unthinking automaton iconized in popular culture, the zombie Dionisio belongs to a category of zombies that, according to Emily Maguire, can be described as the "sentient zombie" or the "sentient undead."[49] Popularized in recent media, the sentient undead, Maguire explains, occupy a "liminal position" that is "closer to life than to death: the undead protagonist is conscious of his or her inhumanity/nonhumanness, along with the marginality of his position." Likewise, Dionisio has exceptionally high cognitive capabilities, as evidenced by his position as a scientist and chief executive at the Santo Domingo division of an Eli Lilly laboratory. Importantly, he does not betray the signs of putrefaction emblematic of the popular zombie. Given his "acomodada posición social" (comfortable social posi-

ALTERED STATES 127

tion) made possible by a hefty inheritance his deceased parents left him, he has been able to protect his body from decay through cosmetic concealment and dissimulation.[50] And it is because of this corporeal privilege that Dionisio the zombie can "pass" as a living being, so to speak, without detection in everyday Dominican life, even while he struggles to conjure an emotional life that allows him to relate to other living, human beings.

I concur with Maguire that the zombie's "flexible liminality," as a sentient undead, makes possible a "deeper exploration of life on the border of humanity, offering a nuanced—if sometimes contradictory—subject position from which to examine the biopolitical borders of the citizen in the Dominican Republic and Haiti.[51] However, I pursue a slightly different line of inquiry that further problematizes the shifting ontologies of existence within this Dominican-Haitian biopolitical border through a reading of the zombie narrative as an allegory for *passing*. While, in the passing narrative, a person engages in dissimulation in order to assume a fictive public identity, Cabiya's novel discloses how life itself is redefined as a category of identity such that zombification becomes a metaphor for what I define below as "passing life," using the archetypal narrative of racial passing as a frame of reference.

Malas hierbas further dismantles the postulates that undergird a Western ontology of life through disjointed clinical-juridical, philosophical, and sociopolitical narratives about zombification, each of which attempts to account for Dionisio's belief that he is living-dead. Moreover, these three narratives function as intertexts that set up the novel's fourth and main intertext, Dionisio's testimony and account. Readers must piece these narratives together coherently in order to decode the relationship between Dionisio's zombification and his "passing" as a living being. In this latter regard, I read Dionisio as a shape-shifter, to the extent that, in his search for a cure and liberation from living death, he embodies and must "pass" through ontologies of both life and death as they are codified in the discourses of Western medicine, the law, philosophy, and Haitian-Dominican society.

The racial *passing* narrative is resemanticized in the novel's contemporary Haitian and Dominican contexts, where racial difference has functioned metonymically to radically demarcate a dubious distinction between Dominican and Haitian sovereignty, national identity, and juridical status. *Malas hierbas* discloses how this juridical reconceptualization of racial difference in Haiti and the Dominican Republic forms the basis of an insidious political narrative in which Haitians, in particular, are construed as impostor citizens in Hispaniola, forcing them to engage in forms of simulation and dissimulation as a matter of life and death. Cabiya's invocation of the trope of passing signals to the history of internecine conflict in contemporary Hispaniola and the misrepresentation of Haitians as a clandestine, invasive force that needs to be rooted out. Similarly, in Haiti, dissenting citizens have been driven to engage in ontological self-effacement due to political persecution.[52] I find that it is in these survivalist terms that being both alive (and dead) shifts from a physiological marker to a juridical index.[53] Therefore, I invoke the concept of "passing life" to describe Haitians who, rendered impostors, are relegated to a state of ontological and juridical unsettledness and transience that is akin to zombification.

Passing is traditionally defined as the ability to construct and assume a fictive public identity as a member of a social group that does not correspond with one's "real" private identity as a member of another social group to which one was originally assigned, usually by law. As Elaine Ginsberg has noted, passing has been historically associated with a person's ability to disguise racial difference—most notably, Blackness—owing to the privilege of having a bodily phenotype that is misread as "white."[54] However, she continues, to the extent that the logic of passing relies on the faulty presupposition that identity is "natural" or biologically innate, "'passing' has been applied discursively" to other categories of identity that can be emulated through bodily, sartorial, or behavioral dissimulation, including sexuality, gender, and even class. Therefore, Ginsberg explains, the ability to pass has been a matter of "life and death" for some in a political system where whiteness—or the expression of a dominant identity—has conditioned one's membership in a political community and, by extension, the benefits that accrue from being considered a full-fledged citizen.

This racial-juridical logic is further complicated by the fact that this discourse of (skin) color is filtered through a raciolinguistic binary that reflects neither the Dominican nor the Haitian body politic, which, according to Ginetta Candelario, exists within a broad and variegated spectrum of color and are classified within, as Michel-Rolph Trouillot observes, "sociopolitical categories" that destabilize the fixed "somatic referent" of race.[55] In fact, those who visibly betray what we might consider an epidermal Blackness or whiteness could be identified interchangeably as Haitian or Dominican, even if the official discourse of the nation says otherwise. It is the metonymy of skin for the nation-state that partially informs my reading of passing life in Haitian-Dominican contexts of *Malas hierbas*.

A cursory reading of *Malas hierbas* suggests that this racial-juridical logic does not extend to Dionisio, for not only does he pass as a living being, but many aspects of his social and political identity, including his race and juridical status, are also shrouded in mystery. What we call human "life" is, ostensibly, not a social category of identity—insofar as life, unlike race, gender, or sex, cannot be dissimulated. Naturally, the dead cannot pass; they cannot simulate life because they cannot reproduce its vital signs—the medical community's universally accepted measurements of the body's essential, life-sustaining functions, which take place below the skin. Death, as a preliminary physiological definition, is the cessation of these essential functions. Interestingly, in distinguishing life from identity—and in situating life against its negative, death—it becomes clear

ALTERED STATES   129

that a precise definition of life seems patently elusive. Indeed, the meaning of
life is always already deferred by the need to resort to a semiotic discourse that,
while describing subdermal and neural processes, relies on an ocular and
representational logic not far removed from the logic of identity. As Eugene
Thacker argues in *After Life*, this inability to arrive at an immanent definition
of "life itself" constitutes one of the central quandaries of Western philosophy.
Following Heidegger, Thacker shows, ontology paradoxically "thinks of life in
terms of something-other-than-itself," whether theology, biology, the law, or
humanism.[56]

It is precisely this "something-other-than-itself" that Dionisio's "passing life"
makes manifest. The idea of passing as a living being not only refashions the
ontology of life into an identity category, like race and citizenship, but also suggests
that the very categories of identity deemed "natural" are mobilized to mark some
as living and others as dead. Thus, to transform life into an identity means both
to define life and to conceptualize the status of being alive through something
other than "universal" vital signs and mobility. Likewise, death constitutes something other and more than the physiological cessation of these vital functions.
I find it meaningful, then, that Dionisio's autobiographical testimony opens
with the story of his resurrection as a zombie—which, alternatively, constitutes
the story of his birth into a society that has always already marked him as dead.

If success in passing as a member of a social group hinges partially on one's
ability to accurately mimic those for whom one passes, Dionisio connects what
it means to be alive—and, thus, a member of the living—with his ability to conceal his putrefying skin. Having described his miraculous resurrection, he
explains,

> Las costosas fragancias, lociones y cosméticos (especialmente formados para
> nosotros, los muertos vivientes, por laboratorios que hace mucho tiempo
> descubrieron ese nicho del mercado y lo explotan sin misericordia) y demás
> productos de sobrevivencia y camuflaje a los que estoy esclavizado, me garan-
> tizan una considerable libertad de movimiento. Puedo ir y venir a placer sin
> levantar sospechas ni causar aprensión entre mis conciudadanos. Mi vida es
> un simulacro tan perfecto.
>
> (Expensive fragrances, lotions, and cosmetics [specially formulated for us, the
> living dead, by laboratories that long ago discovered that market niche and
> exploit it mercilessly], and all other products of survival and camouflage to
> which I'm enslaved, guarantee me considerable freedom of movement. I can
> go and come as I please without raising suspicions or uneasiness among my
> fellow citizens. My life is such a perfect simulacrum.)[57]

I locate in this description of Dionisio's epidermal concealment a mimicry not
just of life itself but, in particular, of personhood and citizenship. Indeed, in the

legal idiom of Western political thought, the process by which the human is reborn as Man is represented as a form of sartorial concealment—a metaphor for taking on the shroud of thought and reason.[58] Likewise, in *Malas hierbas,* this rebirth corresponds with Dionisio's resurrection as a zombie in full possession of his ratiocinative capacities. It is precisely through the creation of Dionisio's personhood that life moves from a pure ontology of existence to an identity. Furthermore, Dionisio's concealment metaphorically reproduces the process of becoming naturalized as a citizen. However, if the life of the living—human life itself—can be legitimized only through the attainment of legal personhood, passing life in *Malas hierbas* adheres to the consumptive logic of neoliberal citizenship.[59] As Dionisio acquires the "natural" look of life through cosmetics, naturalization as a citizen can be feigned through a performative consumption. In other words, I suggest that passing life also equates with passing citizenship. Thus, the artificiality of material goods overrides the materiality of skin as a signifier of racial-juridical difference because skin (color) alone cannot be trusted to tell the truth about who is a citizen and who is not. Globalization, emblematized by the presence of the multinational, U.S.-based pharmaceutical company Eli Lilly in Dominican territory, has made it such that purchasing power now distinguishes the dead from the living, the formerly enslaved from the ostensibly free citizen. In a postcolonial Haitian-Dominican context, the plantation laboratory is replaced by the laboratory of the largest producer of psychotropic medication today, and the meaning of slavery as a logic of production is resemanticized as the illusory narcotic of freedom as consumption.[60] This illusion, as I later explain, forms the basis of Dionisio's psychotic delusion.

In his (re)birth as a legal person and citizen, Dionisio's passing life is akin to shape-shifting—possessing or taking on the body of another being through supernatural rituals deemed to exceed Western reason. In *The Law Is a White Dog,* Colin Dayan productively syncretizes "myth and legal practice" to delineate a connection between shape-shifting and the everyday, state-sanctioned rituals by which the law dispossesses the living of their self-identity or, alternatively, renders them what she calls "depersonalized persons."[61] Recalling Orlando Patterson's definition of slavery as social death, Dayan underscores that slavery did not divest the enslaved of their personhood but instead made their personhood into a property malleable to the dictates of the law. Dayan reframes this civil death—"the state of a person who though possessing *natural life* has lost all *civil* rights."[62] Against the grain of contemporary political philosophy, Dayan underscores that life itself does not confer the right of personhood. To the contrary, through a reading of literature in which the defilement and theft of a *buried* corpse is ruled unlawful, she observes that "when a body has been worked on and bettered, possessed or occupied by another's labor and thus owned, it gains legal recognition."[63] In these terms, the biologically dead may possess as many, or even more, legal rights as the living to the extent that their

ALTERED STATES   131

bodies have undergone the rituals of mortuary vestment. Second, in a manner not unlike the spells that are both cast upon and cast by shape-shifters such as zombies, ghosts, and goblins, "shedding and taking on different skins," the law appropriates and transforms living humans who bear the mark of juridical abjection into legal persons, who "have no fixed definitions, but instead take on changing capacities variously granted by the state such as legal rights, freedoms, duties, and obligations."[64]

Taking to heart Dayan's engagement with the supernatural through the lens of the law, I want to hesitate on the parallels between shape-shifting and passing. Passing—in most, though not all, cases—is a marginal human's response to legal discourses that have failed to recognize their personhood and thus have rendered them utterly abject under the law, like an unclaimed and unworked corpse. Passing, then, enables those marked as dead to assume a shape and acquire a definition intelligible to the law. But, as Sara Ahmed stresses, the act of passing is related to the verb "to pass," which entails "the literal act of moving through space (in which there is no departure or arrival)."[65] In other words, passing begets an interminable movement without fixity of form or definition because one can never become the person for whom one passes.

Similarly, what I am calling passing life betrays the very indeterminacy of life itself: Dionisio takes on a fictive form of life called "citizenship" that grants him neither specificity nor completeness enough to liberate him from living death. In contemplating the incompleteness and lack of fixity that characterize Dionisio's passing life, I return to Eugene Thacker, who links shape-shifting with the inability to define life: "There is a sense in which the major problem concerning life has to do not with its definition, . . . but with the very plasticity of life, a shape-shifting quality exhibited in all the different ways in which we use the concept to correlate to the different phenomena that are deemed to be living."[66] Thacker suggests that life passes as many things—it takes on so many permutations, constantly on the move in the terrain of philosophy, that through its overabundance of definitions, it is transfigured into a "nameless thing."[67]

Curiously, my reading of Dionisio as a shape-shifter is informed precisely by the multifarious definitions of life proffered in Cabiya's text—and notably by the fact that Dionisio is simultaneously unnamed and named as two distinct characters. Following the passage wherein he describes the stealthy concealment of his skin, Cabiya's zombie protagonist invokes the name "Dionisio" not to identify himself but instead to designate another character—a philosopher of life who owns a bar (in reality, the insane asylum) where a collective of zombies (in reality, other persons suffering psychotic disorders) congregate to relieve themselves of "la tensión que nos produce pasarnos el día pretendiendo estar vivos" (the tension occasioned by having to spend the day pretending to be alive).[68] As I have previously noted, the protagonist's name is withheld until the novel's end, when it is disclosed by the law. By rendering him nameless in the majority of the text,

Cabiya casts Dionisio in two different roles: first, a nameless zombie scientist and, second, a dispassionate philosopher named Dionisio. In the end, readers realize that Dionisio the philosopher is, in fact, the zombie scientist, split from himself. Effectively, Cabiya recapitulates the disciplinary splitting of medicine or the science of life from the philosophy of life.

Through this splitting, *Malas hierbas* introduces, as a separate intertext, a disquisition concerning what philosophy of mind calls the "phenomenal zombie" or "p-zombie," to which the novel gestures explicitly in "P-Zed," a chapter that is part of the novel's philosophical section titled "Vacuus." Indeed, as the noted philosopher of mind, David Chalmers elaborates, the concept of the p-zombie emerges from a thought experiment that aims to theorize the possibility of human existence without consciousness. The p-zombie is physiologically alive—awake, breathing, and even possessing a certain level of sentience—but, at the same time, lacks the "real conscious experience" of being fully alive.[69] The p-zed concept defines death as the cessation of conscious experience, which in medical discourse does not constitute a vital sign of human life. Philosophy of mind calls this conscious experience of life "qualia," which denotes the phenomenal quality of life—that which cannot be reduced to physical sensations or rational thought. Put another way, qualia entails the ability to qualitatively describe "what it is like" to have a subjective experience—for example, what it is like to be a living human being. Indeed, in splitting from himself, Dionisio the philosopher introduces the notion of qualia to Dionisio the scientist, who, nevertheless, doubts its conceptual relevance in the search for a cure, suggesting that qualia does not wholly account for his condition.

Yet the intercalation of philosophy of mind in Cabiya's text not only elucidates what Thacker calls the plasticity or shape-shifting quality of life's meanings but also counterbalances Dionisio's clinical diagnosis of Cotard's delusion. On the one hand, by providing another plausible explanation for Dionisio's condition, these philosophical speculations have a cognitive function insofar as they prompt readers to consider the very question of what it is like to be alive. On the other hand, by introducing Dionisio's madness at the end of the novel as a clear-cut condition of possibility, Cabiya seems to foreclose the very speculative nature of *Malas hierbas*.

READING *MALAS HIERBAS* SOCIOGENICALLY

Still, both the clinical diagnosis and philosophical theory of zombification are inextricable from the novel's Dominican and Haitian sociopolitical contexts, to which I now turn my attention. Indeed, to read the novel's clinical and philosophical intertexts absent of this grounding is to fall back into the very universalist characterization of life itself that the example of Dionisio's passing life patently disallows. That is to say, Dionisio's zombification, even as *Malas hierbas* represents it through a variety of disciplinary discourses, nevertheless temporarily renders him a "nameless thing." In making sense of what these shifting theories of life (and death) suggest about Dionisio's condition, I find instructive Sylvia Wynter's admonition about the limitations of strictly philosophical, psychoanalytic, and neurobiological explanations of both human consciousness and delusional thinking: such explanations fail when they do not account for the role of cultural discourses.

Wynter explicitly interpolates theories of conscious experience drawn from Chalmers's work and philosophy of mind, writ large, and constructs a parallel conversation with the Haitian narrative of zombification to advance a "transcultural" reading of human consciousness. She mediates this transcultural parallel through Fanon, who in *Black Skin, White Masks* made the now classic assertion, "Alongside phylogeny and ontogeny, there is sociogeny."[70] To be clear, in this pronouncement, Fanon aimed to show that our sense of "what it is like" to be human is informed not only by the mere fact of our biological birth into a species (phylogeny and ontogeny) but also by anti-Black language encoded in dominant Western narratives. In a brilliant move that rigorously bridges scientific empiricism and cultural theory, Wynter extends Fanon's original claim to demonstrate that cultural narratives (*mythoi*), in Katherine McKittrick's words, "are therefore always formulaically patterned so as to co-function with the endogenous neurochemical behavior regulatory system of our human brain."[71] In other words, anti-Black narratives neurochemically restructure the mind, generating positive or negative sensations that signal what constitutes a "normal" human or an "aberration."[72] In these terms, Wynter reframes "qualia"—the subjective experience of what it is like to be human—vis-à-vis what she calls the "sociogenic principle."

Turning her attention to Haiti, Wynter observes how the threat of zombification was used as a disciplinary mechanism to regulate what were considered "antisocial behaviors."[73] She gives an example from *Passage of Darkness*, ethnobotanist Wade Davis's controvertible study on the administration of plant- and animal-based toxins to induce zombification as punishment.[74] In an earlier work, *The Serpent and the Rainbow*, Davis describes how zombification was meted out as a system of justice under the Duvalier regime to castigate citizens perceived as disloyal to their local communities and, by extension, the state.[75] (Not incidentally, it would appear that Davis's text also constitutes source material to *Malas hierbas*, which literally means "poisonous weeds"—that is, unwanted, uncultivated, and invasive plants that blend or, one could argue, *pass* alongside cultivated plants, interfering with their ability to thrive.) In the fear that the threat of zombification prompts in Haitians, Wynter locates a parallel with Fanon's diagnosis of the Black Caribbean subject's fear of being perceived as acting Black, which produces a neurological effect similar to that of the toxins that cause zombification:

> What Fanon enables us to see by analysis is not only the way in which the culturally imposed symbolic belief system of the French bourgeois *sense of self* also structures the *sense of self* of the colonized French Caribbean middle class Negro, but also that it is a *sense of self* for which the notion of "acting like a nigger," and thereby lapsing into non-being, that—like the threat of zombification for the Vodunist—serves as the internalized sanction system which motivates his/her behaviors, thereby functioning in the same way as a "garrison controls a conquered system." In this context, a transcultural perspective on two quite different injunctions related to two quite different *senses* of the *self*, yet functioning to the same end, enables us to recognize that the qualitative mental states which correlated with aversive sensations, or fear of behaving, in the one case, in such an antisocial way as to make the threat of zombification real, and in the other as to make "negrification" real, are of the same objectively instituted and subjectively experience modality, even where the cultural conception of identity, or what it is like to be human, is different.[76]

The narratives that shape the Afro-Caribbean subject's cultural and social education into the human community suggest that they must act *contra natura*, against the (Black) self to secure and ensure their humanity within the very Western construct that renders them aberrant. This self-imposed injunction, in Fanon's broader work, forms the basis of the Caribbean subject's autophobic delusion.

Overall, Fanon's analysis of French Caribbean subjects' failure to conceptualize a sense of self, which Wynter expands upon in her sociogenic principle, provides a critical framework for my reading of Dionisio's delusion of zombification: the fact that he misreads himself as dead in order to, paradoxically, pass as a living being emphasizes the necessity of grounding his conscious experience in the cultural and social milieu of everyday Caribbean life. *Malas hierbas* discloses the sociogenic underpinnings of Dionisio's delusion vis-à-vis what Cabiya describes as the "curatorial" handiwork of Isadore, whom the author identifies in the novel's prefatory matter as the owner and compiler of the "scrapbook."[77] In the body of the novel, we learn that Isadore is one of Dionisio's three research assistants; notably, she specializes in Caribbean ethnobotany and, in particular, pharmacopeia—a role that recapitulates Wade Davis's work on zombie toxins. Out of the three assistants, Isadore shares a marked yet unexplainable affinity with Dionisio the scientist. They engage in a substantive dialogue on the nature of zombification—without him revealing his secret identity—by way of a sweeping survey of zombie tropes in Western literature, film, and media.[78] Importantly, it is through Isadore, a second-generation Dominican citizen of Haitian descent, that we learn of Dionisio's diagnosis. The Dominican police reveal it to her only in the wake of his death, which she has witnessed. Isadore's duality as a Haitian-Dominican subject plays a vital role in Cabiya's zombie narrative: the list of poisonous plants she annotates in her scrapbook, combined with the police transcripts of her interrogation and her accounts of zombification in Haiti, suggest that she authors Dionisio's birth as a zombie in the Dominican Republic as a means of processing and representing her own exclusion as a (Black) Dominican citizen of Haitian descent. Through Isadore's testimony, Cabiya highlights long-standing historical discourses—on both sides of the island—that cast Haitian subjects as impostors and mimics. This impostor narrative structures the ontology of living death that forms the basis for Dionisio's delusion.

Dominican political and legal responses to Haitian transmigrants have consolidated this impostor narrative, as Moya Pons shows in a series of three groundbreaking essays—"La matriz transnacional haitiana (I)," "La matriz transnacional haitiana (II)," and "La matriz transnacional dominico haitiana (III)"—published in 2010 in *Diario Libre,* one of the principal daily newspapers in the Dominican Republic. Moya Pons elucidates how Haitian-Dominican subjects known as *ambas-fils*, who blur the national, racial, linguistic, and cultural "prototypes" of Dominican and Haitian identity, must navigate a complex geopolitics of belonging.[79] Their name is a portmanteau that, more than likely, originates from the fusion of the Spanish word *ambas* (both) and the French *fils* (children)—in other words, children of both sides of the island. The *am-bas-fils* remain elusive for Dominican social theorists because of their capacity to pass undetected. Notably, from 1961 to 2000, the *am-bas-fils* engaged in "clandestine migration" from Haiti to the Dominican Republic, going back and forth between the two counties and eventually settling in Dominican territory.[80] What stands out in the Dominican historian's account of the *am-bas-fils* is the public perception of their ability to pass. This narrative was buttressed by the Dominican government— heightened during the era of Rafael Trujillo, the Dominican dictator who, in 1937, mandated the slaughter of those identified as Haitians residing on the Dominican side of the Haitian-Dominican borderland: it is said that, through cunning, the *am-bas-fils* "elude" Dominican border checkpoints "comprando el favor de los comandantes militares y los caciques políticos" (buying the favor of military commanders and political heads), thereby assimilating into a country notoriously consumed with detecting Haitianness.[81] Such a view of the racial-juridical flexibility of the *am-bas-fils* signifies, even today, beyond the group in question to influence perceptions of Haitian-Dominican legality, as the Dominican police officer's interrogation of Isadore in *Malas hierbas* shows. In mobilizing this rhetoric of Haitian unreadability and dissimulation, the Dominican government tacitly implicates not only the *am-bas-fils* but also naturalized and natural-born Dominican citizens of Haitian parentage as impostors—or, in other words, as subjects who "pass" through the racial-juridical borders of Dominican society as though they were Dominican citizens.

I find two features of Moya Pons's description of the *am-bas-fils* particularly striking and relevant to *Malas hierbas*. First, his assertion that little is known about them connects their epistemological opacity to their undetectability as immigrants. Second, I find in his description of their ability to elude both detection and knowability a kinship with the shape-shifter. In particular, we might consider the ways in which the *am-bas-fils*, as juridical shape-shifters, must also play dead, so to speak—that is, they must render themselves illegible as Haitians—in order to move or pass along the borders of Dominican existence. In these terms, I see in Dionisio a specter of the *am-bas-fils*, a man about whom little is known and yet who, through epidermal concealment, is able to pass as alive and, by extension, pass as a citizen.

The *am-bas-fils* impostor narrative appears to haunt *Malas hierbas* in the sections that constitute transcripts of Isadore's interrogation by the Dominican police, who call into question her national identity and the legitimacy of her status as a Dominican citizen. Isadore promptly rebuffs one of the officers by stating, "Mi pasaporte, detective, es el mismo que el suyo. . . . Pero quizás eso no es lo que le importa saber, sino el lugar de nacimiento de mis padres, porque el mío, como usted, sin duda, sabe ya, es el mismo que el suyo" (My passport, detective, is the same as yours. . . . But perhaps that's not what you really want to know but, rather my parents' birthplace, since mine, as you well know, is that same as yours).[82] The police officers' questions about Isadore's status are not simply standard procedure. Their queries—and her rightful correction that they are, in fact, asking about her parents' origins—allude to the revival of protracted debates about the status and legitimacy of second-generation Dominican citizens of Haitian descent, culminating with the issuance of "La Sentencia."[83]

I have argued that the philosophical intertext and Dionisio's clinical diagnosis of Cotard's delusion work in tandem to both destabilize and ground the novel's science-fiction premise. If that is the case, then the police interrogation of Isadore's status and, by extension, her pledged allegiance to the Dominican nation further corroborate the extent to which the discourse of Dominican law structures the clinical discourse of Dionisio's diagnosis. I contend that by establishing this correlation, *Malas hierbas* invites readers to assume a critical stance toward Dionisio's diagnosis—not because it isn't valid, but rather because it gestures toward a history of anti-Haitian contempt—iconized notoriously by Trujillo and consolidated with the Sentencia—that has partially undergirded Dominican national discourses.[84] And from a sociogenic perspective, one aspect of Dionisio's delusion could be understood as a neurological adaptation to anti-Haitianism.

Since Cabiya's text intentionally effaces Dionisio's juridical status and national identity, making him a blank slate—even as he takes on the shroud of legal personhood and citizenship—I maintain that his relationship with Isadore and Isadore's sociogenic narration links Dionisio's zombification to the

ALTERED STATES

Haitian-Dominican context. Specifically, in the chapter immediately following Dionisio's story of his resurrection and his life as an Eli Lilly executive, the novel introduces Isadore, who narrates her encounter with a clandestine network of Haitian exiles. As she tells us, they represent Haiti's elite: they are Tonton Macoutes, former high-ranking military officials in the regime of Jean-Claude "Baby Doc" Duvalier, who ruled over Haiti from 1971 to 1986.[85] As a paramilitary force installed by Baby Doc's father and political predecessor, François "Papa Doc" Duvalier, during his reign of terror (1957–1971), the Macoutes enforced the Duvaliers' reign of terror—and, according to popular lore, did so using voudun sorcery. For example, legend has it that Papa Doc, dubbed the Vampire of the Caribbean, enlisted the services of *hougans* (voudun priests) to make unwilling Haitian citizens conform to his will by turning them into zombies. Following in his father's footsteps, Baby Doc obtained the nonconsensual loyalty of many Haitian citizens through similar tactics of mind control. However, as Peter Hallward chronicles in *Damming the Flood*, the Macoutes were disbanded following the overthrow of Baby Doc in 1986 and again in 1994 after the election of Haitian priest Jean-Bertrand Aristide to Haiti's presidency. In the wake of these events, Hallward explains, the Dominican Republic granted the Macoutes asylum, legal immunity, and even military training, with the hope that they would eventually depose the democratically elected Aristide and reestablish their power.[86] Using the sociopolitical upheavals of Duvalierist Haiti as one of its critical reference points, *Malas hierbas* depicts these elites as impostors who, ensconced in the upscale gated communities of Santo Domingo, have striven not only to assimilate into Dominican life but also to exceed its standards, since class privilege accrues to their light skin and *mulato* identity. That Dionisio is able to pass as a living being because of an inheritance from his unnamed parents, who were "una pareja opulenta" (an affluent couple), suggests that he bears some type of kinship with these Haitian elites—although to what extent the novel leaves unclear.[87] Cabiya interrupts Dionisio's Dominican-based narration of his zombification throughout the novel and intercalates it with Isadore's seemingly unrelated accounts of both these Haitian elites and those touched by zombification in Haiti, as I consider below. This further positions Dionisio's Dominican existence in relationship to Haitian Blackness and, in doing so, discloses the obverse side of the zombie narrative as an ontology of passing life.

PLAYING DEAD

Most tellingly, the impostor narrative tragically takes over Isadore's story of the aforementioned Haitian exiles. Recalling her close friendship with her classmate Valerie, Isadore reveals that both Valerie and her mother were hacked to death by the family's patriarch, Simònides Myrthil, a retired colonel in the Macoutes. As it turns out, Myrthil's violent actions were also the result of psychotic disorder—Capgras delusion, which causes those affected to believe their loved ones have been replaced by identical impostors. It is also not happenstance that Isadore learns of the colonel's disorder from the same Dominican police officers who reveal to her (and readers) Dionisio's disorder, which lands him in the asylum-cum-zombie-bar where he meets Colonel Myrthil. But whereas the police questioning of Isadore's status reveals long-held perceptions of Haitians as impostors in the Dominican Republic, Myrthil's actions, I contend, represent the internalization of narratives about Haitian impostors consolidated by Haiti's Baby Doc regime. The impostor narrative thus circulates from one side of the island to the other. This is a significant intervention on Cabiya's part, for it contests what Dixa Ramírez calls "enshrining anti-Haitianism as the heart of Dominican nationalism."[88] Instead, the novel's transnational displacement of the impostor narrative across borders, via the representation of economically ascendant subjects who share an autophobic relationship to Haitianness qua Blackness, discloses that the Dominican Republic and Haiti share not only the island of Hispaniola but an intertwined colonial inheritance and a history of state violence against Haitians made manifest in the aspiration for neoliberal belonging and membership. As I have previously elucidated, this is also thematically pervasive in *Le Peuple des terres mêlées*.[89]

Turning her attention to the Haitian side of the island, Isadore shares the story of her grandfather Papa Vincent—a *hougan* who must simulate death in order to survive the Tonton Macoutes—to reveal the role of the Duvalierist state in buttressing this ontology. *Malas hierbas* revisits this dark period in recent Haitian history through a memory in Isadore's scrapbook that presents an account of Papa Vincent's survival and escape from the famed Citadelle, where he finds himself imprisoned in a dungeon alongside other dissident *hougans* who refused to use their powers in service of the Duvalierist state. Witnessing the fate of his cellmates, tortured and then left for dead to rot in the sun, Papa Vincent befriends a young man named Placide, with whom he devises an escape plan:

> No tuvieron que pensar mucho para concluir que de la Citadelle solo podrían salir muertos. Así que pusieron manos a la obra. No tuvieron tiempo para pensar a que uno de sus compañeros de celda muriera y poner en ejecución la clásica y literaria apropiación de su mortaja. En todo caso, habría sido necesario que murieran dos, no uno. . . . Debían, pues, simular su propia muerte.

> (They didn't have to think very hard to conclude that the only way they could leave the Citadel was as dead mean. And so they set to work. They didn't have time to wait for one of their cellmates to die in order to employ the classical and literary appropriation of his shroud. In any case, it would have been necessary for two of them to die, not just one. . . . Thus, they would have to simulate their own deaths.)[90]

The simulation would be carried out through Papa Vincent's sorcery, which would put both of them in a comatose state, suspending all their vital functions and thereby tricking the guards into removing their lifeless bodies from the dungeon and leaving them unattended outside with the other cadavers. After a few days, Papa Vincent's spell would wear off, and outside the Citadelle, the two would be free to make their getaway.

Undoubtedly, Cabiya's text aims to establish a parallel between Isadore's account of Papa Vincent's self-induced zombification and Dionisio's autophobic delusion of zombification. On the one hand, like Dionisio, Papa Vincent and Placide simulate alternative bodily and physiological states in order to survive, pass through, and pass out of the hold of confinement and social death imposed upon Haitian citizens. On the other hand, neither Papa Vincent nor Placide labor under the delusion that they are really dead. The voudun priest and his acolyte instead engage in something more akin to "playing dead"—a behavioral mechanism employed by nonhuman animals as a form of defensive mimicry against predation. In this light, I find it telling that, by "playing dead," Placide and Papa Vincent are simulating the cadavers of tortured cellmates, for it suggests that they are not merely simulating death in and of itself but rather imitating death as a form of juridical subjectivity. That is, they are mimicking the juridical conformity demanded of and enacted by citizens in compliance with Haiti's Duvalierist state; this conformity is the mode of shape-shifting that Colin Dayan has called "civil death." While it certainly can be said that Dionisio, Papa Vincent, and Placide all embody forms of civil death, I maintain that Dionisio's civil death gives way to the mimetic delusion called "passing life" because of his positionality as an ontological border subject. He is a figurative *am-bas-fils* who is caught between two identitarian narratives: one that demands that Haitian citizens "play dead" and another that requires Haitians to conceal themselves in a milieu that has always already marked them as impostors. Put another way, Dionisio is a living being who must engage in an autophobic annihilation of his selfhood in order to reconfigure himself as a living being in accordance with the dictates of the state.

Caillois's reading of the relationship between mimicry and psychiatric delusions in his classic essay, "Mimicry and Legendary Psychastenia," is instructive here: it illuminates Dionisio's position as a border figure who must play dead while simultaneously passing as a living being. Analyzing animals' defensive mimicry, Caillois complicates the long-held notion that mimetic behavior in animals is simply the simulation of one by another. Instead, Caillois offers an alternative definition of mimicry as a "disturbance in the perception of space."[91] In these terms, he suggests that mimicry is not a matter of dissimulation and feigning resemblance but rather entails destabilizing both the representation of and angular relations of space between the mimicking subject (an insect, for example), what is being mimicked (a plant, for example), and the beholder (the predator), such that, from the beholder's perspective, the planes of difference collapse. For Caillois, interpreting mimicry from the vantage point of spatial relations provides a segue to decoding what he calls *legendary psychasthenia*. Though the term is no longer used in psychoanalytic practice, psychasthenia defined a psychological disorder characterized by obsessive compulsions, phobias, and delusions. As Caillois explains, for those suffering from these forms of psychosis—as in the case of schizophrenics, to cite the example he provides—the boundary between the body and the space around it collapses, such that they perceive themselves as "becoming the space."[92] In effect, as in animal mimicry, psychasthenic subjects assimilate into their spatial surroundings so that they come to resemble them. Mimicry, in the case of a psychotic disturbance, Caillois concludes in the same passage, entails "depersonalization by assimilation to space," a process that is "accompanied by the decline in the personality and feeling of life." Put another way, to become the space that one inhabits requires a loss of one's sense of self that is akin to death because the space is perceived as a threat to the self.

I find in Caillois's expanded classification of mimicry and its relationship to psychosis a corollary to Dayan's definition of shape-shifting as a state-sanctioned ritual by means of which the law reconfigures the living as "depersonalized persons." If the law depersonalizes the self by "working on the body" in a manner that unfixes it from any coherent self-definition, it does so by effacing the boundaries between the body and the nation. Moreover, if passing is a form of dissimulation that facilitates access to and movement across previously forbidden spaces, it is made possible through the passing subject's depersonalization. Combining and extending these definitions to *Malas hierbas*, we see that Dionisio does not merely simulate life but rather assimilates himself into the border between two geopolitical spaces that render Haitians both socially and civically dead. That is, he comes to resemble a space that requires the very death of Haitianness—and, I would add, of the Blackness associated with it—as an ontology of existence. Thus, what is being depersonalized is Dionisio's proximity to Haitianness qua Blackness, which is represented in the text as an autobiographical and racial-juridical lacuna.

HOW TO SET A HAITIAN-DOMINICAN SUBJECT FREE

While Cabiya dedicates the greater part of *Malas hierbas* to an exploration of the ontology of living-death through Dionisio's predicament, ultimately, the author's text is a search for an emancipatory philosophy of life—one in which those born and marked as dead in Hispaniola and the Caribbean, writ large, articulate and embody a freedom that is not rooted in an illusion of neoliberal citizenship. If Dionisio embodies passing life through the concealment of his skin—which, as I have argued, is a metaphor for the attainment of legal personhood—Cabiya's text proposes that the way out of this illusory life is through the exposure of his skin to the touch of the other, specifically the (Black) Haitian Other he has disavowed in himself. The parallels to *Le Peuple des terres mêlées* are clear. The ethics of the flesh attain primacy; exposing the skin to the touch of others becomes the act that penetrates the imposed madness of derealization (whether it is state-imposed as in *Le Peuple des terres mêlées* or self-imposed as in *Malas hierbas*). Splitting from himself, Dionisio the scientist describes his awakening to Dionisio the philosopher of life as the moment in which he *feels* toward Isadore. In this moment, he reflects, "Por unos instantes, que al mismo tiempo fueron eternos y fugaces, estuve *vivo*; fui normal" (For a few instants, which were both eternal and fleeting, I was *alive*; I was normal).[93] To be clear, Dionisio describes this moment of feeling as the culmination of two previous erotic encounters with his two other research assistants—Patricia Julia and Mathilde, both Dominican women. But there is something about Isadore's look, her specific acknowledgment as a Haitian woman of him, and her touch of his hand that make them the final agents in his awakening. If Isadore is the "author" of his zombification, she is his bridge to life, for we see her live openly as a Dominican citizen without renouncing her Haitianness. And this freedom becomes the condition of possibility for Dionisio's liberation from a state of living death.

Through the touch of the Other whom he has disavowed in himself, he learns for the first time that living is the capacity to put himself in the place of another. In this moment, the zombie, as a purely rational being, dies. Thus, Dionisio passes across and through the threshold of living death into life insofar as his sentience is expanded from pure reason to feeling. No longer constrained, he moves from post-Cartesian, interiorized rationality to a world-oriented affect that we might call empathy. It is at this critical juncture of *Malas hierbas* that Cabiya fleetingly elucidates a Caribbean philosophy of life based on affective relationality, which bespeaks Lauro and Embry's assertion that freedom for the zombie comes with the forfeiture of the "already illusory sense of the individual" borne of the Enlightenment and consolidated with our current neoliberal order.[94] In this post-colonial liberation, the Caribbean zombie narrative comes full circle, for the zombie finds freedom and life not within the discourse of sovereignty or personhood proffered by Western modernity but rather within a Caribbean ethic of proximity that disavows biopolitical and racial-juridical borders. Forfeiting his individuality, Dionisio tells us, "Dentro de mi cuerpo se agitó una persona extraña, una persona que pretendía cosechar percepciones. Una especie de invasor, aunque ese invasor era yo mismo" (Inside my body a strange person was stirring, a person who was trying to reap perceptions. An invader of sorts, though that invader was none other than myself).[95] Effectively, rejecting the interiority of the individual, Dionisio opens himself to an affective vulnerability that is like an encounter with a stranger. It is perhaps no coincidence that Dionisio likens this awoken being to an "invader," the very term used to describe Haitian being on the Dominican side of Hispaniola, as depicted in *Le Peuple des terres mêlées*. Interestingly, having welcomed the invader within, Dionisio is able to see his delusion, realizing that he, in fact, "never was" (dead) in the coffin in which he was born as a zombie in the novel's opening. Indeed, the empty coffin, like the slave ship described by Christina Sharpe in *In the Wake*, was but a hold in which we can, perhaps, now lay to rest the poisonous narratives that delimit Haitian existence.[96]

Coda

LOVING BEYOND (SOVEREIGNTY)

At this present moment, the world and the planet seem terrifyingly inhospitable and increasingly uninhabitable. The threat of societal collapse and uncertainty—the ghosts of intolerance, fascism, and other political ghouls presumably vanquished by the North Atlantic ideals of liberalism—loom large and near. Political violence, repression, and instability have fueled an unprecedented global refugee crisis that has exposed the limits of cosmopolitan hospitality. As massive waves of strangers arrive before the law, at the threshold of seemingly more stable Western nation-states, the law moves swiftly to shore up the state's integrity against the wrong types of guests who are deemed unwelcomed. If, as I have previously discussed, unconditional hospitality entails the act of hostage taking or hostage becoming, in one instance, this act appeared literalized and inverted by the creation of detention sites for migrants held hostage indefinitely the U.S-Mexico border. Yet the world also bears witness to a growing critical mass of internally displaced persons—citizens who must flee their homes while remaining politically estranged within their homelands and, therefore, are not considered refugees by international law. According to the United Nations High Commissioner for Refugees, internally displaced persons account for more than half of the world's forcibly dislocated migrant population.[1] Against this backdrop, the viability of citizenship as a form of political membership, a universally recognized juridical status, and a guarantor of human rights is continually fragmented under the duress of the nation-state that ostensibly guarantees it and the international political community that recognizes it.

Often described as a laboratory, wrought by dispossession and the violent meeting of strangers, the Caribbean can teach us much about how the distinctions between the citizen/native and foreigner/stranger become blurred and collapse onto one another. Although *Caribbean Inhospitality* centers representations of citizens and subjects who are strangers at home, including intergovernmental

143

homelands, this book's four case studies of Barbados, Puerto Rico, Cuba, and Hispaniola also signal how citizens' internal estrangement precedes and structures the nation-state's inhospitality toward foreigners. As this book demonstrates, the Caribbean bears witness to other, more insidious forms of internal displacement that were narratively and discursively instituted by Columbus's arrival in the present-day Bahamas in 1492 and fueled by colonialism, neocolonialism, and neoliberalism, operating under the nomenclature of "hospitality." *Caribbean Inhospitality* is, therefore, a book about colonial inheritances that remain concealed and unsettled as residue within postcolonial legality. It traces the way an idea, narrativized by Columbus, replicates itself from the past into the present, and into the nation-state project, in these rather insidious ways that I call "inhospitality," which undermine the emancipatory possibilities of sovereignty and citizenship, two North Atlantic universals that were conceptually inherited by the Caribbean.

These seemingly innocuous manifestations of internal and external displacement-as-hospitality disclose how moments of crisis in the Caribbean's recent history have been instrumentalized and maximized as "opportunity." Since 2021, for example, Cuba has witnessed the largest mass migration in the island's history—exceeding the 1980 Mariel exodus—due in large part to the Cuban government's gradual loosening of restrictions on emigration. Yet as Cubans relinquish and sell their homes, ongoing (and inescapable) foreign investment on the island foretells the arrival of a new crop of foreign "guests" who will more than likely assume the role of hosts in vacant properties. We might also take a cue from *B-Roll,* a video collage by Puerto Rican visual artist Sofía Gallisá Muriente.[2] In Gallisá Muriente's experimental film, anonymous male voices accented in North American English speculate on Puerto Rico's economic potential and its capacity to yield high financial returns for foreign investors, even as many of those "foreigners" are, in fact, fellow (non–Puerto Rican) citizens from the U.S. mainland. An assemblage of footage excerpted from promotional videos produced by Puerto Rico's Tourism Company and the Department of Economic and Commercial Development, *B-Roll* invites a sobering and critical commentary on the real estate and investment boom made possible by changes to Puerto Rico's tax code and exploited by North Americans, among others, in the aftermath of Hurricane Maria. The 2017 hurricane's devastation of the island's human ecology and infrastructure upon which Puerto Ricans depended for their livelihood is notably absent from the video's shots of an urban and natural landscape teeming with productivity and signs of material and environmental wealth. As the title of Gallisá Muriente's piece suggests, *B-Roll* underscores how the lived experiences of Puerto Ricans impacted by a legal code that benefits nonnative visitors are cut away and minimized to produce a one-sided narrative whose objective is to lure those who can take advantage of, according to one of the voices, the island's "renaissance." In real life, Puerto Rico

CODA

has seen as surge of Airbnb rentals and housing whose prices are not commensurate with Puerto Ricans' wages. The island has also witnessed an influx of North Americans who relate to Puerto Ricans not as fellow U.S. citizens but as hosts. In notable instances, these North American hosts have made the island's public beaches inhospitable to native Puerto Ricans.

In this light, I was once asked what would be viable alternatives to citizenship and nation-state sovereignty. What other forms of belonging and membership are possible, if, as one reading of these Caribbean texts might suggest, the most universal and recognized form of political belonging and membership has been condemned to failure? Even as postnationalist projects and entities dominate our global landscape, nation-state sovereignty and the identification of citizenship do not appear to being going anywhere anytime soon, even as nation-states become more hostile to an increasingly larger body of citizens through technologies of capture and dispossession.

While the works studied in *Caribbean Inhospitality* present a dire situation—a pessimism that seems inescapable—they invite a larger conversation about how to conceive and live freedom in ways that extend beyond the boundaries of this book. Indeed, the myth of Caribbean hospitality that this book unsettles has historically been concomitant to the Caribbean's formation as a place of escape and freedom (political, economic, and sexual)—from pirates to tourists—to the detriment of Caribbean peoples. How, then, might we live otherwise and love otherwise, beyond and within the constraints of nation-state sovereignty?

In the final chapters of this book, I suggested that the novels *Le Peuple des terres mêlées* and *Malas hierbas* allow us to imagine otherwise. But they do so by turning their eyes to the as-of-yet-unfulfilled promise of Haiti, a meeting place of strangers removed from the gaze of Columbus. In these texts, Caribbean citizens find comfort in their strangeness, a position from which they act as liminal yet sovereign citizens beyond the consent of the nation-state. I am reminded of Jean-Luc Nancy's essay "L'Intrus," which defines the stranger not on the basis of knowledge but rather as an approaching: the stranger is one who comes and whose coming never ceases. In his words, "Once he [the stranger] has arrived, if he remains foreign, and for as long as he does so—rather than simply 'becoming naturalized'—his coming will not cease; nor will it cease being some respect an intrusion."[3] In the context of the postcolonial Caribbean, I find that citizens' strangeness intrudes upon the meaning and power of the sovereign nation-state, a political community inherited from the legacy of European colonialism. In intruding upon the law of the sovereign, in standing at its doorway, I see the condition of possibility of a Caribbean community that is yet to come.

Acknowledgments

Although this book is attributed to a single author, it was birthed and shaped in dialogue with a transnational community of teachers, mentors, colleagues, readers, editors, friends, and a chosen family who have supported and nurtured my vision with encouragement, wisdom, and care. This book was birthed and molded in various contexts, in Wisconsin, the Caribbean, and California, in the midst of a global pandemic marked by isolation, loss, and uncertainty, all of which shaped my nagging questions about home, estrangement, and citizenship in what seems like our darkest times.

Thank you to the Rutgers University Press, the staff, and the editors and publisher of the Critical Caribbean Studies Series, Yolanda Martínez-San Miguel, Carter Mathes, and Kathleen López, for valuing this book and the relevance of its ideas at a time marked by global displacement and uncertainty. There are not enough words of gratitude I can offer to my editor, Kimberly Guinta, for holding steadfast to the vision of this project and for being my editorial doula. Thank you to Emma-li Downer, Michelle Witkowski, and the unseen staff who worked on the various moving parts of the book's production. I am especially grateful to visual artists Abigail Hadeed and Annalee Davis for granting me permission to reproduce their artwork for this book. Many thanks to Ben Brewer for providing the indexing.

Immense gratitude to Guillermina De Ferrari, who mentored me with unparalleled attentiveness, care, and a commitment to my scholarly development; Luis Madureira and the late Tejumola "Teju" Olaniyan were generous and kind teachers who were instrumental to my intellectual formation in critical theory and postcolonial studies. Many thanks to Victor Goldgel Carballo, Jim Sweet, and Jerome Kamal for asking important questions that helped shape this book.

The inimitable hospitality of Caribbean writers, artists, scholars, and friends who received me with wisdom and care is imprinted in this book. In the

Dominican Republic, Luz María Borges and Elizabeth Aponte Borges welcomed this stranger to their home and were a fount of knowledge on Haitian-Dominican relations; Cecilia de la Cruz also provided a dwelling place. In Puerto Rico, Mayra Santos Febres guided me to a rich community and archive of writers and artists, while the late Antonia "Güelin" Rodríguez and Ana María González generously opened their homes and gave me respite so that I could research the archives at the University of Puerto Rico–Río Piedras. Endless gratitude to the unnamed scholars and intellectuals in Cuba who helped me navigate various cultural institutions in Havana and directed me to resources that would be instrumental to my research.

Heartfelt thanks go to colleagues, students, and staff in the Latin American and Iberian Cultures and the Comparative Literatures Departments at the University and the Comparative Studies in Literature and Culture Program at the University of Southern California, where I have been welcomed in a nurturing, supportive, and vibrant intellectual community: Erin Graff Zivin generously read early versions of this book and has been a faithful champion; Ronald Mendoza-de Jesús has been a trusted accomplice, friend, and esteemed reader of my work in various stages; Sherry Velasco, Roberto Díaz, Julián Gutiérrez Albila, and Samuel Steinberg have provided inestimable support and direction toward my success. Neetu Khanna provided enthusiastic and supportive feedback on selections from this book and gave me community in a writing group. Outside my home department, colleagues and friends across USC, in particular Melissa Daniels-Rauterkaus, Reighan Gillam, Veli Yashin, Edwin Hill, Lydie Moudileno, Karen Tongson, and Sara Kessler, created a welcoming, supportive community.

Beyond USC, I am grateful to Zakiyyah Jackson, Emily Maguire, Christina León, Sandra Ruiz, Tiffany Florvil, Kyla Wazana Tompkins, Yomaira Figueroa, Nohora Arrieta Fernández, María del Rosario Acosta, Jacques Lezra, Miguel Vásquez, and colleagues in the Seminario Crtítico-Político Trasnacional working group at the Universidad Complutense de Madrid—thank you for your camaraderie, feedback, listening ear, and the small and large ways you have supported me in this process.

I am incredibly grateful to my chosen family who have been my refuge and champions and have anchored me in love and faith in all circumstances. In particular Verónica González and Hugo Campuzano, Carla Peralta, Haydee Núñez, Eliza Solowiej, and Claudia Cecarelli, you were there from the beginning and have faithfully remained; Venita Lockett, you have modeled love in every phase of my journey. Thank you Leigh Vierstra, Jara Ríos, Nora Díaz, and Marcela Guerrero for being my second home in Madison. Keisha Watson, thank you from the bottom of my heart, for always being present from afar. Thanks to Talia Guzmán González for your friendship across the years and guidance in Puerto Rico. There are mentors and teachers who have held my vision with their dark wisdom: immense gratitude to Heather LaFace and My Beloved Mentor.

ACKNOWLEDGMENTS

Thank you, my dear Morten, for your faithful companionship and your unwavering belief in me when the words seemed few and the world felt uninhabitable.

To Ganesha, Saraswati, and their infinite wisdom.

———

Earlier sections of chapter 2 and chapter 4 appear as *"Literatura Nullius*: The Untranslatability of Eduardo Lalo and the Multirelation of the Puerto Rican Intellectual," *Small Axe* 45 (November 2014), published with permission by Duke University Press; and "Passing Life, Playing Dead: Zombification as Juridical Shapeshifting in Pedro Cabiya's *Malas hierbas," Journal of Latin American Cultural Studies* 30, no. 1 (2021), published with permission by Taylor and Francis Group.

Notes

INTRODUCTION

1. In *Poétique de la Relation*, Édouard Glissant describes the slave ship as the first womb that holds the enslaved African in a state of abeyance. Glissant, *Poétique de la Relation* (Paris: Éditions Gallimard, 1990). Glissant, *Poetics of Relation*, trans. Betsy Wing (Ann Arbor: University of Michigan Press, 1997). Paul Gilroy recasts the image of the ship a transhistorical, "micro-cultural and micro-political system" that is constitutive of modernity's circuitry. Gilroy, *The Black Atlantic: Modernity and Double Consciousness* (Cambridge, MA: Harvard University Press, 1993), 5.

2. Marina Reyes Franco, *Trópico es político: arte caribeño bajo el régimen de la economía del visitante* (New York: Americas Society, 2022), 66, 20. All translations are mine, unless noted otherwise.

3. A variegated field of voices and disciplines, postcolonial studies can be said to cohere, as Leela Gandhi observes, around a shared "theoretical resistance to the mystifying amnesia of the colonial aftermath." Gandhi, *Postcolonial Theory: A Critical Introduction* (New York: Columbia University Press, 2019), 4. Abraham Acosta revisits Latin American and Latin Americanist resistance to postcolonial theory, noting the error in reducing the postcolonial to "independence, autonomy, or even emancipation." Acosta, *Thresholds of Illiteracy: Theory, Latin America, and the Crisis of Resistance* (New York: Fordham University Press, 2014), 29.

4. Noteworthy is Glissant's theory of "Relation," a nonidentitarian and "transversal" mode of solidarity enacted, as prime but not sole instance, by Caribbean people's unity, not by genealogical legitimacy but rather by the "shared knowledge" of dispossession. Glissant, *Poetics of Relation*, 8. Also noteworthy is Antonio Benítez-Rojo's notion of the "repeating island" as rhythmic metaphor—elaborated by way of postmodernist thought and deconstruction—for the repetition of cultural forms, such as the rhythms of music and performance, across the Caribbean's linguistically and geopolitically diverse and fragmented landscape. Benítez-Rojo, *The Repeating Island: The Caribbean and the Postmodern Perspective*, trans. James E. Maraniss (Durham, NC: Duke University Press, 2001).

5. Shalini Puri, *The Caribbean Postcolonial: Social Equity, Post/Nationalism, and Cultural Hybridity* (New York: Palgrave Macmillan, 2004), 1.

6. Puri, 5.

7. Brian Meeks, *After the Postcolonial Caribbean: Memory, Imagination, Hope* (London: Pluto Press, 2023), 17.

8. David Scott, *Refashioning Postcolonial Criticism: Criticism after Postcoloniality* (Princeton, NJ: Princeton University Press, 1999), 141, 134.

9. Roberto González Echevarría, *Myth and Archive: A Theory of Latin American Narrative* (Cambridge: Cambridge University Press, 1990), 188.

10. Jamaica Kincaid, *A Small Place* (New York: Farrar, Straus and Giroux, 1988), 3, 13.

11. Jacques Rancière, *The Politics of Aesthetics*, trans. Gabriel Rockhill (New York: Continuum, 2004), 12.

12. Kincaid, *Small Place*, 3, 9.

13. Kincaid, 34.

14. Étienne Balibar, "Bourgeois Universality and Anthropological Differences," in *Citizen Subject: Foundations for Philosophical Anthropology*, trans. Steven Miller (New York: Fordham University Press, 2017), 277. Marx's critique centers on the question of whether such rights can be imputed to the Jew who is not secularized or emancipated from religion, but it opens a larger debate on the reality of political emancipation. Karl Marx, "On the Jewish Question," in *Early Writings*, trans. Rodney Livingstone and Gregor Benton (New York: Penguin, 1991), 211–242.

15. Joshua Chambers-Letson, *A Race so Different: Performance and Law in Asian America* (New York: New York University Press, 2013).

16. Erin Graff Zivin, "Beyond Jameson: The Metapolitics of Allegory," *Yearbook of Comparative Literature* 61 (2015): 160.

17. Michel-Rolph Trouillot, "North Atlantic Universals: Analytical Fictions, 1492–1945," *South Atlantic Quarterly* 101, no. 4 (Fall 2002): 839–858.

18. Sankaran Krishna, "Postcolonialism and Its Relevance for International Relations in a Globalized World," in *Race, Gender, and Culture in International Relations: Postcolonial Perspectives*, ed. Randolph Persaud and Alina Sajed (New York: Routledge, 2018), 19.

19. Mervyn Frost discusses the complexities of state personhood in relation to individual personhood in *Ethics in International Relations: A Constitutive Theory* (Cambridge: Cambridge University Press, 2009).

20. Trouillot, "North Atlantic Universals," 847.

21. Balibar, "Bourgeois Universality and Anthropological Differences," 277, 283.

22. Aníbal Quijano, "Colonialidad del poder y clasificación social," *Journal of World-Systems Research* 1, no. 2 (Summer/Fall 2000): 342, 366–367.

23. Margarita Zamora, *Reading Columbus* (Berkeley: University of California Press, 1993), 63. Zamora's intentional capitalization connotes the Dominican friar's exegetical intervention on the text.

24. Zamora, 64.

25. Zamora examines the transformations in how colonial texts are classified in view of the historical situatedness of their readership. Margarita Zamora, "Historicity and Literariness: Problems in the Literary Criticism of Spanish Colonial Texts," *MLN* 102, no. 2 (March 1987): 334–346.

26. Cristóbal Colón, *Los cuatro viajes*, ed. Consuelo Varela (Madrid: Alianza Editorial, 2004), 142.

27. Christopher Columbus, *The Journal of Christopher Columbus (During His First Voyage, 1492–1493)*, trans. Clements Markham (Farnham: Cambridge University Press, 2010), 130.

NOTES TO PAGES 10–13

28. Gayatri Chakravorty Spivak, *A Critique of Postcolonial Reason: Toward the History of the Vanishing Present* (Cambridge, MA: Harvard University Press, 1999), 211.

29. Jacques Derrida, *Of Hospitality*, trans. Anne Doufourmantelle (Stanford, CA: Stanford University Press, 2000), 81.

30. The vicissitudes of Columbus's dubious confrontation with the Caribe are chronicled by Diego Álvarez Chanca, the physician to Columbus's fleet during his second voyage. Álvarez Chanca's portrait of interethnic and interinsular warfare between the Caribe and their island neighbors weds strangeness to the anthropological—and, therefore, racialized difference. See Christopher Columbus, *Select Letters of Christopher Columbus: With Other Original Documents, Relation to This Four Voyages to the New World*, ed. Richard Henry Major (Cambridge: Cambridge University Press, 2010).

31. Zakiyyah Iman Jackson, *Becoming Human: Matter and Meaning in an Antiblack World* (New York: New York University Press, 2020), 126.

32. Sylvia Wynter, "Columbus, the Ocean Blue, and Fables That Stir the Mind: To Reinvent the Study Letters," in *Poetics of the Americas: Race, Founding, and Textuality*, ed. Bainard Cowan and Jefferson Humphries (Baton Rouge: Louisiana State University Press, 1997), 151–152.

33. Wynter, 142.

34. Wynter, 143.

35. Wynter's conceptualization of the regulating function of storytelling draws upon Francisco Varela and Humberto Maturana's notion of "autopoesis," which describes how biological systems are self-organizing and autonomously functioning. See Sylvia Wynter and Katherine McKittrick, "Unparalleled Catastrophe for Our Species? Or, to Give Humanness a Different Future: Conversations," in *Sylvia Wynter: On Being Human as Praxis* (Durham, NC: Durham University Press, 2015), 9–89.

36. Linden Lewis, "The Dissolution of the Myth of Sovereignty in the Caribbean," in *Caribbean Sovereignty, Development and Democracy in an Age of Globalization*, ed. Linden Lewis (New York: Routledge, 2012), 69–70.

37. Colin Dayan, *Haiti, History, and the Gods* (Berkeley: University of California Press, 1998), 8.

38. Aaron Kamugisha, *Beyond Coloniality: Citizenship and Freedom in the Caribbean Intellectual Tradition* (Bloomington: Indiana University Press, 2019), 38.

39. Trouillot, "North Atlantic Universals," 839.

40. Denise Ferreira da Silva, *Unpayable Debt* (London: Sternberg Press, 2022), 46.

41. While recapitulating some of the ideas espoused previously in "To Perpetual Peace," in *The Metaphysics of Morals* Kant delineates his notion of cosmopolitan right by resolving the distinction between the right of the state (*civitas*) and the right of the nations (*gens* or peoples) in terms that anticipate the distinction and suturing of the citizen and the human being. Immanuel Kant, *The Metaphysics of Morals*, trans. Mary Gregor (Cambridge: Cambridge University Press, 2017). Peter Niesen analyzes how Kant's theory of hospitality enables a contradictory critique of European colonialism and imperialism that does not fully resolve the settler's claim to territory. Niesen, "Colonialism and Hospitality," *Politics and Ethics Review* 3, no. 1 (2007): 90–108.

42. Kant, "To Perpetual Peace: A Philosophical Sketch," in *Perpetual Peace and Other Essays on Politics, History, and Morals*, trans. Ted Humphrey (Indianapolis: Hackett, 1983), 118, line 358.

43. Kant, 118, emphasis original.

44. Kant, 118.

45. Kant, 119, line 358.

46. Kant, 118, line 358.

47. Niesen, "Colonialism and Hospitality," 97.

48. Kant, "To Perpetual Peace," 118, line 358.

49. Niesen keenly notes that in the second section of *Perpetual Peace*, Kant allows for the coercion of those who live in what he calls a "state of lawlessness" to "enter with me into a state of civil law or remove himself," which suggests a limitation to the principle of common ownership. Kant, "To Perpetual Peace," 111–112, line 349; Niesen, "Colonialism and Hospitality," 94–95.

50. Robert Bernasconi, "Kant's Third Thoughts on Race," in *Reading Kant's Geography*, ed. Stuart Elden and Eduardo Mendieta (Albany: State University of New York Press, 2011), 294–295.

51. Bernasconi, 299.

52. Kant, "To Perpetual Peace," 118, line 358.

53. Quoted in Bernasconi, "Kant's Third Thoughts on Race," 302.

54. Immanuel Kant, *Critique of Judgement*, trans. Werner Pluhar (Indianapolis: Hackett, 1987), 160:293; Rizvana Bradley and Denise Ferreira da Silva, "Four Theses on Aesthetics," *E-Flux Journal*, September 2021, https://www.e-flux.com/journal/120/416146/four-theses-on-aesthetics/.

55. Jacques Derrida, "Hostipitality," trans. Barry Stocker and Forbes Morlock, *Angelaki: Journal of the Theoretical Humanities* 5, no. 3 (2000): 13.

56. Derrida elaborates the proprietary nature of hospitality in his "Troisième séance" from Derrida, *Hospitalité: Volume I (1995–1996)* (Paris: Éditions Du Seuil, 2021), 81–109.

57. Derrida, *Of Hospitality*, 55.

58. W. E. B. Du Bois, *The Souls of Black Folk* (New York: Oxford University Press, 2007), 8.

59. Carl Schmitt, *The Concept of the Political*, trans. George Schwab (Chicago: University of Chicago Press, 2007).

60. Juliet Hooker, *Theorizing Race in the Americas: Douglass, Sarmiento, Du Bois, and Vasconcelos* (New York: Oxford University Press, 2017).

61. Georg Simmel, *Sociology: Inquiries into the Construction of Social Forms*, vol. 1, trans. Anthony Blasi, Anton Jacobs, and Matthew Kanjirathinkal (Boston: Brill, 2009), 601.

62. Balibar, "Bourgeois Universality and Anthropological Differences," 287.

63. Édouard Glissant, *Poétique de la Rélation* (Paris: Éditions Gallimard, 1990); Glissant, *Poetics of Relation*.

64. Glissant, *Poetics of Relation*, 9.

65. Glissant, *Poétique de la Relation*, 147, 204, 37; Glissant, *Poetics of Relation*, 131, 190, 25. The demand for the "right to opacity" is conditioned precisely by what Glissant calls "the experience of the abyss" or "the unknown"—that is, the genealogical and natal dispossession for which Caribbean people cannot account.

66. Glissant, *Poétique de la Relation*, 20; Glissant, *Poetics of Relation*, 8.

67. Glissant, *Poetics of Relation*, 190.

68. An example to consider is Sandra Berman's rereading of Glissant in a way that allows creolization to evolve into a "global" and translatable world literary principle. Berman, "Translation as Relation and Glissant," *Comparative Literature and Culture* 16, no. 3 (2014): 9. In another instance, James Clifford famously asserted that "we are all

NOTES TO PAGES 22–28

Caribbeans now in our urban archipelagos" to describe a universal condition of geopolitical and existential displacement that characterizes the modern and postmodern world. Clifford, *The Predicament of Culture: Twentieth-Century Ethnography, Literature, and Art* (Cambridge, MA: Harvard University Press, 2021), 173. Stephan Palmié has considered how contemporary theory extracts "the historically-situated cultural vocabulary of Latin America and the Caribbean" and "elevates them to the status of generalized descriptive of analytical instruments." Palmié, "Creolization and Its Discontents," *Annual Review of Anthropology* 35 (2006): 435.

69. Frantz Fanon, *The Wretched of the Earth*, trans. Richard Philcox (New York: Grove Press, 2005), 1.

CHAPTER 1 — DELIBERATIVE MISDIRECTION

1. Derek Walcott, "The Antilles, Fragments of Epic Memory: The 1992 Nobel Lecture," *World Literature Today* 67, no. 2 (Spring 1993): 266.

2. See Guillermina De Ferrari's "The Ship, the Plantation, and the Polis: Reading Gilroy and Glissant as Moral Philosophy," *Comparative Literature Studies* 49, no. 2 (2012): 186.

3. Walter Rodney, *The Groundings with My Brothers* (1969; London: Verso, 2019), 4.

4. Celia Britton, *Edouard Glissant and Postcolonial Theory: Strategies of Language and Resistance* (Charlottesville: University of Virginia Press, 1999), 90.

5. Édouard Glissant, *Le discours antillais* (Paris: Éditions Gallimard, 1997), 650. All translations are mine unless noted otherwise.

6. Glissant, 639.

7. Aristotle, *Art of Rhetoric*, trans. John Henry Freese (Cambridge, MA: Harvard University Press, 2007), 15, line 1355b.

8. Glissant, *Le discours antillais*, 644.

9. Hannah Arendt, *The Human Condition* (Chicago: University of Chicago Press, 1958), 199.

10. Walter Ong, *The Presence of the World: The Word and the Sensorium* (New Haven, CT: Yale University Press, 2016), 6.

11. Ong, 7.

12. Fiona Borthwick, "Categorising the Senses, Blurring the Lines: Kant, Derrida, Experience," *Journal of the British Society for Phenomenology* 37, no. 2 (2006): 186.

13. It is Kant, primarily, who contributes to the schematic ordering of the senses within Western modernity. Notably, in his *Anthropology from a Different Point of View*, he attributes to sight the quality of illumination (light) that confers upon the eyes "the immediate representation of a given object, without admixture of notable sensation." Immanuel Kant, *Anthropology from a Pragmatic Point of View* (Cambridge: Cambridge University Press, 2016), 48.

14. Jacques Rancière, *The Politics of Aesthetics*, trans. Gabriel Rockhill (New York: Continuum, 2004), 12, emphasis mine. In book 3 of *The Politics*, Aristotle argues that in the sphere of good politics or what he calls "justice," there is "a distribution of equal amounts to those who are equal." By this he means that the decision about who gets to share in the political good, and the proportion in which they share, is determined by the "contributions they make." Aristotle, *Politics*, trans. R. F. Stalley (Oxford: Oxford University Press, 2020), 1282b.

15. Jacques Rancière, "The Aesthetic Dimension: Aesthetic, Politics, Knowledge," *Critical Inquiry* 36, no. 1 (Autumn 2009): 3.

16. Rancière, *Politics of Aesthetics*, 13, emphasis mine.

17. Jamaica Kincaid, *A Small Place* (New York: Farrar, Straus and Giroux, 1988), 3, 13.

18. Kincaid, 4.

19. Although Urry contends that tourism inheres within a constellation of social practices that "involve the notion of 'departure,' of a limited breaking with established routines and practices of everyday life and allowing one's *senses to engage with a set of stimuli* that contrast with the everyday and the mundane," his faithfulness to a Foucauldian reading of clinical gaze—and its relationship to deviant pleasure—delimits his social analysis of tourism to an ocular logic. John Urry, *The Tourist Gaze: Leisure and Travel in Contemporary Societies* (London: Sage, 1990), 2.

20. Barbados, Guyana, Jamaica, and Trinidad and Tobago were the four original signatories of the Treaty of Chaguaramas, which established CARICOM. Today, fifteen countries have full membership in the community, while another five possess associate membership.

21. Kathy McAfee, *Storm Signals: Structural Adjustment and Development Alternatives in the Caribbean* (Boston: South End, 1991), 176.

22. Annalee Davis, *Migrant Discourse* (Experimental documentary, 2006), https://www.youtube.com/watch?v=yA_VGjiy6AQ&t=232s.

23. John Connell and Chris Gibson, "Ambient Australia: Music, Meditation, and Tourist Places," in *Sound, Society, and the Geography of Popular Music*, ed. Ola Johansson and Thomas L. Bell (London: Routledge, 2016), 67, 70.

24. Connell and Gibson, 68, 71.

25. Catherine Elwes, *Installation and the Moving Image* (New York: Columbia University Press, 2015), 207.

26. Michel Chion, *Audio-Vision: Sound on Screen*, trans. Claudia Gorbman (New York: Columbia University Press, 2019), 249.

27. Chion, 5.

28. Chion, 98.

29. Annalee Davis, "Annalee Davis" (2021), https://annaleedavis.com.

30. Michelle Stephens, "Cosmopolitan Creoles and Neoliberal Mobility in Annalee Davis's *On the Map*," in *Negative Cosmopolitanism: Cultures and Politics of World Citizenship after Globalization*, ed. Eddy Kent and Terri Tomsky (Montreal: McGill-Queen's University Press, 2017), 152.

31. Glissant, *Le discours antillais*, 17.

32. Jean Bernabé, Patrick Chamoiseau, and Raphäel Confiant, *Éloge de la Créolité / In Praise of Creoleness*, trans. M. B. Taleb-Khyar (Paris: Éditions Gallimard, 1993), 87.

33. "Revised Treaty of Chaguaramas Establishing the Caribbean Community Including the CARICOM Single Market Economy" (opened for signature July 4, 2001), *Treaty Series: Treaties and International Agreements Registered or Filed and Recorded with the Secretariat of the United Nations* 2259, no. 40269 (2006): 27, https://treaties.un.org/doc/Publication/UNTS/Volume%202259/v2259.pdf.

34. "Revised Treaty of Chaguaramas," 28.

35. Stephens, "Cosmopolitan Creoles," 150.

36. Stephens, 154.

37. Stuart Hall and Pnina Werbner, "Cosmopolitanism, Globalisation and Diaspora," in *Anthropology and the New Cosmopolitanism: Rooted Feminist and Vernacular Perspectives*, ed. Pnina Werbner (Oxford: Berg, 2008), 351; Karen Fog Olwig, "Cosmopolitan

Traditions: Caribbean Perspectives," *Social Anthropology / Anthropologie Sociale* 18, no. 4 (2010): 421.

38. Notably, Davis cites Walter Rodney's work on the history of anti-immigrant sentiment initially directed against Indian indentured laborers by Afro-Barbadian and Afro-Guyanese plantation laborers, who joined forces, fearing that Indian migrants were an economic threat.

39. Annalee Davis, *On the Map* (Experimental documentary, 2006–2007), https://annaleedavis.com/archive/on-the-map-documentary-film.

40. Roland Barthes, *Mythologies*, trans. Annette Lavers (New York: Hill & Wang, 1972), 120.

41. Barthes, 114.

42. Barthes, 143.

43. Barthes, 118.

44. Barthes uses the image of a "young Negro in a French uniform saluting, with his eyes uplifted" to the French flag on the cover of *Paris-Match* as one of two key examples of the mythification. For Barthes, this example of myth's form makes manifest how it deforms and distorts the history that makes this Black man into a subject of France vis-à-vis France's policy of assimilation in its overseas colonies. The man in uniform unquestionably saluting the tricolor thus becomes an *alibi* for French (post)coloniality.

45. Barthes, *Mythologies*, 132.

46. Barthes, 119.

47. Ian Gregory Strachan, *Paradise and Plantation: Tourism and Culture in the Anglophone Caribbean* (Charlottesville: University of Virginia Press, 2002), 27.

48. Strachan, 116.

49. Strachan, 3.

50. Krista Thompson, *An Eye for the Tropics: Tourism, Photography, and Framing the Caribbean Picturesque* (Durham, NC: Duke University Press, 2006), 5.

51. Thompson, 307.

52. Pierre Schaeffer, *Treatise on Musical Objects: An Essay across Disciplines*, trans. Christine North and John Dack (Oakland: University of California Press, 2017), 66.

53. Salomé Voegelin, *Listening to Noise and Silence: Towards a Philosophy of Sound Art* (New York: Continuum, 2010), 13.

54. Derek Walcott, "The Sea Is History," in *Selected Poems*, ed. Edward Baugh (New York: Farrar, Straus and Giroux, 2007), 137–139.

55. Dionne Brand, *A Map to the Door of No Return: Notes to Belonging* (Toronto: Vintage Canada, 2011), 56.

56. Aimé Césaire, *Notebook of a Return to the Native Land* (Middleton, CT: Wesleyan University Press, 2001), 11.

57. Elizabeth DeLoughrey and Tatiana Flores, "Submerged Bodies: The Tidalectics of Representability and the Sea in Caribbean Art," in *Liquid Ecologies in Latin American and Caribbean Art*, ed. Lisa Blackmore and Liliana Gómez (New York: Routledge, 2020), 165.

58. Édouard Glissant, *Poetics of Relation*, trans. Betsy Wing (Ann Arbor: University of Michigan Press, 1997), 6.

59. *The Birds*, directed by Alfred Hitchcock, screenplay by Evan Hunter (Universal Pictures, 1963).

60. David Humbert, "Desire and Monstrosity in the Disaster Film: Alfred Hitchcock's *The Birds*," *Contagion: Journal of Violence, Mimesis, and Culture* 17 (2010): 96.

61. Chion, *Audio-Vision*, 20.

62. Adriana Cavarero, *For More Than One Voice: Toward a Philosophy of Vocal Expression*, trans. Paul A. Kottman (Stanford, CA: Stanford University Press, 2005), 185.

63. As Annalee Davis shared with me in an email, "During the course of making *On the Map* and *Migrant Discourse*, we recorded sounds which were edited in as background to these four interviews during the post-production phase." Davis, "Inquiry about Migrant Discourse and Trans/Plant" (email, February 12, 2021).

64. Ana Lydia Vega, *Encancaranublado y otros cuentos de naufragio* (San Juan: Editorial Antillana, 2001), 57.

65. Vega, 57.

66. Aníbal González, "Ana Lydia Pluravega: Unidad y multiplicidad caribeñas en la obra de Ana Lydia Vega," *Revista Iberoamericana* 162–163 (June 1993): 190.

67. Ricardo Gutiérrez Mouat, "Dismembering the Nation: Ana Lydia Vega's Falsas Crónicas Del Sur," *Journal of Latin American Cultural Studies* 10, no. 1 (2001): 119, 120.

68. Elizabeth Hernández and Consuelo López Springfield, "Women and Writing in Puerto Rico: An Interview with Ana Lydia Vega," *Callaloo* 17, no. 3 (Summer 1994): 823.

69. Sylvia Wynter, "Beyond the Word of Man: Glissant and the New Discourse of the Antilles," *World Literature Today* 63, no. 4 (Autumn 1989): 638.

70. Yarimar Bonilla, *Non-Sovereign Futures: French Caribbean Politics in the Wake of Disenchantment* (Chicago: University of Chicago Press, 2015), xii.

71. The seemingly unsettled nature of Puerto Rico's juridical definition formed the basis of a 1967 plebiscite held by Puerto Rico's Legislative Assembly and five U.S. congressional plebiscites (in 1993, 1998, 2012, 2017, and 2020), convened to solicit Puerto Ricans' consensus on the future of the island's status: whether for statehood, independence, or the continuation of the ELA, which I discuss in further detail in chapter 2. While each plebiscite has yielded distinctive outcomes—most notable among them the election of "none of the above" in 1998 by a majority—the status of Puerto Rico remains unchanged.

72. Bonilla, *Non-Sovereign Futures*, xiii, xiv, emphasis original.

73. Anthony Payne, "Seaga's Jamaica after One Year," *World Today*, November 1981, 438.

74. Vega, *Encancaranublado y otros cuentos de naufragio*, 53.

75. Vega, 56.

76. Vega, 53.

77. Vega, 55.

78. Vega, 56.

79. Vega, 53.

80. Vega, 54.

81. Vega, 54.

82. Vega, 53.

83. Vega, 55.

84. Jean-Luc Nancy, *Intoxication*, trans. Philip Armstrong (New York: Fordham University Press, 2016), 4, 8.

85. Guillermina De Ferrari, *Vulnerable States: Bodies of Memory in Contemporary Caribbean Fiction* (Charlottesville: University of Virginia Press, 2007), 8.

86. Vega, *Encancaranublado y otros cuentos de naufragio*, 54.

87. Aristotle, *Art of Rhetoric*, 429–459, lines 1415a–1418b.

88. Without question, it is the German philosopher Jürgen Habermas's idea of "deliberative democracy" that has had the most sustained influence and spawned the most prolific

subsequent responses on the political philosophy of Western democratic communicative rationality in the twentieth and twenty-first centuries. For example, while Habermas has argued that the aim of deliberative democracy is to harmonize individual perspectives to achieve agreement on the basis of universalizable principles, critics of Habermasian deliberation, most notably Chantal Mouffe, rightly note that liberal democratic claims to "universal consensus based on reason" engage in a denial of the antagonistic, conflictive dimension of politics—the "passions" (6)—making it powerless to confront and respond to very real violence that arises from antagonistic politics. Mouffe, *Agonistics: Thinking the World Politically* (London: Verso, 2013), 3.

89. Danielle Allen, *Talking to Strangers: Anxieties of Citizenship since* Brown v. Board of Education (Chicago: University of Chicago Press, 2009), 87.

90. Glissant, *Poetics of Relation*, 8.

91. Jacques Derrida, *Of Hospitality*, trans. Anne Doufourmantelle (Stanford, CA: Stanford University Press, 2000), 15.

92. Rodney, *Groundings with My Brothers*, 68.

93. Rodney, 69.

94. See "The West Indies Federation," Our Community, CARICOM, https://caricom.org/the-west-indies-federation/.

95. Although Lewis's statement is in reference to British historian Herman Miravale's suggestion in his *Lectures on Colonisation and Colonies*, it reflects a growing desire for self-determination throughout the Caribbean beginning in the nineteenth century.

96. Yolanda Martínez-San Miguel and Katerina Gonzalez Seligmann, "Con-Federating the Archipelago: Introduction," *Small Axe* 24, no. 1 (March 2020): 37.

97. Martínez-San Miguel and Gonzalez Seligmann, 37.

98. Alison Donnell offers an illuminating reading of how artists' and intellectuals' alignment with the West Indian Federation nourished the "boom of West Indian literature." Donnell, "West Indian Literature and Federation: Imaginative Accord and Uneven Realities," *Small Axe* 24, no. 1 (March 2020): 80.

99. Glissant, *Caribbean Discourse: Selected Essays*, trans. J. Michael Dash (Charlottesville: University of Virginia Press, 1989), 222.

100. Nick Nesbitt, *Caribbean Critique: Antillean Critical Theory from Touissant to Glissant* (Liverpool: Liverpool University Press, 2017), 145.

CHAPTER 2 — DISORIENTED CITIZENSHIP

1. To be clear, it is always a crossover *to* the presumed universality of the English-speaking market.

2. In the aftermath of viewers' backlash, CBS retroactively added Spanish-language closed captions to replays of Bad Bunny's performance.

3. Eduardo Lalo, "El Estado Libre Asociado y la glosolalia," *80 grados* (blog), June 29, 2012, https://www.80grados.net/el-estado-libre-asociado-y-la-glosolalia/. All translations are mine unless noted otherwise.

4. César Ayala and Rafael Bernabe contend that creating the illusion of Puerto Ricans' popular consent to the ELA was key to giving Puerto Rico the appearance of sovereignty as a neocolonial state. Ayala and Bernabe, *Puerto Rico in the American Century: A History since 1898* (Chapel Hill: University of North Carolina Press, 2007), 172.

5. Notably, in *Imagined Communities* Benedict Anderson proposed that reading enables citizens scattered across the world to imagine themselves as members of a shared political

community. Anderson, *Imagined Communities: Reflections on the Origin and Spread of Nationalism* (London: Verso, 1983).

6. Sara Ahmed, *Queer Phenomenology: Orientations, Objects, Others* (Durham, NC: Duke University Press, 2006), 119.

7. Ahmed, 78.

8. I frame counterreading as a corollary to what Paul Gilroy denominates as the Black Atlantic "counternarrative that defiantly reconstructs its own critical, intellectual, and moral genealogy in a partially hidden public sphere of its own." Gilroy, *The Black Atlantic: Modernity and Double Consciousness* (Cambridge, MA: Harvard University Press, 1993), 38.

9. For a critical review of Oswald Spengler's influence in early twentieth-century Latin American thought and literature, see Anke Birkenmaier, "Scenarios of Colonialism and Culture: Oswald Spengler's Latin America," *MLN* 128, no. 2 (2013): 256–276.

10. Antonio Pedreira, *Insularismo* (1934; Guaynabo, PR: Editorial Plaza Mayor, 2001), 49.

11. Pedreira, 45.

12. Pedreira, 49.

13. Pedreira, 97.

14. Pedreira, 107. The *ethos* conceived as an orientation appears similarly in Michel Foucault's *Care of the Self*, wherein, by way of Plutarch, he regards the *ethos* as a "guiding" and "setting straight" of the soul. Foucault, *The History of Sexuality*, vol. 3: *The Care of the Self*, trans. Robert Huxley (New York: Vintage, 1990), 90–92.

15. Pedreira, *Insularismo*, 107.

16. Luis Felipe Díaz, "Tránsitos y traumas en el discurso na(rracional) puertorriqueño," in *Globalización, nación, posmodernidad: estudios culturales puertorriqueños*, ed. Luis Felipe Díaz and Marc Zimmerman (San Juan: LACASA, 2001), 255–256.

17. Pedreira, *Insularismo*, 107.

18. Pedreira, 132.

19. Pedro Malavet, *America's Colony: The Political and Cultural Conflict between the United States and Puerto Rico* (New York: New York University Press, 2004), 43.

20. Juan Flores, *Divided Borders: Essays on Puerto Rican Identity* (Houston: Arte Público Press, 1995), 202.

21. Immanuel Kant, "To Perpetual Peace: A Philosophical Sketch," in *Perpetual Peace and Other Essays on Politics, History, and Morals*, trans. Ted Humphrey (Indianapolis: Hackett, 1983), 118.

22. Immanuel Kant, *Critique of Judgment*, trans. Werner Pluhar (Indianapolis: Hackett, 1987), 160.

23. Hector Hoyos reads representative instances of the Latin American novel as a global form that both discloses the form in which globalization takes shape and critiques ideologies of globalization. Hoyos, *Beyond Bolaño: The Global Latin American Novel* (New York: Columbia University Press, 2015), 7, 12.

24. Ignacio Sánchez Prado considers how the contemporary global novel tracks these misalignments and "(dis)alignments between Latin America and its shifting location in the capitalist system and in world literature." Sánchez Prado, "The Persistence of the Transcultural: A Latin American Theory of the Novel from the National-Popular to the Global," *New Literary History* 51, no. 2 (Spring 2020): 349.

25. Julio Ramos, *Divergent Modernities: Culture and Politics of Nineteenth-Century Latin America*, trans. John D. Blanco (Durham, NC: Duke University Press, 2001), xxxvi.

NOTES TO PAGES 59–65

26. Doris Sommer and Alexandra Vega-Marino, "Introduction: Either And," in Giannina Braschi, *Yo-Yo Boing!* (Pittsburgh: Latin American Literary Review Press, 1998), 11–18.

27. Sommer and Vega-Marino, 11.

28. Braschi, 129; Jorge Duany, "Nation and Migration: Rethinking Puerto Rican Identity in a Transnational Context," in *None of the Above: Puerto Ricans in the Global Era*, ed. Frances Negrón-Muntaner (New York: Palgrave Macmillan, 2008), 52, 51.

29. Ellen Jones, "'I Want My Closet Back': Queering and Unqueering Language in Giannina Braschi's *Yo-Yo Boing!*," *Textual Practice* 34, no. 2 (2020): 284.

30. This critique is reflected in Alberto Moreiras, *The Exhaustion of Difference: The Politics of Latin American Cultural Studies* (Durham, NC: Duke University Press, 2001).

31. Christopher González, *Permissible Narratives: The Promise of Latino/a Literature* (Columbus: Ohio State University Press, 2017), 92.

32. José L. Torres-Padilla, "When Hybridity Doesn't Resist: Giannina Braschi's *Yo-Yo Boing!*," in *Complicating Constructions: Race, Ethnicity, and Hybridity in American Texts*, ed. David S. Goldstein and Audrey B. Thacker (Seattle: University of Washington Press, 2000), 292, 293.

33. I adopt the term "translingual" from Francisco Moreno-Fernández, "*Yo-Yo Boing!* Or Literature as a Translingual Practice," in *Poets, Philosophers, Lovers: On the Writing of Giannina Braschi*, ed. Frederick Luis Aldama and Tess O'Dwyer (Pittsburgh: University of Pittsburgh Press, 2020), 63.

34. Braschi, *Yo-Yo Boing!*, 142.

35. Braschi, 87.

36. Erin Graff Zivin, *Anarchaeologies: Reading as Misreading* (New York: Fordham University Press, 2020), 12.

37. Frances Negrón-Muntaner, "Introduction," in Negrón-Muntaner *None of the Above*, 1.

38. Erin Graff Zivin, "Beyond Jameson: The Metapolitics of Allegory," *Yearbook of Comparative Literature* 61 (2015): 160.

39. J. Hillis Miller, *The Ethics of Reading* (New York: Columbia University Press, 1987), 24.

40. Miller, 25.

41. Braschi, *Yo-Yo Boing!*, 143.

42. Jonathan Rosa, *Looking Like a Language, Sounding Like a Race: Raciolinguistic Ideologies and the Learning of Latinidad* (New York: Oxford University Press, 2019), 7.

43. Édouard Glissant, *Le discours antillais* (Paris: Éditions Gallimard, 1997), 426.

44. Braschi, *Yo-Yo Boing!*, 142.

45. Pascale Casanova, *The World Republic of Letters* (Cambridge, MA: Harvard University Press, 2004), xiii.

46. Casanova, 36.

47. Braschi, *Yo-Yo Boing!*, 142.

48. Braschi, 167.

49. Emily Apter, *The Translation Zone: A New Comparative World Literature* (Princeton, NJ: Princeton University Press, 2006), 12.

50. Jacques Derrida, "Des Tours de Babel," in *Psyche: Inventions of the Other*, vol. 1 (Stanford, CA: Stanford University Press, 2007), 208.

51. United Nations Conference on the Law of Treaties, "Vienna Convention on the Law of Treaties, 23 May 1969" (1980), https://treaties.un.org/doc/Publication/UNTS/Volume %201155/v1155.pdf.

52. Braschi, *Yo-Yo Boing!*, 167.

53. Italo Calvino, *Invisible Cities*, trans. William Weaver (New York: Harcourt Brace Jovanovich, 1974), 21.

54. Lalo, *Los países invisibles*, 173.

55. A transcription of Lalo's speech first appeared in online journal *80 grados* and has since been reproduced in *Intervenciones*, an anthology of Lalo's shorter writing on politics, culture, and the status question in Puerto Rico. Eduardo Lalo, *Intervenciones* (Buenos Aires: Corregidor, 2018); Eduardo Lalo, "El 'Hermoso Hoy,'" *80 Grados* (blog), August 13, 2013, https://www.80grados.net/el-hermoso-hoy-de-eduardo-lalo/.

56. Lalo, *Los países invisibles*, 126.

57. Lalo, 60.

58. Glissant, *Le discours antillais*, 426.

59. Within the context of his *Poétique* and *Le discours antillais*, Glissant writes about the imposition of monolingual French, against Creole, in its overseas department of Martinique.

60. Lalo, *Los países invisibles*, 31.

61. Pedreira, *Insularismo*, 101.

62. Emily Apter, *Against World Literature: On the Politics of Untranslatability* (London: Verso, 2006), 15.

63. Lalo, *Los países invisibles*, 176.

64. Lalo, 21.

65. Walter Mignolo, "Canons A(Nd)Cross-Cultural Boundaries (Or, Whose Canon Are We Talking About?)," *Poetics Today*, no. 12 (1991): 6.

66. Lalo, *Los países invisibles*, 60.

67. Anthony Padgen, "The Law of Continuity: Conquest and Settlement with the Limits of Kant's International Right," in *Kant and Colonialism: Historical and Critical Perspectives*, ed. Katrin Flikschuch and Lea Ypi (Oxford: Oxford University Press, 2014), 34; Andrew Fitzmaurice, "The Genealogy of Terra Nullius," *Australian Historical Studies* 129 (2007): 1–15.

68. For a salient analysis of the problem of translating and "placing" Nuyorican and diasporic Puerto Rican literature, see Yolanda Martínez-San Miguel, "Boricua (between) Borders: On the Possibility of Translating Bilingual Narratives," in Negrón-Muntaner, *None of the Above*, 195–210.

69. Lalo, *Los países invisibles*, 61, emphasis original.

70. Eduardo Lalo, *Simone* (Buenos Aires: Ediciones Corregidor, 2011); Lalo, *Simone* (Chicago: University of Chicago Press, 2015).

71. César A. Salgado, "Eduardo Lalo o la ciudadanía que nos falta," in Eduardo Lalo, *Intervenciones* (Buenos Aires: Ediciones Corregidor, 2018), 17.

72. Ana María Marsán, "Entrevista a Eduardo Lalo," *Katay: Revista Crítica de Literatura Latinoamericana*, September 6, 2008.

73. Casanova, *World Republic of Letters*, 32.

74. Mariano Siskind, *Cosmopolitan Desires: Global Modernity and World Literature in Latin America* (Evanston, IL: Northwestern University Press, 2014), 7.

NOTES TO PAGES 73–79

75. While Siskind admits his unwillingness to wholly abandon the ethical and political possibilities of "the cosmopolitan dream," he calls for a renewed, "revised and dislocated" vision of cosmopolitan hospitality that contends with the world's violent unworlding. Siskind, "Towards a Cosmopolitanism of Loss: An Essay about the End of the World," in *World Literature, Cosmopolitanism, Globality,* ed. *Gesine Müller and Mariano Siskind* (Berlin: De Guyter, 2019), 207.

76. Eduardo Lalo, *La inutilidad* (San Juan: Ediciones Callejón, 2004), 125–26; Eduardo Lalo, *Uselessness,* trans. Jill Levine (Chicago: University of Chicago Press, 2017), 125.

77. Marcy Schwartz offers an indispensable account of Latin American writers' sustained engagement with Paris in the twentieth century. In particular, she explores how, paradoxically, Paris offered a paradigm of political and cultural modernity that was deployed as a "battleground" against (Spanish) European domination. Schwartz, *Writing Paris: Urban Topographies of Desire in Contemporary Latin American Fiction* (Albany: State University of New York Press, 1999).

78. Lalo, *La inutilidad,* 23.

79. James Clifford, *Writing Culture: The Poetics and Politics of Ethnography* (Berkeley: University of California Press, 1986), 112–113.

80. Lalo, *La inutilidad,* 66.

81. Edward Said, *Orientalism* (New York: Vintage Books, 1979), 48–49.

82. Ahmed, *Queer Phenomenology,* 114.

83. Pedro L. San Miguel problematizes Lalo's subaltern self-fashioning in *Intempestivas sobre Clío: Puerto Rico, el Caribe y América Latina* (San Juan: Ediciones Laberinto, 2019).

84. Lalo, *La inutilidad,* 132, emphasis original; Lalo, *Uselessness,* 132, emphasis original.

85. Lalo, *La inutilidad,* 122; Lalo, *Uselessness,* 122. Jill Levine's English translation of the novel removes the last past of the protagonist's statement in Spanish. I have appended to Levine's translation in brackets.

86. Carlos Pabón, *Nación postmortem: Ensayos sobre los insoportables tiempos de ambigüedad* (San Juan: Callejón, 2002), 19–21.

87. Arturo Torrecilla, *La ansiedad de ser puertorriqueño: etnoespectáculo e hiperviolencia en la modernidad líquida* (San Juan: Ediciones Vértigo, 2004).

88. Lalo, *La inutilidad,* 122; Lalo, *Uselessness,* 122.

89. Lalo, *La inutilidad,* 10; Lalo, *Uselessness,* 4.

90. Pedreira, *Insularismo,* 79.

91. Lalo, *La inutilidad,* 182; Lalo, *Uselessness,* 185.

CHAPTER 3 — FREELANCE PERSONHOOD

1. Esther Whitfield, *Cuban Currency: The Dollar and Special Period Fiction* (Minneapolis: University of Minnesota Press, 2008), 2.

2. In "Reinscribing the Aesthetic," James Buckwalter-Arias explores the complicated entanglement of "aesthetic ideology and market ideology" in the period's Cuban literary production. Buckwalter-Arias, "Reinscribing the Aesthetic: Cuban Narrative and Post-Soviet Cultural Politics," *PMLA* 120, no. 2 (March 2005): 372. See also Whitfield's important study on how what she calls "special period fiction" engages in a sustained reflection and critique of "Cuba's cultural currency." Whitfield, *Cuban Currency.*

3. Guillermina De Ferrari, *Community and Culture in Post-Soviet Cuba* (New York: Routledge, 2014), 25; Buckwalter-Arias, "Reinscribing the Aesthetic," 365.

4. Charles W. Mills, "The Political Economy of Personhood," *On the Human: A Project of the National Humanities Center*, April 4, 2011, https://nationalhumanitiescenter.org/on-the-human/2011/04/political-economy-of-personhood/#n3.

5. Désirée Díaz, *Ciudadanías liminales: Vida cotidiana y espacio urbano en la Cuba postsoviética* (Leiden: Almenara Press, 2021), 21, 30.

6. Margarita Mateo Palmer, "La narrartiva cubana contemporánea: las puertas del siglo XXI," *Anales de la Literatura Hispanoamericana* 32 (2002): 52. The ethical imperatives of post-Soviet Cuban aesthetics have formed a notable thematic in the scholarship on Special Period culture. Notably, Odette Casamayor-Cisneros, in *Utopía, distopía e ingravidez: Reconfiguraciones cosmológicas en la narrativa postsoviética cubana* (Madrid: Iberoamericana Vervuert, 2013), argues that the writing of this period can be characterized by an "ethical weightlessness"—a sense that one cannot organize oneself presently in history due to a systematic collapse of the revolution's cosmology and its norms. Alternatively, in *Community and Culture in Post-Soviet Cuba* Guillermina De Ferrari argues that underlying the aesthetic paradigm of Cuban literary and visual production during the Special Period is an ethical upheaval of the revolutionary social contract, which demanded citizens' ideological adherence to the socialist state, in search of "new aesthetic paradigms" amid this ethical crisis. De Ferrari, *Community and Culture in Post-Soviet Cuba*, 25.

7. Ariana Hernandez-Reguant, "Writing the Special Period: An Introduction," in *Cuba in the Special Period: Culture and Ideology in the 1990s*, ed. Hernandez-Reguant (New York: Palgrave Macmillan, 2009), 5–6.

8. Hernandez-Reguant, 6.

9. The term is a portmanteau of "free" and "lance," the weapon used by medieval mercenaries. Its earliest usage is attributed to Walter Scott in *Ivanhoe*. For an exposition of the etymology of the term and its modern translation, see Merriam-Webster, "The Surprising History of 'Freelance,'" https://www.merriam-webster.com/wordplay/freelance-origin-meaning.

10. John Locke, *Second Treatise of Government*, ed. Ian MacPherson (Indianapolis: Hackett, 1980), §27, 19.

11. In their critical rereading of Locke, Charles Mills and Colin Dayan note that both legal precedent and political economy suggest that personhood is decoupled from the human. Rather, a person designates a legal name and moral status that, encompassing nonpersons, describes an entity who can be accountable for their actions before the law. Mills, "Political Economy of Personhood"; Dayan, *The Law Is a White Dog: How Legal Rituals Make and Unmake Persons* (Princeton, NJ: Princeton University Press, 2013), 89. I expound on the idea of personhood as a decoupling of the person from the body in a discussion of *Se alquila un planeta* in the third section of this chapter. I also explore how personhood is constructed in a reading of Haitian-Dominican narrative in chapter 4.

12. For example, Onur Ulas Ince examines how Locke provides the liberal justification for colonial dispossession. Ince corroborates that Locke's theory of property is "necessarily enmeshed" with the "historical practices of capital accumulation." Ince, *Colonial Capitalism and the Dilemmas of Liberalism* (Oxford: Oxford University Press, 2018), 48.

13. Velia Cecilia Bobes, *La nación inconclusa: (Re)constituciones de la ciudadanía y la identidad en Cuba* (Mexico: FLASCO, 2007), 123. All translations are mine, unless otherwise noted. I cite English editions when available.

14. Ley No. 60—also known as the Ley de Reforma Urbana (Law of Urban Reform)—prohibited the commercialization of housing for financial gain. Other key reforms like the 1989 Ley No. 65 banned "the enhancement of personal property interests through investment or speculation." Debra Evenson, *Law and Society in Contemporary Cuba* (The Hague: Kluwer, 2003), 207.

15. Bobes, *La nación inconclusa*, 126; Vicky Unruh, "Introduction: 'Compañero, Respect Your Vocation!' Improvisations for a Workaday Crisis," *PMLA* 127, no. 4 (October 2012): 735. In particular, Unruh perceptively draws attention to the fact that Article 1 of the Cuban constitution opens with the declaration, "Cuba is a socialist state of workers."

16. Ricardo Pérez, "The Promise of Globalization: Sustainable Tourism Development and Environmental Policy in Cuba," in *Cuba in a Global Context: International Relations, Internationalism, and Transnationalism*, ed. Catherine Krull and Louis A. Pérez (Gainesville: University Press of Florida, 2014), 170–171.

17. Pérez, 166.

18. Aaron Kamugisha, *Beyond Coloniality: Citizenship and Freedom in the Caribbean Intellectual Tradition* (Bloomington: Indiana University Press, 2019), 58.

19. Jacques Derrida, *Hospitalité: Volume I (1995–1996)* (Paris: Éditions Du Seuil, 2021), 89.

20. Derrida, 91.

21. Derrida, 91.

22. Yoss, *Se alquila un planeta*, Kindle ed. (Brooklyn: Restless Books, 2001); Yoss, *A Planet for Rent*, trans. David Frye (Brooklyn: Restless Books, 2014), 11, 156.

23. Yoss, *Se alquila un planeta*, loc. 160 of 4681; Yoss, *A Planet for Rent*, 10.

24. As John Rieder explains, a representative work like Wells's *War of the Worlds* wages an "ethical critique" of the British Empire through "political analogy" and a reversal of the frame of reference: the European colonizer is cast as an invading Martian, whereas the racialized Other appears as a mere human. Rieder, *Colonialism and the Emergence of Science Fiction* (Middleton, CT: Wesleyan University Press, 2008), 132–133, 135. This inverted gaze is similarly sustained in 1950s alien invasion films, like *Invasion of the Body Snatchers*, which, according to Robert Kolker, in its representation of aliens who take on human form, emplots the new enemy Other, communists—and, broadly, the Soviet Union—to the ascendancy of U.S. military and economic hegemony. Kolker, *Politics Goes to the Movies: Hollywood, Europe, and Beyond* (London: Routledge, 2018), 106.

25. Yoss, *Se alquila un planeta*; Yoss, *A Planet for Rent*, 13.

26. Guillermo Cabrera Infante, *Tres tristes tigres* (Barcelona: Seix Barral, 2005), 17.

27. Jeanine Murray-Román, *Performance and Personhood in Caribbean Literature: From Alexis to the Digital Age* (Charlottesville: University of Virginia Press, 2016), 105.

28. David Shook, "Exorcising Cuba's Future: A Conversation with Yoss," *World Literature Today* 91, no. 2 (April 2017): 54.

29. Shook, 55.

30. Whitfield, *Cuban Currency*, 10.

31. Castro further consolidated the state's position in a 2002 constitutional reform, in which he declared that "el socialismo y el sistema politico y social revolutiocionario" (socialism and the revolutionary social and political system) were "*irrevocable.*" Josep M. Colomer, "La dictadura (ir)revocable," in *La transición invisible: Sociedad y cambio politico en Cuba*, ed. Velia Cecilia Bobes and Rafael Rojas (Mexico: Océano, 2004), 119, emphasis original. Castro's mandate not only gave the state license to shore up its

governmental power but also positioned citizens who no longer had faith in the country's socialist rhetoric at odds with the political practices of the state.

32. Gregory Claeys, *Dystopia: A Natural History* (Oxford: Oxford University Press, 2017), 7.

33. Jacqueline Loss, "Is the Post- in Post-Soviet the Post- in Post-Guevarian? Introduction to 'Diálogo Crítico: Cuba Post-Soviética,'" *Revista de Estudios Hispánicos* 43, no. 1 (January 2009): 85.

34. Rieder, *Colonialism and the Emergence of Science Fiction*, 2.

35. Rieder, 148.

36. Rieder, 15.

37. José Quiroga, *Cuban Palimpsests* (Minneapolis: University of Minnesota Press, 2005), 3, 5. Quiroga's text explores time and memory in Cuba by way of "sites" that are not limited to "concrete, physical space" but also include literary, visual, cinematic, and sonic texts.

38. Madina Tlostanova, *Postcolonialism and Postsocialism in Fiction and Art: Resistance and Re-existence* (Cham: Palgrave Macmillan, 2017), 98.

39. Tlostanova, 3.

40. Wendy Brown similarly qualifies this space-shifting capacity of neoliberalism—its capacity as a mutable logic to be "disunified and nonidentical with itself in space over time" and interact and intersect with "extant cultures and political traditions" and take "diverse shapes." Brown, *Undoing the Demos: Neoliberalism's Stealth Revolution* (Cambridge, MA: MIT Press, 2015), 21.

41. Yoss, *Se alquila un planeta*, loc. 38 of 4681; Yoss, *A Planet for Rent*, 3.

42. Mimi Sheller and John Urry, "Places to Play, Places in Play," in *Tourism Mobilities: Places to Play, Places in Play*, ed. Mimi Sheller and John Urry (London: Routledge, 2004), 1–3.

43. Sheller and Urry, 3.

44. Mimi Sheller, "Demobilizing and Remobilizing Caribbean Paradise," in Sheller and Urry, *Tourism Mobilities*, 14.

45. Sheller, 18.

46. Yoss, *Se alquila un planeta*, loc. 116 of 4681; Yoss, *A Planet for Rent*, 8.

47. Yoss, *Se alquila un planeta*, loc. 293 of 4681; Yoss, *A Planet for Rent*, 18.

48. De Ferrari, *Community and Culture in Post-Soviet Cuba*, 2–3.

49. Bobes, *La nación inconclusa*, 129–130.

50. Coco Fusco, "Hustling for Dollars: Jineterismo in Cuba," in *Global Sex Workers: Rights, Resistance, and Redefinition*, ed. Kamala Kempadoo and Jo Doezema (New York: Routledge, 1998), 154; Rosalie Schwartz, *Pleasure Island: Tourism and Temptation in Cuba* (Lincoln: University of Nebraska Press, 1997), 86.

51. Amalia L. Cabezas, "Between Love and Money: Sex, Tourism, and Citizenship in Cuba and the Dominican Republic," *Signs* 29, no. 4 (Summer 2004): 993.

52. Yoss's dystopian representation of *jineterismo* is prefigured by the likes of Cuban writer Zoé Valdés's 1995 semiautobiographical bestseller *La nada cotidiana* (Barcelona: Ediciones Salamdra, 2002) and Spanish director and screenwriter Icíar Bollaín's acclaimed 1999 film *Flores de otro mundo* (Alta Films, 1999), both of which explore the vicissitudes of migrant Cuban and Dominican women who engage, implicitly or explicitly, in sex work and other illegal labor to secure marriage, financial stability, and, importantly, legal status in Spain. Valdés's novel, especially, demystifies Cuban sex and

NOTES TO PAGES 92–101

reframes the conversation in a chapter on a migrant *jinetera* who lives practically as a hostage to an aging Spanish man for whom she feels no affection and with whom she derives no sexual pleasure but who, through marriage, has passed on to her Spanish citizenship and, most importantly, material security.

53. Kamala Kempadoo, "Women of Color and the Global Sex Trade: Transnational Feminist Perspectives," *Meridians: Feminism, Race, Transnationalism* 1, no. 2 (2001): 39.

54. Brenda Farnell, *Dynamic Embodiment for Social Theory: "I Move Therefore I Am"* (New York: Routledge, 2012), 19.

55. Zakiyyah Iman Jackson, *Becoming Human: Matter and Meaning in an Antiblack World* (New York: New York University Press, 2020), 141–142.

56. Yoss, *Se alquila un planeta*, loc. 321 or 4681; Yoss, *A Planet for Rent*, 20.

57. Marcel Mauss, "A Category of the Human Mind: The Notion of Person, the Notion of Self," in *The Category of the Person: Anthropology, Philosophy, History*, trans. W. D. Halls (Cambridge: Cambridge University Press, 1985), 15.

58. Mauss, 14.

59. Angela Naimou, *Salvage Work: U.S. and Caribbean Literatures amid the Debris of Legal Personhood* (New York: Fordham University Press, 2015), 19–20.

60. Lindsay B. Gezinski, Sharvari Karandikar, Alexis Levitt, and Roxane Ghaffarian, "'Total Girlfriend Experience': Examining Marketplace Mythologies on Sex Tourism Websites," *Culture, Health, and Society* 18, no. 7 (2016): 793, emphasis added.

61. Gezinski et al., 793, emphasis added.

62. Yoss, *Se alquila un planeta*, loc. 63 of 4681; Yoss, *A Planet for Rent*, 5.

63. Yoss, *Se alquila un planeta*, loc. 77 of 4681; Yoss, *A Planet for Rent*, 5.

64. Yoss, *Se alquila un planeta*, loc. 564 of 4681; Yoss, *A Planet for Rent*, 35.

65. Yoss, *Se alquila un planeta*, loc. 77 of 4681; Yoss, *A Planet for Rent*, 5–6.

66. Yoss, *Se alquila un planeta*, loc. 348 of 4681; Yoss, *A Planet for Rent*, 21.

67. Tlostanova, *Postcolonialism and Postsocialism*, 9, emphasis added.

68. Rocío Zambrana, *Colonial Debts: The Case of Puerto Rico* (Durham, NC: Duke University Press, 2021), 40, 44.

69. Yoss, *Se alquila un planeta*, loc. 77 of 4681; Yoss, *A Planet for Rent*, 6.

70. Colin Dayan, *Haiti, History, and the Gods* (Berkeley: University of California Press, 1998), 56.

71. Yoss, *Se alquila un planeta*, loc. 131 of 4681; Yoss, *A Planet for Rent*, 9, emphasis added.

72. Yoss, *Se alquila un planeta*, loc. 469 of 4681; Yoss, *A Planet for Rent*, 29.

73. Yoss, *Se alquila un planeta*, loc. 77 of 4681; Yoss, *A Planet for Rent*, 6, emphasis added.

74. Quoted in Mills, "Political Economy of Personhood"; Dayan, *Law Is a White Dog*, 89.

75. Emily Martin, *Bipolar Expeditions: Mania and Depression in American Culture* (Princeton, NJ: Princeton University Press, 2007), 41–42.

76. Yoss, *Se alquila un planeta*, loc. 92 of 4681; Yoss, *A Planet for Rent*, 6.

77. Gaceta Oficial de la República de Cuba, Ley No. 62, Código Penal § (1989).

78. Cabezas, "Between Love and Money," 1006.

79. Gaceta Oficial de la República de Cuba, Ley No. 62, emphasis added.

80. Iván de la Nuez, "El Hombre Nuevo and el otro futuro," in *Cuba y el día después: doce ensayistas nacidos con la revolución imaginan el futuro* (Barcelona: Mondadori, 2001), 10. The title of de la Nuez's work is a reference to the "New Man," Ernesto "Che" Guevara's messianic archetype of the revolutionary Cuban citizen who would be reborn

and redeemed from the "original sin" of capitalism. Che Guevara, *El socialismo y el hombre en Cuba* (Mexico: Editorial Grijalbo, 1971), 14.

81. De la Nuez, "El Hombre Nuevo," 11, 12.

82. Fidel Castro, *Palabras a los intelectuales* (Montevideo: Comité de intelectuales y artistas apoyo a la Revolución, 1961), 12.

83. De la Nuez, "El Hombre Nuevo," 15.

84. De la Nuez, 13.

85. Arturo Arango, "Cuba, los intelectuales ante un futuro que ya es presente," *Revista Temas*, no. 64 (December 2010): 80.

86. Arango, 87.

87. Orlando Luis Pardo Lazo, "Reportaje al pie de la horda," *Voces*, no. 1 (August 2010): 3.

88. Beatriz Calvo Peña, "Internet, comunidad y democracia: La blogosfera cubana teje su propia 'isla virtual,'" in *Buena Vista Social Blog: Internet y libertad de expresión en Cuba*, ed. Beatriz Calvo Peña (Valencia: Aduana Vieja, 2010), 158.

89. Judith Butler, *Notes toward a Performative Theory of Assembly* (Cambridge, MA: Harvard University Press, 2015), 11.

90. Rafael Rojas, *El estante vacío: literatura y política en Cuba* (Barcelona: Editorial Anagrama, 2009), 12.

91. Paloma Duong, "Bloggers Unplugged: Amateur Citizens, Cultural Discourse, and Public Sphere in Cuba," *Journal of Latin American Cultural Studies* 22, no. 4 (2013): 376.

92. Duong, 378.

93. The predicament of the Alternative Cuban Blogosphere eerily recalls the plight of the late Reinaldo Arenas, who, although living on the island, had to send his manuscripts abroad to get them published, even amid threats by the state against his livelihood. In one telling passage from his biography, *Antes que anochezca* (Before night falls), Arenas describes in detail his clandestine meetings with friends at the historic Hotel Nacional—a magisterial tourist space from which Cuban citizens were excluded. There, he would entrust his manuscripts to a Cuban friend who had been living in exile and who, later, would submit them for publication to an editor in Europe. Arena's literary career was engendered in the face of myriad physical, professional, and political displacements and alienation. Arenas, *Antes que anochezca* (Barcelona: Tusquets, 1992), 141.

94. Thank you to Morten Bay Christensen for his guidance on the workings of internet infrastructure.

95. John Perry Barlow, "A Declaration of the Independence of Cyberspace" (Electronic Frontier Foundation, 2005), https://www.eff.org/cyberspace-independence.

96. Daniel Kreiss, "A Vision of and for the Networked World: John Perry Barlow's 'A Declaration of the Independence of Cyberspace' at Twenty," in *Media Independence: Working with Freedom or Working for Free?*, ed. James Bennett and Niki Strange (London: Routledge, 2014), 120.

97. Kreiss, 120.

98. Claudia Cadelo, "Líderes de una revolución alternativa," *Voces* 1 (2011): 6.

99. Yoani Sánchez, *Cuba libre: Vivir y escribir en La Habana* (Mexico: Debate, 2010), 13.

100. The colloquial neologism "internaut," an amalgam of "internet" and "astronaut," was popular in the 1990s and early 2000s and is rooted in the term "Arpanaut," used for users of the Internet's predecessor, ARPANET. Sánchez uses it here as a metaphor for her displacement in the blogosphere. Patrice Flichy, *The Internet Imaginaire* (Cambridge, MA: MIT Press, 2007).

NOTES TO PAGES 107–113

101. Tom Phillips, "Cuban Blogger Appeals to Brazil's President for Help to Leave the Island: Dissident Yoani Sánchez Denied Exit Visa since 2004 Plea to Dilma Roussef Issued via YouTube," *Guardian*, January 26, 2012.

102. Yoani Sánchez, "Un pasaporte, un salvaconducto," *Generación Y* (blog), April 8, 2010, https://web.archive.org/web/20101203035534/http://www.desdecuba.com/generation y/?p=1632.

103. Gaceta Oficial de la República de Cuba, Ministerio de Justicia, "Decreto-Ley No. 349/2018" (2018), https://www.ministeriodecultura.gob.cu/images/jdownloads/pol%C3 %ADticas_p%C3%BAblicas/marco_normativo/decreto349.pdf.

104. Michael Chanan's *Cuban Cinema* (Minneapolis: University of Minnesota Press, 2002) chronicles the evolution of Cuban cinema, from its early prerevolutionary era to its institutionalization under ICAIC.

105. Alexis Triana, "El 349, un Decreto en torno a la circulación del arte," *Granma*, November 29, 2018, https://www.granma.cu/cultura/2018-11-29/el-349-un-decreto-en -torno-a-la-circulacion-del-arte-29-11-2018-22-11-31?fbclid=IwARopiCs6QCXNVvrJoi2 OKaP4G1S9Qnprk5JqWlFEGQGEQ7NM9Qr-ettPwcs.

106. Gaceta Oficial de la República de Cuba, Ministerio de Justicia, "De las Telecomunicaciones, las Tecnologías de la Información y la Comunicación y el Uso del Espectro Radioeléctrico," Decreto-Ley No. 35/2021 § (2021), 2583, https://www.gacetaoficial.gob.cu /es/gaceta-oficial-no-92-ordinaria-de-2021.

107. Redacción Nacional, "Decreto-Ley 35: el derecho de Cuba y de todos los cubanos," *Granma*, August 20, 2021, https://www.granma.cu/cuba/2021-08-20/decreto-ley-35-el -derecho-de-cuba-y-de-todos-los-cubanos-20-08-2021-00-08-06.

108. 27N, "Manifiesto del 27N," Facebook, April 12, 2021, https://www.facebook.com /search/top/?q=27N%20Manifiesto.

109. Jacques Derrida, "Hostipitality," trans. Barry Stocker and Forbes Morlock, *Angelaki: Journal of the Theoretical Humanities* 5, no. 3 (2000): 9.

CHAPTER 4 — ALTERED STATES

1. Joaquín Balaguer, *La sla al revés* (1983; Santo Domingo: Ediciones de la Fundación Corripio, 1990), 182.

2. Balaguer, 159.

3. Balaguer, 129.

4. The late María Elena Martínez's groundbreaking work *Genealogical Fictions* historicizes the legal permutations of citizenship rooted in "vecindad," lineage, and racialized fictions of blood purity that were translated from early modern Spain to New Spain (which includes present-day Mexico). María Elena Martínez, *Genealogical Fictions: Limpieza de Sangre, Religion, and Gender in Colonial Mexico* (Stanford, CA: Stanford University Press, 2008).

5. Silvio Torres-Saillant, "Dominican Literature and Its Criticism: Anatomy of a Troubled Identity," in *A History of Literature in the Caribbean*, vol. 1: *Hispanic and Francophone Regions*, ed. James Arnold, J. Michael Dash, and Julio Rodríguez-Luis (Amsterdam: John Benjamins, 1994), 56.

6. Indeed, the dispute over the Haitian-Dominican borderland made news as recently as 2023, when Dominican president Luis Abinader moved to close all Dominican land, sea, and air borders with Haiti over the latter's decision to construct a canal that would tap into the waters of the river that separates them.

7. For example, while Kant allows for the right of a political community to peacefully deny entry to a stranger, he asserts that humans have the right to a common possession of the earth, a right that would potentially call into question the state's refusal of the stranger's passage as a denial of their humanity. Seyla Benhabib considers the human recognition as a moral implication of Kant's hospitality principle. Benhabib, *The Rights of Others: Aliens, Residents, and Citizens* (New Haven, CT: Yale University Press, 2004).

8. Gloria Anzaldúa, *Borderlands/La Frontera: The New Mestiza* (San Francisco: Aunt Lute Books, 1987), 25.

9. Aníbal Quijano, "Coloniality of Power, Eurocentrism, and Latin America," *Nepantla: Views from South* 1, no. 3 (2000): 533–580.

10. Hannah Arendt, *The Origins of Totalitarianism* (San Diego, CA: Harcourt, 1968), 297; Giorgio Agamben, *Homo Sacer: Sovereign Power and Bare Life*, trans. Daniel Heller-Roazen (Stanford, CA: Stanford University Press, 1998), 127–128.

11. Frantz Fanon, *Black Skin, White Masks*, trans. Richard Philcox (New York: Grove Press, 2008), 91.

12. Frantz Fanon, *Peau noire, masques blanques* (Paris: Éditions du Seuil, 1992), 92.

13. Maurice Merleau-Ponty, *Phenomenology of Perception*, trans. Donald A. Landes (New York: Routledge, 2012), xi.

14. Michael Baud, "'Constitutionally White': The Forging of a National Identity in the Dominican Republic," in *Ethnicity in the Caribbean: Essays in Honor of Harry Hoetnik*, ed. Gert Ostindie (Amsterdam: Amsterdam University Press, 2005), 131.

15. Ernesto Sagás, *Race and Politics in the Dominican Republic* (Gainesville: University Press of Florida, 2000), 66–67; Francisco Moscoso Puello, *Cartas a Evita* (Santo Domingo: Editora Cole, 1997), 10.

16. Sybille Fischer, *Modernity Disavowed: Haiti and the Cultures of Slavery in the Age of Revolution* (Durham, NC: Duke University Press, 2004), 234–235, 232.

17. David Theo Goldberg, *The Racial State* (Malden, MA: Blackwell, 2002).

18. Charles Wade Mills, *The Racial Contract* (Ithaca, NY: Cornell University Press, 1997), 13.

19. Notably, in June 2015 Cabiya took to his Facebook page to condemn the Dominican state's move to deport Dominicans of Haitian descent, on the basis of the 2012 "La Sentencia," passed by the Constitutional Tribunal of the Dominican Republic.

20. The work of sociologist Jorge Duany details Dominicans' confinement to the periphery of Puerto Rican society owing to anti-Black discrimination.

21. René Philoctète, *Massacre River*, trans. Linda Coverdale (New York: New Directions Books, 2005).

22. Basilio Belliard, "Presentación," in *Palabras de una isla / Paroles d'une île*, ed. Gaston Saint-Fleur and Basilio Belliard (Santo Domingo: Ediciones de Cultura, 2012), 13–14.

23. René Philoctète, *Le Peuple des terres mêlées* (Paris: CareOf Publishing, 2020), 56; Anne Eller, "'Awful Pirates' and 'Hordes of Jackals': Santo Domingo/the Dominican Republic in Nineteenth-Century Historiography," *Small Axe: A Caribbean Journal of Criticism* 18, no. 2 (July 2014): 86.

24. Philoctète, *Le Peuple des terres mêlées*, 25; Philoctète, *Massacre River*, 66.

25. Philoctète, *Le Peuple des terres mêlées*, 55; Philoctète, *Massacre River*, 83.

26. Ann Laura Stoler, *Carnal Knowledge and Imperial Power: Race and the Intimate in Colonial Rule* (Berkeley: University of California Press, 2002), 23.

NOTES TO PAGES 120–127

27. George Steinmetz, *The Colonial Origins of Modern Social Thought: French Sociology and the Overseas Empire* (Princeton, NJ: Princeton University Press, 2023), 4.

28. Stoler, *Carnal Knowledge and Imperial Power*, 19.

29. Emily Senior, *The Caribbean and the Medical Imagination, 1764–1834: Slavery, Disease and Colonial Modernity* (Cambridge: Cambridge University Press, 2018), 90.

30. Bernardo Vega, *Trujillo y Haití Vol. 1 (1930–1937)* (Santo Domingo: Fundación Cultural, 1988), 319.

31. Robin Derby, "Haitians, Magic, and Money: Raza and Society in the Haitian-Dominican Borderlands, 1900 to 1937," *Comparative Studies in Society and History* 3, no. 3 (1994): 521.

32. Derby, 522.

33. Philoctète, *Le Peuple des terres mêlées*, 84; Philoctète, *Massacre River*, 123. Perhaps Philoctète is too generous in giving the impression that border guards allowed Haitians to pass out of philanthropic sentiment. In fact, Dominican historian Bernardo Vega clarifies, border officials were known to collude with the heads of the major sugar factories—in exchange for a fee—to introduce illegal Haitian labor into the country, so as to avoid paying the required tariffs levied against them by the state. Vega, *Trujillo y Haití*, 286.

34. Paul Ricoeur, *Memory, History, Forgetting*, trans. Kathleen Blamey and David Pellaeur (Chicago: University of Chicago Press, 2004), 415.

35. Ricoeur, 445.

36. Philoctète, *Le Peuple des terres mêlées*, 56; Philoctète, *Massacre River*, 85.

37. Philoctète, *Le Peuple des terres mêlées*, 76; Philoctète, *Massacre River*, 110.

38. Philoctète, *Le Peuple des terres mêlées*, 20–21; Philoctète, *Massacre River*, 31.

39. Frank Moya Pons, *El batey: estudio socioeconómico de los bateyes del Consejo Estatal de Azúcar* (Santo Domingo: Fondo para Avance de las Ciencias Sociales, 1986), 18.

40. Philoctète, *Massacre River*, 101.

41. Kaiama L. Glover, *Haiti Unbound: A Spiralist Challenge to the Postcolonial Canon* (Liverpool: Liverpool University Press, 2010), 232.

42. Édouard Glissant, *Poétique de la Relation* (Paris: Éditions Gallimard, 1990), 18, 20.

43. This tendency toward a postracial and posthuman reading of flesh is exemplified most notably by Cary Wolfe, a prominent theorist of the posthuman, in *Before the Law: Humans and Animals in a Biopolitical Frame* (Chicago: University of Chicago Press, 2012). Arguing that biopolitics acts fundamentally on "the flesh," Wolfe defines flesh as "the communal substrate shared by humans with other forms of life in and through which 'the body' is both sustained and threatened" (50).

44. Hortense J. Spillers, "Mama's Baby, Papa's Maybe: An American Grammar Book," *Diacritics* 17, no. 2 (Summer 1987): 206.

45. Alexander G. Weheliye, *Habeas Viscus: Racializing Assemblages, Biopolitics, and Black Feminist Theories of the Human* (Durham, NC: Duke University Press, 2014), 43.

46. Maurice Merleau-Ponty, *The Visible and the Invisible*, trans. Alphonso Linguis (Evanston, IL: Northwestern University Press, 1968), 139.

47. Weheliye, *Habeas Viscus*, 44.

48. Pedro Cabiya, *Malas hierbas* (New York: Zemí Book, 2011), 9.

49. Emily Maguire, "The Heart of a Zombie: Dominican Literature's Sentient Undead," *Alambique: Revista Académica de Ciencia Ficción y Fantasía* 6, no. 1 (2018): 1.

50. Cabiya, *Malas hierbas*, 21.

51. Maguire, "Heart of a Zombie," 2, 1.

52. This view of Haiti as a postimperial force lying in wait to invade eastern Hispaniola is consolidated by Dominican writer and politico Joaquín Balaguer's *La isla al revés*, an essay that canonizes anti-Haitian ideology.

53. Similarly, Jossianna Arroyo identifies a survivalist narrative in her arresting account of what she calls the "performative dead" in Puerto Rican and Cuban social and cultural texts. Arroyo, "Cities of the Dead: Performing Life in the Caribbean," *Journal of Latin American Cultural Studies* 27, no. 3 (2018): 331–356. Arroyo is particularly concerned with how the living erect performative funerary tableaus of the dead to make sense of the extreme violence that assuages them.

54. Elaine Ginsberg, *Passing and the Fictions of Identity* (Durham, NC: Duke University Press, 1996), 2–3.

55. Ginetta Candelario, *Black Behind the Ears: Dominican Racial Identity from Museums to Beauty Shops* (Durham, NC: Duke University Press, 2007), 26; Michel-Rolph Trouillot, *Haiti: State Against Nation: The Origins and Legacy of Duvalierism* (New York: Monthly Review Press, 1990), 113.

56. Eugene Thacker, *After Life* (Chicago: University of Chicago Press, 2010), x.

57. Cabiya, *Malas hierbas*, 21; Pedro Cabiya, *Wicked Weeds*, trans. Jessica Powell (Simsbury, CT: Mandel Vilar Press, 2016), 4.

58. Jacques Derrida's "The Animal That Therefore I Am," *Critical Inquiry* 28, no. 2 (2002): 369–418, traces how the Judeo-Christian myth of humans' evolution into clothed beings informs the transformation of the human from state of nature into man, metaphorically robed in language, consciousness, and reason, the Western European discourse of modernity.

59. Néstor García Canclini elucidates how the practice of citizenship in Latin America shifts in the neoliberal era from civic participation to "capacity to appropriate commodities." García Canclini, *Consumers and Citizens: Globalization and Multicultural Conflicts* (Minneapolis: University of Minnesota Press, 2001), 15.

60. As Sylvia Wynter cautions, in a neoliberal society the recognition of human life is also contingent on the capacity to accumulate capital in the name of freedom. Sylvia Wynter and Katherine McKittrick, "Unparalleled Catastrophe for Our Species? Or, to Give Humanness a Different Future: Conversations," in *Sylvia Wynter: On Being Human as Praxis* (Durham, NC: Durham University Press, 2015), 10.

61. Colin Dayan, *The Law Is a White Dog: How Legal Rituals Make and Unmake Persons* (Princeton, NJ: Princeton University Press, 2013), 42, 36.

62. Dayan, 44.

63. Dayan, 35.

64. Dayan, 26, 25.

65. Sara Ahmed, *Strange Encounters: Embodied Others in Post-coloniality* (London: Routledge, 2000), 128.

66. Thacker, *After Life*, 4.

67. Thacker, 3.

68. Cabiya, *Malas hierbas*, 22; Cabiya, *Wicked Weeds*, 5.

69. David Chalmers, *The Conscious Mind: In Search of a Fundamental Theory* (New York: Oxford University Press, 2007), 4, 94.

70. Fanon, *Black Skin, White Masks*, xv.

71. Wynter and McKittrick, "Unparalleled Catastrophe for Our Species?," 11.

NOTES TO PAGES 133–137

72. Sylvia Wynter, "Towards the Sociogenic Principle: Fanon, Identity, the Puzzle of Conscious Experience, and What It Is Like to Be 'Black,'" in *National Identities and Sociopolitical Changes in Latin America*, ed. Mercedes Durán-Cogan and Antonio Gómez-Moriana (New York: Routledge, 2001), 60.

73. Wynter, 34.

74. Wade Davis, *Passage of Darkness: The Ethnobiology of the Haitian Zombie* (Chapel Hill: University of North Carolina Press, 1988).

75. Wade Davis, *The Serpent and the Rainbow* (New York: Warner Books, 1985), 19, 89.

76. Wynter, "Towards the Sociogenic Principle," 34.

77. Cabiya, *Malas hierbas*, 9.

78. See Kerstin Oloff's illuminating interview with Pedro Cabiya, where he describes early literary depictions of "pre-zombies" and provides a blueprint for his critique of the modern Western construct of the human. Oloff, "'Lo humano es una historia, un cuento de hadas': entrevista a Pedro Cabiya," *La Habana Elegante* 51 (Primavera-Verano 2012), http://www.habanaelegante.com/Spring_Summer_2012/Entrevista_Oloff.html.

79. Frank Moya Pons, "La matriz transnacional dominico haitiana (III)," *Diario Libre*, June 26, 2010, https://www.diariolibre.com/opinion/lecturas/la-matriz-transnacional -dominico-haitiana-iii-FPDL251062.

80. Frank Moya Pons, "La matriz transnacional haitiana (II)," *Diario Libre*, June 19, 2010, https://www.diariolibre.com/opinion/lecturas/la-matriz-transnacional-haitiana-ii -IPDL250109.

81. Frank Moya Pons, "La matriz transnacional haitiana (I)," *Diario Libre*, June 12, 2010, https://www.diariolibre.com/opinion/lecturas/la-matriz-transnacional-haitiana-i -IODL249100.

82. Cabiya, *Malas hierbas*, 59; Cabiya, *Wicked Weeds*, 29.

83. Notably, these debates brought into view the fact that the Dominican Constitution of 1966 denies the right of citizenship to children born on Dominican soil to foreigners "in transit." Tribunal Constitucional de la República Dominicana, "Sentencia TC/0168/13" (2013), 11, https://www.tribunalconstitucional.gob.do/consultas/secretar %C3%ADa/sentencias/tco16813/. In doing so, the constitutional proviso effectively relegated second-generation Dominicans of Haitian descent to a state of transience. In 2013 and 2015, following the novel's publication, this constitutional proviso drew the global attention of legal scholars and intellectuals (among them Pedro Cabiya), who noted that it deliberately targeted the Dominican-born offspring of Haitian migrant workers.

84. Torres-Saillant has argued that "insofar as Haitians are seen as homogenously Black," anti-Haitianism mobilizes Dominican citizens' affect around a "declared contempt for blackness." Torres-Saillant, "Dominican Literature and Its Criticism," 55. However, Lorgia García-Peña has pushed back against the universalizing brushstroke of anti-Blackness with which the Dominican Republic has been labeled, emphasizing, instead, the need for a nuanced situating of anti-Haitianism both as a "contra*diction*" within the Dominican archive and as "the result of a colonial bequeath that was in turn and upheld by the United States to preserve its own imperial ventures." García-Peña, *The Borders of Dominicanidad: Race, Nation, and Archives of Dominicanidad* (Durham, NC: Duke University Press, 2016), 1–3, 15.

85. Cabiya, *Malas hierbas*, 37.

86. Peter Hallward, *Damming the Flood: Haiti, Aristide, and the Politics of Containment* (London: Verso, 2007), 121–129.

87. Cabiya, *Malas hierbas*, 32.

88. Dixa Ramírez, *Colonial Phantoms: Belonging and Refusal in the Dominican Americas from the 19th Century to the Present* (New York: New York University Press, 2018), 43.

89. Pedro San Miguel explores the mirroring of these intertwining histories in "An Island in the Mirror: The Dominican Republic and Haiti," in *The Caribbean: A History of the Region and Its Peoples*, ed. Stephan Palmié and Francisco A Scarano (Chicago: University of Chicago Press, 2011), 568.

90. Cabiya, *Malas hierbas*, 198; Cabiya, *Wicked Weeds*, 129.

91. Roger Caillois, "Mimicry and Legendary Psychasthenia," trans. John Shepley, *October* 31 (Winter 1984): 27.

92. Caillois, 30.

93. Cabiya, *Malas hierbas*, 218; Cabiya, *Wicked Weeds*, 144.

94. Sarah Juliet Lauro and Karen Embry, "A Zombie Manifesto: The Nonhuman Condition in the Era of Advanced Capitalism," *Boundary 2* 35, no. 1 (2008): 94.

95. Cabiya, *Malas hierbas*, 181; Cabiya, *Wicked Weeds*, 117.

96. Christina Sharpe, *In the Wake: On Blackness and Being* (Durham, NC: Duke University Press, 2016), 21

CODA

1. United Nations High Commissioner for Refugees, "Who We Protect: Internally Displaced Persons," https://www.unhcr.org/us/about-unhcr/who-we-protect/internally-displaced-people.

2. Sofía Gallisá Muriente, *B-Roll* (Video collage, 2017), https://sofiagallisa.com/B-Roll-2.

3. Jean-Luc Nancy, "L'Intrus," *CR: The New Centennial Review* 2, no. 3 (Fall 2002): 1.

Index

Abinader, Luis, 169n6
Acosta, Abraham, 151n3
aesthetics, 1–3, 15, 19, 27, 34, 57–58, 60, 79–80, 82, 86, 88, 101–102, 114, 164n6; aesthetic practices, 3, 20, 108; of hospitality, 8
Africa, 13, 34; African, 36; Black Africans 1, 17, 54, 119–120; diaspora 1, 38; enslaved Africans, 23, 25, 38, 70, 151n1; North Africans, 13–14; *race africaine*, 119; races, 54. *See* decolonization; enslavement
Agamben, Giorgio, 115
Ahmed, Sara, 54, 64, 66, 75, 131
allegory, 5–6, 30, 33, 44, 57, 61, 74, 81, 87, 91, 96–98, 123, 127
Allen, Danielle, 48
Alternative Cuban Blogosphere (Blogósfera Cubana Alternativa), 2, 21, 80–82, 84, 101–104, 108, 168n93; *hostigamiento* (house arrest), 21, 110–11; paperlessness (undocumentation), 103–104, 107–108
Americas, 9, 12, 63
Anderson, Benedict, 54, 159n5
Anglo (British) Caribbean, 42, 49
anti-Black, 115–116, 133, 170n19, 173n82
anticolonial, 43
Antigua, 4, 23
Antillanité, 3, 50
Anzaldúa, Gloria, 113
Aparicio, Frances, 36
Apple Mail, 106
Apter, Emily, 65
Arabs, 13–14
Arabic, 100

Arango, Arturo, 101–102
Arenas, Reinaldo, 168n93
Arendt, Hannah, 26, 40, 115
Aristide, Jean-Bertrand, 137
Aristotle, 25, 28–29, 40, 47, 155n14
ARPANET, 106, 168n100
Arroyo, Jossianna, 172n52
Asia, 13, 34; Asian woman, 72; indentureship of Asian peoples, 1, 23, 25
Ayala, César, 159n4

Babel, 59, 62, 65–66
Bad Bunny (Benito Antonio Martínez Ocasio), 51–52, 159n2
Bahamas, 36, 144
Balaguer, Joaquín, 112, 172n51
Balibar, Étienne, 5, 8, 17, 120
Barbados, 7, 12, 19, 26, 30–31, 34–36, 38–40, 144, 156n20; Afro-Barbadians, 35, 157n38; Barbadians, 31, 35–36
Barlow, John Perry, 106–107
Barthes, Roland, 35–37, 157n44
Baud, Michael, 115
Belafonte, Harry, 44
Belliard, Basilio, 118
Benhabib, Seyla, 170n7
Benítez-Rojo, Antonio, 151n4
Berman, Sandra, 154n68
Bernabé, Jean, 34, 159n4
Bernasconi, Robert, 14–15
biopolitics, 113, 115, 119, 171n42; biopolitical borders, 127, 141
Birkenmaier, Anke, 160n9
Bisquet, Katherine, 110

INDEX

Black American, 16
Black Antilleans, 115
Black bodies, 115, 124–125
Black Caribbean, 133
Black Dominican, 135
Black enslavement of. *See* enslavement
Black Haitian, 118, 141
Blackness, 11, 15–16, 62, 98, 128; epidermal, 128; in relation to Whiteness, 15, 115. *See also* Haitian Blackness
Bobes, Velia Cecilia, 83
body, 21, 37, 46, 77, 82, 84, 88–100, 106, 108, 114–115, 127–128, 130, 140, 141, 164n11, 171n42; citizen's body, 84, 114; consciousness of, 115, 125; disembodiment, 20, 114, 106; embodiment, 89, 92, 101, 105–106, 127, 140; *Invasion of the Body Snatchers* (1956 film), 86, 165n24; in relation to "flesh," 125
body-politic, 113, 121, 122, 128, 145
Bollaín, Icíar, 166n52
Bonilla, Yarimar, 43–44
Borthwick, Fiona, 155n12
Bradley, Rizvana, 15
Brand, Dionne, 38
Braschi, Giannina: *El imperio de los sueños*, 59; misreading, 20, 56, 58, 61; opacity, 59–60; *United States of Banana*, 59; *Yo-Yo Boing!*, 2, 20, 54–64, 66
Brathwaite, Kamau, 34
Brazil, 74, 107
Britton, Celia, 24–25
Brown, Wendy, 166n40
Buckwalter-Arias, James, 79, 163n2
Butler, Judith, 103

Cabezas, Amalia, 92, 99
Cabiya, Pedro: critic of Dominican government policy toward Haitians, 170n18, 173n81; on literary depiction of "prezombies," 173n76; *Malas hierbas*, 2, 21–22, 113–114, 117, 123, 126–128, 13–32, 134–141
Cabrera Infante, Guillermo, 86
Cadelo, Claudia, 81, 101–104, 107
Caillois, Roger, 139–140
Calvino, Italo, 66–67, 69
Calvo Peña, Beatriz, 103
Candelario, Ginetta, 128
canon, 20, 34, 58, 61, 66, 68–71, 87; Caribbean literary, 53; Latin American literary, 53; as law, 66, 70; noncanonical, 69–71; U.S. literary, 53, 71; of world literature, 53, 57

Caribe Indians, 10
Caribbean Community and Common Market (CARICOM), 7, 19, 29–31, 33–35, 49–50, 63, 156n20
Caribbean discourse, 19, 34, 36–37, 47–48, 65
Caribbeanness, 19, 26, 33, 46, 50
Caribbean Single Market Economy (CSME), 29, 49
Caribbean unity/regional harmony (myth of), 19, 23–24, 26, 29, 30, 33–37, 40–42, 43, 45–46, 49
Casamayor-Cisneros, Odette, 164n6
Casanova, Pascale, 63, 67, 71, 73
Castillo Pérez, Maykel "Osorbo," 110
Castro, Fidel, 83, 101, 109, 165n31
Cavarero, Adriana, 40
CBS (television broadcaster), 51, 159n2
Césaire, Aimé, 38, 45
Chalmers, David, 132–133
Chambers-Letson, Joshua, 6
Chamoiseau, Patrick, 34
Chanca, Diego Álvarez, 153n30
Chávez-Silverman, Susana, 36
Chion, Michel, 33, 40
Christensen, Morten Bay, 168n94
citizen, 8, 12, 16, 18, 91, 98, 102, 105, 107, 128, 130, 136; Caribbean, 6, 8, 30; definition of, 28, 40; distinction from "stranger," 2, 5, 17, 143, 153n41; relation to category of "human being," 21, 115, 125
citizen-stranger, 17
citizen-subject, 40, 80
citizenship, 8, 12–21, 18, 30, 67–68, 72–73, 80, 82, 85, 92, 112–113, 115, 129, 131, 143; definition of, 6, 43; neoliberal, 130, 140; personhood and, 7, 16, 129, 136; practice(s) of, 2–3, 5, 22, 53–54, 167n58; and sovereignty, 4, 6, 7, 12, 16–17, 19, 21, 62, 65, 144, 145
Claey, Gregory, 87
class, 8, 13, 14, 28, 81, 83, 89, 128, 134, 137
Clifford, James, 74, 154n68
Colón, Cristóbal (Columbus, Christopher), 1, 9, 11, 36, 144–145, 153n30; *Diario del primer viaje*, 9–10; *Relaciones*, 10
coloniality, 12, 23, 36, 49, 118; decoloniality, 22; of flesh, 124; neoliberal, 86–87, 96; of power, 8, 114; of race, 14, 75, 115
Colomer, Josep M., 165n31
Confederación Antillana (Antillean Confederation), 49

Confiant, Raphäel, 34
constitution, 7, 13, 16, 54, 109; cosmopolitan/world, 15–16, 56; multiracial, 25. *See also* Cuba; Dominican Republic; Haiti
Connell, John, 31–32
consciousness, 21–22, 98–100, 115, 117, 118, 123, 125, 132–134; perception, 113; self-consciousness, 113. *See also* body
cosmopolitanism, 14, 16, 19, 25, 34–35, 53, 62–64, 73, 163n75; Derrida's theory of, 15, 84; Kant's theory of, 13–15, 56, 58, 64, 153n41. *See also* constitution; hospitality
COVID-19, 1, 111
Creoleness (*Creolité*), 34
Creolization, 3, 35, 154n68
Cuba, 7, 20–21, 41, 67, 79–84, 86–94, 96–111, 165n15; 11J protests, 111; Foreign Investment Act, 83; Ministry of Culture, 108, 110; Ministry of Justice, 108; Movimiento San Isidro (MSI), 110; Office of Immigration, 107; Policía Nacional, 110; postsocialist, 20, 80, 82, 86, 88, 91, 96; socialist, 7; Special Period, 20, 79, 83–87, 92, 101; 27N (27 de Noviembre) collective, 110–111, 169n108
Cuban citizen, 80, 83–84, 167n80
Cuban citizenship, 83, 91, 102, 107
Cuban constitution, 83, 165n15, 165n31
Cuban revolution, 79–80, 83, 87, 101

Dajabón River, 117, 169n6
Dash, J. Michael, 36
Davis, Annalee: ambient soundscapes, 26, 30–33, 37–41; demythification of Caribbean unity, 37; *Migrant Discourse*, 2, 19, 26–34, 37–38, 41–42, 50, 158n63; *On the Map*, 34–36, 157n39, 158n63
Davis, Wade, 133–134
Dayan, Colin, 12, 18, 97, 130–131, 139–140, 164n11
"Declaration of the Rights of Man and Citizen," 67, 115
decolonial, 4, 49; politics, 22, 44; theory/thought, 19, 22, 44
decoloniality, 22
decolonization, 34, 49, 71, 73; African, 44; of British Caribbean, 42
De Ferrari, Guillermina, 46, 79, 91, 147, 164n6
de la Nuez, Iván, 101–102, 167n80
DeLoughrey, Elizabeth, 38
demythification. *See* Davis, Annalee

denaturalization, 112, 119, 121, 124
depersonalization, 2, 81, 100, 103, 114, 118, 130, 140
Derby, Robin (Lauren), 121
dermal politics, 21
Derrida, Jacques, 10, 19, 48, 65, 84, 93, 107, 111, 172n57; on the etymology of hospitality, 10; on Kant, 15–16
Dessalines, Jean-Jacques, 116
Díaz, Désirée, 80
Díaz, Luis Felipe, 55
disenchantment, 82, 101–102
disorientation, 20, 53–57, 79
displacement, 2, 22, 33, 38, 81, 105, 107, 126, 168n93, 168n100; displacement-as-hospitality, 144; existential, 155n68; internal displacement, 143–144; transnational, 20, 138
Dominican body-politic, 113, 121–122, 128
Dominican citizen, 118, 127, 134–136, 141
Dominican citizenship, 112, 120–122, 173n81
Dominican constitution, 116, 170n18, 173n81
Dominican Republic, 7, 21, 112–118, 126–127, 135, 137–138, 173n82; Elías Piña (province), 117–119, 121, 123–124; Haitian occupation of, 118; *programas de domincanización*, 117; U.S. occupation of, 115–116
Dominican whiteness, 116, 122–123, 128
Donnell, Alison, 159n98
Duany, Jorge, 59, 170n19
Du Bois, W.E.B., 16, 110
Duong, Paloma, 104
Duvalier, François ("Papa Doc"), 137–139
Duvalier, Jean-Claude ("Baby Doc"), 126, 133, 137–139
dystopia, 38–39, 80–81, 85–87, 90, 100, 166n52

ecology, 9, 19, 26, 30, 37, 46; human, 9, 144; racial, 21; spatial, 88
economic agreements/associations, 7, 29, 41
economic anxiety, 35, 157n38
economic exploitation, 29, 83, 96–97, 124
economic sovereignty, 24, 29
Eli Lilly (corporation), 126, 130, 137
Eller, Anne, 119
Elwes, Catherine, 32
emancipation, 12, 17, 74–75, 77, 99, 140, 152; digital, 104, 106; emancipatory

possibility, 6, 82, 144; Latin-American, 4, 42, 49
Embry, Karen, 141
Enlightenment, 13, 17, 55, 141; post-Enlightenment, 13, 21
enslavement, 56, 99, 129–130; Black enslavement, 14, 36, 116, 124, 125; enslaved Africans 1, 23, 25, 38, 54, 70, 151n1
environment, 26, 30, 37, 95, 98, 102; environmental diversity/wealth, 1, 144; tourist environment, 99
estrangement, 2–3, 6, 8, 16, 30, 48, 77, 111, 115; self-estrangement, 2, 113–114
Europe, 9, 13, 34, 52, 62–63, 66–68, 71, 74, 168n93; early Modern, 9; European colonialism/imperialism, 3, 6, 13, 25, 36, 71, 87–88, 106, 116, 120, 145, 153n41, 165n24; European inhospitality, 12, 15; European thought, 4, 11, 13–14, 18, 172n57; hegemony of, 10, 29; as universal, 8, 11; (Westphalian) nation-state form, 8, 11–12, 116
Evenson, Debra, 165n14

Facebook, 110, 170n18
Fanon, Frantz, 21–22, 115; racial-epidermal schema, 125; sociogeny, 133
Farnell, Brenda, 92
Ferreira da Silva, Denise, 12, 15
Fischer, Sybille, 116
flesh (*chair*), 114, 118, 124–125, 141, 171n42
Flores, Juan, 56, 74
Flores, Tatiana, 38
Foucault, Michel, 88, 156n19
France, 25, 43, 74–75, 157n44
freelance, 81, 83, 87, 102, 106, 108; etymology of, 21, 82, 164n9; personhood, 81, 83–84, 94, 99, 101, 104, sex work ("social work," *jineterismo*), 81, 85, 90–91, 93–95, 98, 100
French Caribbean, 24–25, 43, 134
Frost, Mervyn, 152n19
Fusco, Coco, 166n50

Gallisá Muriente, Sofia, 144
Gandhi, Leela, 151n3
García Canclini, Néstor, 172n58
García-Peña, Lorgia, 173n82
geography, 3, 10, 14, 32–33, 37–38; imperial, 50, 68–69; national, 100; political, 54
Gezinski, Lindsay B., 94
Gibson, Chris, 31–32

Gilroy, Paul, 151n1, 160n8
Ginsberg, Elaine, 128
Glissant, Édouard, 19, 34, 38, 50, 47, 57, 151n1, 154n68; on the abyss, 124, 154n65; on monolingualism, 61, 68, 162n59; on opacity, 17, 154n65; Relation, 17–18, 48, 151n4; on verbal delirium, 24–25
Glover, Kaiama L., 124
globalization. *See* neoliberalism
Gmail, 106
Goldberg, David Theo, 116
González, Aníbal, 158n66
González, Christopher, 59
González Echevarría, Roberto, 4
Gonzalez Seligmann, Katerina, 49
Graff Zivin, Erin, 6, 60–61
Grammy Awards, 51–52
Guadeloupe, 25, 43–44; Gosier (commune), 25
guest, 1, 99–100, 143–144; as client, 87, 98, 106; European "guest," 36; worker, 93–94
guest/host distinction, 9, 14–15, 88–90, 93; *hostigamiento*, 111
guest/stranger distinction, 2, 16, 84
Gutiérrez Mouat, Ricardo, 43
Guyana, 7, 31, 39, 156n20; Afro-Guyanese, 35, 157n38; Guyanese citizens/nationals, 30, 33; Guyanese migrants, 31, 35–36; Guyanese subjects (of *Migrant Discourse*), 26, 31–34, 37–41

Habermas, Jürgen, 158n87
Hadeed, Abigail, 1, 147
Haiti, 7, 12, 112–130, 132–142; constitution of, 116; Duvalierist, 137–139, Haitian citizenship, 116, 127
Haitian Blackness, 116, 123, 137–138, 140, 173n82
Haitianness, 116, 121, 135, 138, 140, 141
Haitian Revolution, 49
Hall, Stuart, 35
Hallward, Peter, 137
harmony, 33, 43; multilingual, 24; multiracial, 24, 49
Havana, 86, 105, 110
Heidegger, Martin, 129
Hernández, Elizabeth, 158n68
Hernandez-Reguant, Ariana, 81
Hitchcock, Alfred, 39–40
Hispaniola, 9–10, 124, 125, 140, 144; division between Haiti and Dominican Republic, 112, 115, 117–118, 138, 142, 172n51

INDEX

home, 1–2, 4, 16, 26, 19, 23, 53, 71, 75–76, 106, 107; as alienated ("home"), 2–3, 17, 55, 66, 91, 110–111; and the logic of hospitality, 14–16, 86, 88, 90–91
Hooker, Juliet, 16
hospitality: aesthetics of, 4, 8; aporia of (hospitality/inhospitality), 9, 14–16, 30, 86, 88, 100, 114; Caribbean, 1–2, 10–12, 13, 22, 25, 33, 36–37, 40–41, 49, 104, 144–145; cosmopolitan, 19, 25, 47, 56, 58, 143, 163n75; interplanetary, 85, 88–91; logic of, 2, 13, 19, 27, 33, 113; myth/illusion of, 3, 5, 10, 42, 45, 47, 85, 113; racialization of, 1, 14–17, 48, 97; rhetoric of 25, 48; socialist, 87; unconditional, 22, 36, 111, 115, 143. *See also* Derrida, Jacques; Kant, Immanuel
host. *See* hospitality
host (internet server), 102, 105–106
Hoyos, Hector, 160n23
Humbert, David, 157n60
Hurricane Maria, 20, 144

Ince, Onur Ulas, 164n12
inhospitality. *See* hospitality
Instituto Cubano del Arte e Industria Cinematográficos (ICAIC), 108
imperialism. *See* Europe
Indigenous peoples, 9, 17, 23, 25, 70, 71, 75
Instituto Científico Domínico-Alemán (the German-Dominican Scientific Institute), 120
International Monetary Fund (IMF), 44

Jackson, Zakiyyah Iman, 11, 93
Jamaica, 24, 41–42, 44, 105, 156n20; Jamaica Labour Party (JLP), 44; People's National Party (PNP), 44
Jones, Ellen, 59
José Martí International Airport, 111

Kamugisha, Aaron, 12, 84
Kant, Immanuel, 16, 28, 84, 113, 155n13, 170n7; condemnation of inhospitality, 13–14; geography, 62, 64; *Perpetual Peace*, 13–15, 56, 153n41, 154n49
Kempadoo, Kamala, 92
Kincaid, Jamaica, 4–5, 23, 25, 28
Kolker, Robert, 165n24
Kreiss, Daniel, 106
Krishna, Sankaran, 152n18

Lalo, Eduardo: disorientation, 53–57; illegibility of, 19–20, 52, 58, 72; *La inutilidad*, 20, 53, 57, 71–77; no-canon's-land, 70–71; *Los países invisibles*, 20, 53, 58, 66, 67–71; *Simone*, 72; on the visibility/invisibility of Puerto Rican literature, 58, 63, 66–68, 71, 74, 77
las Casas, Bartolomé de, 9–10
Latin American criticism and theory, 3, 18, 22, 57–59, 65
Latin American independence, 4, 42, 49, 125
Latinx, 51, 65
Lauro, Sarah Juliet, 141
Lavastida, Hamlet, 110–111
law: juridical universality, 2, 5, 7–8; international, 4, 7, 13–14, 52, 143; *nomos*, 80, 83; onto-juridical, 1, 113; racial-juridical, 21, 55, 112–114 ,116–120, 123, 128, 130, 135, 140–141
legal discourse, 9, 11, 131
legal fiction, 4–5, 12, 18, 80, 94, 112, 115
legal grammar/grammar of the law, 5, 56, 61, 80, 83
Levant, 34
Lewis, Linden, 12
life and death (border between), 18, 22, 95, 124, 126, 127–133, 135, 138–141. *See also* passing life
Locke, John, 16, 164n11; on the body as property, 82; definition of personhood, 98, 100
López Springfield, Consuelo, 158n68
Loss, Jacqueline, 87
Louis XIV, 90

Maguire, Emily, 126–127
Malavet, Pedro, 55
Man, 48, 55–56, 82, 115, 125, 130
market: black market/illegal, 81, 90, 92, 99, 166n52, 171n32; common, 29, 62, 63 global/international, 6, 13, 20, 80, 83, 96, 114; literary, 21, 61, 63, 65; neoliberal, 34, 65, 87
Markham, Clements, 10
Marsán, Ana María, 162n72
Martí, José, 58
Martin, Emily, 98
Martinique, 24, 41, 43–45, 115
Martínez, María Elena, 169n4
Martinez-San Miguel, Yolanda, 49, 162n68
Martínez Ocasio, Benito Antonio. *See* Bad Bunny
Marx, Karl, 5, 152n14
Mateo Palmer, Margarita, 164n6

Maturana, Humberto, 153n35
Massacre de Perejil ("parsley massacre"),
117–119, 121, 123
Mauss, Marcel, 93
McAfee, Kathy, 156n21
McKittrick, Katherine, 133
Meeks, Brian, 3
Merleau-Ponty, Maurice, 92, 115, 125
mestizaje, 3
metonymy, 76, 93, 127–128
Mignolo, Walter, 70
Miller, J. Hillis, 61
Mills, Charles W., 70, 116, 164n11
Miravale, Herman, 159
mixed-race, 98, 116, 123; *mulato*, 118, 137
modernity, 7–8, 12, 17, 58, 67, 73–74, 114,
151n1, 163n77; literary, 73; neoliberal, 88;
political, 8; Western, 16, 18, 27, 30, 33, 40,
96, 141, 155n13, 172n57
monolingualism, 65; Spanish, 62, 69, 76.
See also Glissant, Édouard
Moscoso Puello, Francisco, 116
Movimiento San Isidro, 110
Moya Pons, Frank, 124, 135
Murray-Román, Jeanine, 86

Naimou, Angela, 94
Naipaul, V. S., 45
Nancy, Jean-Luc, 46, 145
Negrón-Muntaner, Frances, 61
neocoloniality, 7, 64, 69, 74, 85, 144; of
global literary market, 65, 67; Martinique, 24; Puerto Rico, 43, 56, 60, 68,
96, 159n4
neoliberalism, 18, 13, 20, 47, 58, 88, 96,
98–99, 144, 166n40
neoliberalization, 29, 30, 48
Nesbitt, Nick, 50
New World, 4, 6, 8–9, 11, 13, 38, 77, 89, 94
Niesen, Peter, 14, 153n41
noncanonical, 69–71
nonrelationality, 18
nonsovereignty, 44, 115; of Puerto Rico, 7,
53, 54, 57–58, 67
North America, 10, 30, 72, 77, 144–145; and
Europe, 11, 29, 52, 87
North Atlantic Universals, 7, 19, 116, 143–144
Nuyorican, 162n68

Oloff, Kerstin, 173
Olwig, Karen Fog, 35
Ong, Walter, 27
ontology, 12, 88, 127, 129–130, 135, 137–138,
140

Other, 4, 12, 15, 18, 54, 64, 120; Black, 11, 114,
141; racialized, 8, 14, 58, 86, 113, 165n24
opacity. *See* Braschi, Giannina; Glissant,
Édouard
Otero Alcántara, Luis Manuel, 110

Pabón, Carlos, 76
Padgen, Anthony, 162n67
Palmié, Stephan, 155n68
Pardo Lazo, Orlando Luis, 101–103,
105, 107
passing, 21, 127, 129, 140; definition of, 128;
legal discourse of 131
passing life, 127–132; 137, 139–140
Patterson, Orlando, 130
Pedreira, Antonio, 55, 70–72, 76–77; on
monolingualism, 56, 69; on racial
"con-fusion," 54, 62
Peignot, Jérôme, 37
Pérez, Ricardo, 83
performance, 3, 6, 59, 87, 94, 151n4; art,
104, 108, 110; literary, 59, 61–62
persona, 20, 93, 99–100; etymology of, 94;
fictive, 94
persona non grata, 104
phenomenology, 37, 54, 66, 92, 115, 125;
neurophenomenology, 21
Phillips, Tom, 169n101
Philoctète, René: *Le Peuple des terres
mêlées*, 2, 21–22, 113–114, 116–122,
124–126, 138, 141–142, 145; "common
flesh" (Haitian-Dominican flesh), 118,
124–125, 141
place: Caribbean as place of tourism, 19,
89–90, 145; out-of-placeness, 33, 101;
placelessness, 20, 52, 57, 88; relation
to citizenship, 2, 16; relation to
language, 62
Plato, 28
Plutarch, 160n14
Poland, 111
political deliberation, 2, 24, 29–30, 41–42,
44–49, 120–121
postcolonial Caribbean nation-state, 7–9,
24, 88, 96
postcolonial Caribbean sovereignty,
2–3
property, 5, 16, 70, 81, 85–86, 97, 108;
personhood as property, 82–84, 88, 93,
130, 164n11, 165n14; the proper, 16, 20, 88,
90, 93. *See also* citizenship; hospitality;
Locke, John
Puerto Rico, 7, 19, 44, 47, 54, 58, 62–64,
66–67, 74–77, 96, 117, 144, 159n4;

INDEX

economic relationship to the U.S., 43, 47; Estado Libre Asociado (ELA), 20, 43, 51–52, 56, 61; legal status ("status question"), 19–20, 43, 51–53, 55–57, 59–61, 68–72, 162n55; Legislative Assembly, 158n71; Partido Nuevo Progresista (PNP), 76; U.S. Citizenship, 43, 64–65, 73
Puri, Shalini, 3, 59

Quijano, Aníbal, 8, 96, 114
Quiroga, José, 88, 116n37

raciality of inhospitality, 16–17
Ramírez, Dixa, 138
Ramos, Julio, 58
Rancière, Jacques, 4, 6, 8, 19, 29; partition of the sensible, 27–28
Rastafarian, 42, 48–49
Reagan, Ronald, 44
relation. *See* Glissant, Édouard
Reyes Franco, Marina, 1
Ricoeur, Paul, 122
Rieder, John, 87–88, 165n24
Rodney, Walter, 19, 24–25, 48, 49
Rojas, Rafael, 104
Romero Barceló, Carlos, 76–77
Rosa, Jonathan, 62
Royal Caribbean, 1

Said, Edward, 75
Sagás, Ernesto, 116
Salgado, César A., 72
San Miguel, Pedro L., 163n83, 174n87
Sánchez Gómez, José Miguel. *See* Yoss (Sánchez Gómez, José Miguel)
Sánchez, Yoani, 81, 101–108
Santo Domingo, 113, 117, 120, 126, 137
Saussure, Ferdinand de, 35
Schaeffer, Pierre, 37
Schmitt, Carl, 16
Schwartz, Marcy, 163n77
Schwartz, Rosalie, 166n50
Scott, David, 3
Scott, Walter, 164n9
Seaga, Edward, 44
self-authorship, 102
self-determination, 3, 12, 93, 159n95; in Haiti and the Dominican Republic, 115; Puerto Rican, 59, 72
self-proprietorship. *See* freelance
Senior, Emily, 120
sense of belonging, 2, 4
senses (five), 4, 26–28, 30, 32, 36–37, 41, 45, 46; hearing as traditional metaphor for

understanding, 27, 41; partitioning of, 30, 33; sight as privileged metaphor for knowledge, 27–28, 41; smell as condition of judgment, 47
sensorium, 23, 27–28, 30, 33, 37, 46
sex work. *See* freelance
Sharpe, Christina, 142
Sheller, Mimi, 89, 95
Simmel, Georg, 17
Siskind, Mariano, 73, 165n75
sociogeny. *See* Fanon, Frantz; Wynter, Sylvia
Solís, Denis, 110
Sommer, Doris, 59
sonic tourism, 32
Soviet Bloc, 20, 79, 101
Spanish Caribbean, 145
Spanish citizenship, 165n62, 169n4
Spengler, Oswald, 54, 160n9
Spillers, Hortense, 125
Spivak, Gayatri Chakravorty, 10
Steinmetz, George, 120
Stephens, Michelle, 34
Strachan, Ian Gregory, 36
statelessness, 82, 115; stateless person/subject, 81, 85, 92, 107, 103
Stoler, Ann Laura, 120
stranger. *See* citizen
stranger at home, 16–17

Taínos, 9–10, 36, 74–75
taste (*sensus communis*), 15, 109
terra nullis, 14, 64, 70–71
Thacker, Eugene, 129, 131–132
Thompson, Krista, 36
Tlostanova, Madina, 88, 96
Tonton Macoutes, 137–138
Torres-Padilla, José L., 59–60
touch, 46, 121–125, 137, 141
tourist economy, 1–2, 5, 19, 26, 29, 36, 83, 85, 89, 91–92, 96, 98
tourist enclosure, 25
tourist photography, 28, 36–37
Treaty of Chaguaramas, 156n20; revised, 34, 36, 40
Trinidad, 45, 156n20
Tropicana nightclub, 86
Trouillot, Michel-Rolph, 12, 128; on North Atlantic Universals, 6–7, 116
Trujillo, Rafael, 117, 119–123, 126, 135
Trump, Donald, 109

undocumented migrants, 30–34, 37–41
universality, 3, 5, 7–8, 57, 73, 159n1

United Nations, 55; Conferences on the Law of Treaties ("Vienna Convention"), 65; High Commissioner for Refugees, 143

United States, 45, 46, 48, 56–57, 67; Good Neighbor Policy, 86; hegemony, 29, 43, 47, 106, 173n82; intervention in Jamaican economy, 44; relation to Puerto Rico, 51, 52–55, 60, 64, 69, 74, 76, 96; U.S.-Mexico Border, 143. *See* Vieques

unreadability, 53, 65, 135

unworlding, 52, 73, 163n75

Urry, John, 28, 89, 156n19

Varela, Francisco, 153n35

Vega, Ana Lydia: deliberation, 41, 44–49; *Encancaranublado y otros cuentos de naufragio*, 43; "Jamaica Farewell," 2, 19, 23, 26–30, 41–50; pan-Caribbeanism, 42

Vega, Bernardo, 120, 171n32

Vega-Marino, Alexandra, 59

Venezuela, 67, 105

Vienna Convention on the Law of Treatises. *See* United Nations

Vieques, 47

visitor. *See* guest

Voegelin, Salomé, 37

Walcott, Derek, 23, 25, 28, 37–38

Weheliye, Alexander, 125

Wells, H.G., 86, 165n24

Werbner, Pnina, 156n37

Western modernity. *See* modernity

West Indian Federation, 49–50, 159n98

whiteness, 15, 75, 115; juridical, 116

Whitfield, Esther, 163n2

Wolfe, Cary, 171n42

world literature, 53, 56–57

Wynter, Sylvia, 21, 43, 69, 121, 172n59; on myth, 133; on storytelling, 11, 153n35; sociogenic principle, 134

Yoss (Sánchez Gómez, José Miguel): Body Spare, 94–100; planetary tourism/hospitality, 85, 88–91, 98, 100; *Se alquila una planeta*, 2, 21, 80, 82, 85–88, 100, 102, 106, 164n11; "Trabajadora social," 21, 82, 84–101; xenoid, 85–87, 89, 90–100

Zambrana, Rocío, 96

Zamora, Margarita, 9, 152n23, 152n25

About the Author

Natalie Lauren Belisle is assistant professor of Spanish and comparative literature at the University of Southern California in Los Angeles. Her research and teaching engage contemporary Caribbean literature, visual culture and media, and movement practices. She is particularly interested in the relationship between aesthetics and the law, Black ecologies in Latin America, the Caribbean, and its diaspora, theories of existence, and the speculative.

Available titles in the Critical Caribbean Studies series

Giselle Anatol, *The Things That Fly in the Night: Female Vampires in Literature of the Circum-Caribbean and African Diaspora*

Alaí Reyes-Santos, *Our Caribbean Kin: Race and Nation in the Neoliberal Antilles*

Milagros Ricourt, *The Dominican Racial Imaginary: Surveying the Landscape of Race and Nation in Hispaniola*

Katherine A. Zien, *Sovereign Acts: Performing Race, Space, and Belonging in Panama and the Canal Zone*

Frances R. Botkin, *Thieving Three-Fingered Jack: Transatlantic Tales of a Jamaican Outlaw, 1780–2015*

Melissa A. Johnson, *Becoming Creole: Nature and Race in Belize*

Carlos Garrido Castellano, *Beyond Representation in Contemporary Caribbean Art: Space, Politics, and the Public Sphere*

Njelle W. Hamilton, *Phonographic Memories: Popular Music and the Contemporary Caribbean Novel*

Lia T. Bascomb, *In Plenty and in Time of Need: Popular Culture and the Remapping of Barbadian Identity*

Aliyah Khan, *Far from Mecca: Globalizing the Muslim Caribbean*

Rafael Ocasio, *Race and Nation in Puerto Rican Folklore: Franz Boas and John Alden Mason in Porto Rico*

Ana-Maurine Lara, *Streetwalking: LGBTQ Lives and Protest in the Dominican Republic*

Anke Birkenmaier, ed., *Caribbean Migrations: The Legacies of Colonialism*

Sherina Feliciano-Santos, *A Contested Caribbean Indigeneity: Language, Social Practice, and Identity within Puerto Rican Taíno Activism*

H. Adlai Murdoch, ed., *The Struggle of Non-Sovereign Caribbean Territories: Neoliberalism since the French Antillean Uprisings of 2009*

Robert Fatton Jr., *The Guise of Exceptionalism: Unmasking the National Narratives of Haiti and the United States*

Rafael Ocasio, *Folk Stories from the Hills of Puerto Rico/Cuentos folklóricos de las montañas de Puerto Rico*

Yveline Alexis, *Haiti Fights Back: The Life and Legacy of Charlemagne Péralte*

Katerina Gonzalez Seligmann, *Writing the Caribbean in Magazine Time*

Jocelyn Fenton Stitt, *Dreams of Archives Unfolded: Absence and Caribbean Life Writing*

Alison Donnell, *Creolized Sexualities: Undoing Heteronormativity in the Literary Imagination of the Anglo-Caribbean*

Vincent Joos, *Urban Dwellings, Haitian Citizenships: Housing, Memory, and Daily Life in Haiti*

Krystal Nandini Ghisyawan, *Erotic Cartographies: Decolonization and the Queer Caribbean Imagination*

Yvon van der Pijl and Francio Guadeloupe, eds., *Equaliberty in the Dutch Caribbean: Ways of Being Non/Sovereign*

Patricia Joan Saunders, *Buyers Beware: Insurgency and Consumption in Caribbean Popular Culture*

Atreyee Phukan, *Contradictory Indianness: Indenture, Creolization, and Literary Imaginary*

Nikoli A. Attai, *Defiant Bodies: Making Queer Community in the Anglophone Caribbean*

Samuel Ginsburg, *The Cyborg Caribbean: Techno-Dominance in Twenty-First-Century Cuban, Dominican, and Puerto Rican Science Fiction*

Linden F. Lewis, *Forbes Burnham: The Life and Times of the Comrade Leader*

Keja L. Valens, *Culinary Colonialism, Caribbean Cookbooks, and Recipes for National Independence*

Kim Williams-Pulfer, *Get Involved! Stories of Bahamian Civil Society*

Preity R. Kumar, *An Ordinary Landscape of Violence: Women Loving Women in Guyana*

Kezia Page, *Inside Tenement Time: Suss, Spirit, and Surveillance*

Darlène Elizabeth Dubuisson, *Reclaiming Haiti's Futures: Returned Intellectuals, Placemaking, and Radical Imagination*

Natalie Lauren Belisle, *Caribbean Inhospitality: The Poetics of Strangers at Home*